JEAN GABIN

Jean Gabin

The Actor Who Was France

Joseph Harriss

McFarland & Company, Inc., Publishers
Jefferson, North Carolina

LIBRARY OF CONGRESS CATALOGUING-IN-PUBLICATION DATA

Names: Harriss, Joseph, author.
Title: Jean Gabin : the actor who was France / Joseph Harriss.
Description: Jefferson, North Carolina : McFarland & Company, Inc.,
2018 | Includes bibliographical references, filmography, and index.
Identifiers: LCCN 2018040865 | ISBN 9781476676272
(softcover : acid free paper) ∞
Subjects: LCSH: Gabin, Jean, 1904–1976. | Motion picture
actors and actresses—France—Biography.
Classification: LCC PN2638.G15 H37 2018 | DDC 791.4302/8092 [B]—dc23
LC record available at https://lccn.loc.gov/2018040865

BRITISH LIBRARY CATALOGUING DATA ARE AVAILABLE

ISBN (print) 978-1-4766-7627-2
ISBN (ebook) 978-1-4766-3460-9

Front cover image of Jean Gabin circa 1939
(Collection du Musée Jean Gabin)

Printed in the United States of America

*McFarland & Company, Inc., Publishers
Box 611, Jefferson, North Carolina 28640
www.mcfarlandpub.com*

For Claudie and Christopher

Table of Contents

Acknowledgments

I would like to thank the following for their kind response to my requests for interviews and other assistance with this book.

Florence Moncorgé-Gabin welcomed me into her home in Normandy for a frank discussion of her father's career and family life. Her clear-eyed insight into his character helped me understand this man who remained an enigma to many of those who were closest to him. She also facilitated my entrée at the Jean Gabin Museum in Mériel, where the curator, Mrs. Latifa Charef, allowed me the free run of the museum's extensive archives and generously made available most of the photos that appear in these pages.

Claude Gauteur, one of France's preeminent film historians, helped orient my research and refine my viewpoint on Jean Gabin's place in French motion picture history. His books on the actor were one of my primary sources for understanding "the Gabin myth." Other prominent French writers who took time from their own work to discuss with me Gabin as a national icon were Olivier Barrot, who has an encyclopedic knowledge of both French literature and films, Didier Goux, who has reflected at length on how and why the French identify with him, and Alain Paucard, who appreciates more than most how Gabin's films evoke the France that was.

Patrick Glâtre, an active member of the board of the Gabin museum and himself a prolific writer on Jean Gabin, provided useful guidance, especially on Gabin's military service and the wartime FBI investigation of him and Marlene Dietrich. When I followed up on that, the FBI public affairs office patiently explained how and where to find their online documents relating to the investigation. More details on Gabin's military service, especially his role in the liberation of Royan by Free French Forces, was provided by Pierre-Louis Bouchet, a municipal official there who has thoroughly researched the battle against entrenched German forces that destroyed most of his city.

As with any work on French cinema, the Cinémathèque Française in Paris was an invaluable research source both online and in the person of program director Jean-François Rauger, who discussed with me Gabin's place in what the French call the seventh art. I was able to draw on the Cinémathèque's unique film collection to view those of Gabin's films that were difficult to come by otherwise.

My search for documentation was generously aided by Charles L. Zigman, a Los Angeles–based screenwriter and film historian whose book *World's Coolest Movie Star* contains a detailed Gabin filmography. He spontaneously sent me a trove of material dating from Gabin's early years in movies.

Brigitte Bardot and Françoise Arnoul, who played opposite Jean Gabin in some of his most important films, responded promptly and graciously to my requests for interviews. Their keen admiration for him and gratitude for his moral support during filming was still palpable many years after those roles.

A special thanks also goes to Michael Johnson, an American writer and friend who lives in Bordeaux, for his close reading of the manuscript and his helpful suggestions for improvement.

Introduction

An elegant little cushion sat atop the coffin. On it lay the beribboned military and civil decorations of the defunct. Nearby stood the furled flags of the Fusiliers Armored Regiment and the Second Armored Division of the Free French Forces where he had served as a tank commander during the liberation of France in 1945. Amid the trappings of national honors, the crowd of mourners ignored the damp cold of November 1976. They milled behind police barriers, many bearing bouquets, waiting to file by the black-draped coffin of Jean Alexis Gabin Moncorgé. A large photo in *The New York Times*, like those in newspapers the world over, showed the mob scene his funeral created at Paris' Père Lachaise cemetery, final resting place of many of France's most illustrious men and women. The paper's obituary referred to "the craggy and sardonic hero-victim of a hundred French films," and called him "one of the great men of cinema."[1] For most of those gathered at the cemetery that chilly morning, he was much more than a great film actor. He had incarnated a distinct national character, *their* national character.

If Jean Gabin merited the title of great man of cinema, and I believe he did, it's because during the convulsive heart of France's 20th century, he convincingly showed on the big screen what it meant to be French. Today the kind of Frenchman he personified is an endangered species due to the wrenching change caused by the country's accelerating technological evolution, its unsettling tectonic shift from a rural to an urban society, and the forced-march homogenization of globalization in general and the European Union in particular. For many of us who have long known and loved France, his films are a way to recover its unique but fast-fading spirit and flavor.

My own interest in Jean Gabin began when I came to live and work in Paris as a journalist and non-fiction writer many years ago. I had, of course, seen some of his films in America, but I didn't understand his importance until I got to know, or try to know, the French people themselves. I admired his acting enough to seek out his old pictures in the little Left Bank theaters that showed them frequently. Gradually I came to see that studying his characters in those movies was as good a way as any of getting at the notoriously complex and contradictory French identity, an often bewildering mix of preening panache and gruff, earthy common sense.

Taken all together, the characters Jean Gabin portrayed in 95 films over 40-odd years form a mosaic amounting to the French version of the human comedy. His roles ranged from the downtrodden proletarian and drifter with a tragic destiny to gangland bosses, from a grease-covered locomotive engineer to a homburg-wearing, cigar-smoking capitalist, government prime minister to police commissioner to clochard. Not to mention

1

the aging, aching, married male attempting one more fling, tragically, with a frivolous young beauty. His characters bore recognizably French names: Jacques, Pierre, Marcel, André, Lucien, and especially Jean, not the ones fashionable in today's mutating France, like Kevin, Johnny, Jacky or Mehdi. Most of all, he was unmistakably a street-smart Parisian in his way of speaking *titi Parisien* slang, his tough-minded irreverence toward conventional attitudes and middle-class commonplaces, his contempt for sham. He was simply, as the director Julien Duvivier, who did several films with Gabin, said, "the regular guy every Frenchman enjoys drinking a glass of red wine with."[2]

At one time or another during his exceptionally long career he represented the socio-economic archetypes of different periods of France's national existence. That began in the Depression-ridden 1930s when he played a member of a group of unemployed men in *La Belle Équipe* whose attempt to start a restaurant ends in a disaster symbolic of the painful end of the working-class dreams of the utopian Popular Front movement. With angst building in France over the inevitability of another war with Germany, he was the disabused soldier in Jean Renoir's anti-war classic, *La Grande Illusion*, which Orson Welles said was the only film in the world that absolutely had to be saved.[3]

Later, reflecting France's burgeoning post-war prosperity, the three-decade period from the 1950s through the 1970s known as *les Trente Glorieuses*, he was the prosperous, silver-haired businessman and family patriarch of *Les Grandes Familles*. When hippies, drugs, and a different kind of gangland violence respecting none of the old rules of the criminal milieu hit France in the 1960s, he was a taciturn, world-weary police commissioner confronting the new era in *Le Pacha*, or an elderly, rooted Norman farmer in *La Horse* lashing out to save his grandson from vicious drug gangs. As the perceptive French writer Alain Paucard told me, "There's not a single Gabin film where his role doesn't reflect French society. Or, more precisely, there's not a single Frenchman who doesn't see himself in some Gabin role."[4]

Film after film, he was constructing his persona. As it evolved with the times, it remained palpably the Jean Gabin that audiences responded to, leading some to compare the emotion provoked by his on-screen appearance to that of the husky voice of Edith Piaf. The Greece-born director Costa-Gavras, whose film career was mainly in France, once reflected, "The only character he ever created on screen was himself, and that was largely enough.... He represented the Frenchman. By his way of being, by his way of speaking, moving. When you saw Gabin, it was France."[5]

It was he, more than any other French actor, who had the unique universality to personify this variegated, determinedly difficult nation, where *au contraire!* is one of the favorite expressions. Over the years, he became the very image of a certain invincible Frenchness. Just as Brigitte Bardot exemplified the French woman for many, he was the emblematic Frenchman. The "Gabin myth" is a frequent theme in many scholarly studies of him. The Australian film historian Colin Crisp, for example, finds that Gabin, along with the French stars Michèle Morgan and Brigitte Bardot, "are the clearest instances of actors or actresses who came to embody mythic stereotypes, which they subsequently brought ready-made to each new film.... Gabin was the first to impose his cinematic persona on critics and the public."[6]

He never gave any sign during his lifetime that he was aware of bearing this mantle. Until his death at 72 in Paris' American Hospital, he stubbornly remained in his own view nothing more or less than Jean Moncorgé. Born in 1904 in the raffish Paris neighborhood of Montmartre, he was the seventh child of a couple of cabaret entertainers. Left mostly to himself at an early age, he was raised largely by his big sister in a rural village. It was there that the young Jean learned to love the countryside, the *terroir* so dear to many Frenchmen. He hated school, dropping out as a teenager to find work as a day laborer. Under the prodding of his father, a song-and-dance man at the Folies Bergère, he reluctantly tried his hand at a few walk-on parts in music hall revues. That led to silent films, then to talkies.

Jean Gabin became the linchpin of the Golden Age of French cinema, from around 1932 to 1939. In the space of six years he did 12 films, including no fewer than ten now considered classics. Many, precursors of Hollywood's film noir, saw Gabin, his dreams crushed by an impersonal, indifferent society, fated for a tragic end. In the process he became what the prominent French film critic André Bazin called "Oedipus in a flat cap … perhaps the only real tragic character of French cinema."[7] Then, as later in his career, his appeal was largely due to his expressive pale eyes, which directors liked to emphasize with special lighting. Otherwise, his face was more than the sum of its parts: his broken nose with its bulbous tip was too big, his lips too thin. But through the inexplicable magic of charisma it somehow gave him massive presence.

His acting was instinctive. Early on he, like Gary Cooper, understood the importance of underplaying, realizing how much the camera's lens magnified every gesture and change of expression. In fact, in the 1930s some French movie critics thought Gabin might become the Gallic Gary Cooper, whom they considered the model of the average American.[8] In America, on the other hand, film buffs debated for decades about who was his Hollywood equivalent. Bosley Crowther, the eminent film critic of *The New York Times* for 27 years, said flatly in the early 1940s that Gabin was "the Spencer Tracey of French films … obviously one of the best slap-'em-and-kiss-'em actors in the game."[9] That didn't deter a later *Times* reviewer from calling Gabin a sad-eyed James Cagney who brought "a delicate, almost feminine quality to his tough-guy roles."[10] Comparisons to Humphrey Bogart as the epitome of cool weltschmerz were inevitable.

For the Film Society of New York, Jean Gabin was "Everybody's Star," as it entitled its three-week, 17-film retrospective of his career. Held in June and July 2002 at the Society's Walter Reade Theater in Lincoln Center, the film festival made the point that Gabin was one of the world's best-known, best-loved screen actors. More than that, its program declared, "For many people around the world, Jean Gabin was—and still is—French cinema." After savoring his acting in a wide variety of roles, audiences could decide for themselves whether he was indeed, as the Society claimed, "a new kind of screen hero, lifeworn, proudly proletarian, and naturally graceful."[11]

Gabin could and did play virtually anything from somber works of poetic realism to lighthearted comedies and everything in between—he was the best-ever cinematic model of Georges Simenon's stoic, pipe-smoking Inspector Maigret. As actor and man, he was constantly growing, maturing, evolving. That was inevitable, given the trajectory of his life, from pugnacious, pigheaded punk from the wrong side of the tracks, to national idol and one of the 20th century's biggest motion picture stars. His charisma has excited critics to flights of purple prose. The film historian Colleen Kennedy-Karpat calls him "the pinnacle of the French male ideal,"[12] the French *homme de lettres* Gabriel Reuillard says Gabin had "the nobility of a beautiful animal,"[13] while another, Pierre Duvillars, says, "He is the universal man. You only have to see him to want to shake his hand if you are a man, or take him in your arms, if you are a woman."[14]

Many women were ready to take him in their arms. Not for nothing was one of his early films entitled *Gueule d'Amour*, Lady Killer. He habitually courted his leading ladies and was married three times. In *Le Quai des Brumes* the lady was a 17-year-old Michèle Morgan in beret and raincoat, to whom he murmured what became one of the cult lines of French cinema: "You've got beautiful eyes, you know." The popular press immediately dubbed them the dream couple. His tumultuous, well-publicized affairs included several other French actresses, as well as Ginger Rogers and Marlene Dietrich, both of whom he met during his unhappy stint in Hollywood while seeking refuge from France's Nazi occupation. Besides his charisma, muscular physique and bad-boy appeal, Dietrich's connoisseur eye appreciated something else: "Gabin," she once reminisced, "had the most beautiful loins I have ever seen on a man."[15]

Their tortuous, at times torturous relationship lasted six years, covering the entire period of the Second World War. Gabin fled to the United States after the French debacle of 1940, refusing any part of his country's shameful collaboration with the Nazis. In a spontaneous act of selfless patriotism, he chose to leave the palmy life of Hollywood after making two films, and join Charles de Gaulle's Free French as a tank commander liberating his country. That was completely in character for the man who so deeply loved his country that he could be happy nowhere else. But when he returned to civilian life, much of the French public unfairly ignored his service and spitefully remembered only that he had left for Hollywood.

Jean Gabin was unquestionably one of the giants of world cinema. In America, despite the frequent inclusion of his movies in art house film festivals, he has also been one of the most overlooked. Moreover, this intensely reserved, sensitive, complex, and vulnerable man was far from the one-dimensional movie star often depicted by the press of the day. Toward the end of his life, his wife of nearly 30 years admitted that she had given up trying to understand him. To her and to many who knew him, he remained an enigma. And yet he had embodied the national character to the point of becoming, in many ways, the actor who was France.

The question is, how?

The question is, why?

1

The Moncorgés

When Jean Gabin recalled his paternal grandfather, he conjured up the imposing figure of a muscular, Rhadamanthine man with a white beard from the center of which emerged a calabash pipe clamped in his teeth. The teeth rarely seemed to unclamp, so seldom did he speak. His head was large, his craggy features deeply lined by a lifetime of labor in the open air. Like most 19th-century French working men, Ferdinand Moncorgé wore beneath his shirt, summer and winter, a wide flannel strip known as a *petite laine* wrapped around his abdomen. His black, wide-wale corduroy trousers were secured with suspenders and a large leather belt. "What impressed me most when I was about five years old," Gabin told his longtime friend, press agent, and biographer, André Brunelin, "was how much care he took to hold his pants up. Mine, usually too large, were always falling down, with my mother screaming at me not to show my backside. I thought to myself that *grand-père* certainly didn't risk showing his, and decided that any man who used both suspenders and a belt must be respectable."[1]

Grandfather Ferdinand was originally from the village of Mardore, which derives its name from the little Mardoret stream that runs through it, in the hilly Rhône-Alpes region of south-central France. The region has had a rich history. Vestiges of the important Celtic La Tène culture of the European Iron Age can still be found there, Roman legions marched through. Cobblestones of the Gallo-Roman road are still visible—an interesting coincidence in view of Ferdinand's later career path. But the hardscrabble life there in 1839, when was born, was bleak, so as an adolescent he set out for Paris to find a brighter future.

His timing was propitious. Probably the news had arrived in Mardore that the capital was booming, with jobs for anyone who wanted work. Two colossal projects in particular would have been hiring when Ferdinand arrived in Paris. The visionary Emperor Napoleon III was implementing his ambitious plans to modernize the growing capital, then still basically a medieval city in its chaotic layout and woefully inadequate public health infrastructure. He engaged the energetic Georges-Eugène Haussmann, prefect of the Seine Department, which included Paris, to push through his program of wide new boulevards, parks, and other public works. Beginning in 1854, when Ferdinand would have been an able-bodied 15 years old, he could have worked to demolish hundreds of the city's older buildings, making way for the handsome, homogeneous façade still visible in the city center today. Other aspects of the program involved new cobblestone streets, two railroad stations, and a municipal hospital. Napoleon III encouraged innovative architecture such as Victor Baltard's Les Halles produce market, with its cast-iron columns resembling giant umbrellas supporting glass roofing, and the largest theater in the world at that time, Charles Garnier's spectacular Paris Opera.

Ferdinand also could have taken part in Napoleon III's grand effort to make Paris the center of the civilized world with the Paris World's Fair of 1855. Such fairs were often used by London and Paris to vaunt their progress as they vied for leadership in Europe. At times the rivalry was sharp, as when Napoleon Bonaparte's government sponsored the Paris fair of 1798, promising that "the participant who can show that his products and trade have dealt the worst blow to English industry will receive a gold medal."[2] Britain went one up in 1851 with an industrial fair that attracted over 13,000 participants, many housed in Joseph Paxton's magnificent Crystal Palace, the largest enclosure yet constructed, with nearly one million square feet of exhibit space. The fair of 1855 was France's riposte, its innovative glass-and-iron Palais de l'Industrie being even larger than Paxton's. (Paris would go on to hold ever-bigger fairs in 1867, 1878, and 1889, when the thousand-foot Eiffel Tower was the dramatic centerpiece; fair fever reached its climax with the 1900 Paris Universal Exposition, with the Grand Palais, Petit Palais, and the ornate Pont Alexandre III that still form part of the cityscape.)[3]

Both projects required new paved streets, and Ferdinand eventually ended up as a *paveur* laying cobblestones. This gave him the status and job security due a worker of a respected old trade with its specified rules, regulations and traditions. A prudent man, he waited until the relatively advanced age, for the era, of 30 before he felt his socio-economic situation settled enough to start a family. He found a wife in the person of a cook named Rose-Justine, a provincial like himself, who came from the eastern town of Belfort. They married in January 1868, and that September they had a son, Ferdinand Joseph, who would become Jean Gabin's father.

The Moncorgé family lived in central Paris. That meant they bore the brunt of the Franco-Prussian War of 1870, when Napoleon III's Imperial Army was crushed within weeks, leading to a five-month Prussian siege designed to starve the population into submission. The Moncorgés, like other Parisians, were reduced to eating cats, dogs, rats, and the two elephants in the zoo. Hardly had France signed the surrender document in January 1871 than the Radical Socialist revolutionary uprising known as the Paris Commune, led by the politically sympathetic National Guard, was proclaimed. Hastily assembled barricades divided the city for two months as some 30,000 *Communards* held out against 130,000 regular government troops. When the revolt was over, large areas of the city lay in ruin and nearly 20,000 civilians had died at the hands of their countrymen. The aborted movement influenced the thinking of Karl Marx, who considered it a fine example of the dictatorship of the proletariat.[4]

Ferdinand, who identified with working class values but not hotheaded, bloody insurrection, decided it was time to move the family to a safer location. He found it in the peaceful suburb of Boulogne-Billancourt, west of Paris, where he took a house at 19, Route de Versailles. Thanks to his diligence, he rose to the estimable position of *chef paveur de Paris*, and the couple could afford to have another son, Marie August Henri. Ever provident and practical, Ferdinand wanted his elder son to adopt the trade of wheelwright. It was, after all, a logical step up from being a paver and, in the 1880s, all those horse-drawn carts and carriages meant he would always have work and the means to put food on the table. The younger Ferdinand accordingly began his apprenticeship at 14 as a wheelwright in a nearby workshop, learning to build wooden hubs and spokes and to bind them by nailing iron stakes to the rim.

One fateful evening after work, he visited Paris' cafe and theater district on the *grands boulevards*. There he spent his meager pocket money on a balcony seat at the Eldorado music hall on Boulevard de Strasbourg, known for its comedy routines, dance, and popular music. Dating from 1858, the Eldorado was for 60 years one of the city's most famous nightspots. That evening, Ferdinand was particularly smitten with the singer Paulus, then one of the stars of Paris' many *cafés concert*. Then and there he got hooked on show business: he decided to be a cabaret singer like Paulus.

The café concerts, or *caf'conc'* as they were locally known, were one of the most popular forms of entertainment in Paris. During the Belle Epoque it had more than 200 of these little theatres, located mainly between Montmartre and Place de la Bastille; it is estimated that something like 10,000 songs were sung there in a typical year. While the middle and upper classes went to the theater, opera, or operetta, the proletariat could see song and dance routines, acrobats, trained animal acts, and comic sketches for the modest price of a drink—a beer could be had for the equivalent of 30 cents, a coffee for ten. It was a difficult public to please and performers needed a thick skin. If the audience didn't like an act they let it be known with raucous jeers, whistles and catcalls or, in particularly bad cases, thrown coins, cushions, and empty bottles. Female dancers, harassed with calls to show more, sometimes fled to the wings in tears.

When Ferdinand announced his new vocation at home, Moncorgé père predictably begged to differ. A firm believer in the virtue of hard work, he had only scorn for entertainers. Those worthless layabouts, he lectured Ferdinand, had no morals and no pride, the proof being that they were willing to act the fool in public for a few francs. The son persisted, explaining that the trade of wheelwright held no interest for him and he had found his life's work. The father exploded in an angry scene that Jean Gabin later heard described many times. "If you want to play the whore, get out of here and never again set foot in my home," his well-girt grandfather had thundered, underlining the definitive character of the expulsion by using the formal *vous* form of address with his son instead of the usual familiar *tu*.[5] Ferdinand packed his small suitcase with a few belongings, donned his Sunday cap, kissed his weeping mother, said goodbye to his six-year-old brother, and set off down Route de Versailles, virtually penniless, toward Paris. (Ironically, when Ferdinand became a father, his son would also disagree with him over what vocation to choose, but for exactly the opposite reason.)

He learned his trade the hard way. In Belle Epoque France everyone, workers in flat caps and top-hatted toffs, midinette dames and *grandes dames*, wanted fun, craved entertainment. That created heavy demand for singers of popular songs willing to perform in rowdy, smoke-filled, second-rate cafes and cabarets. In exchange, performers got a few francs and the chance to be on a stage accompanied by a pianist or, if lucky, a small orchestra. Ferdinand, filled with the zeal of his new vocation, was more than willing to endure the adversities of apprenticeship, confident there would be constant and increasing demand for what he could offer.

Fin-de-siècle Paris was a beautiful, frivolous city in a frivolous time. The humiliation of the War of 1870, and the consequent loss of the important eastern provinces of Alsace and Lorraine with their mines and industries, had been a psychological and economic shock to the entire country. The city of Paris in particular had been disfigured and its citizens horrified by the self-inflicted carnage and destruction of the Commune. Now France was bouncing back with a vengeance, with plenty of work for all and rising prosperity. It conquered a colonial empire in North and West Africa and in Indochina in the 1880s that would be second only to Great Britain's. Politically too, the country had found a new stability. After a dicey period beginning in 1871 when the National Assembly was dominated by monarchists determined to end the republican form of government as soon as they could decide who would be king, French lawmakers reluctantly founded the Third Republic because, as 74-year-old President Adolphe Thiers said, "it divided us least."[6]

Despite, or perhaps because of, the obvious hypocrisy and injustice, want and misery surrounding them, people were determined to take pleasure where and as they found it. Besides working Paris, Ferdinand hit the circuit of provincial fairs and charity benefits. He learned what worked and what did not, getting ample feedback from the noisy audiences. Gradually he made something of a name for himself, but it was obvious that "Ferdinand Joseph" lacked a certain showbiz zing. One day a friend, noting the vogue among French entertainers to use single names of no more than two syllables, suggested "Gabin." It seems unlikely that either Ferdinand or his friend knew that the name—Saint Gabin's feast day has long been mentioned on the French Catholic calendar on February 19, but few newborns are thus christened—came from Saint Gabinus, brother of early Christianity's obscure third-century Pope Caius. But it fit well enough and he adopted it on the spot. Henceforth his billing would be simply Gabin.

Shortly after he started making the scene virtually singing for his supper, he met a small-time singer and actress named Madeleine Petit, stage name Hélène. Her parents, Louis and Marie-Mathon Dommage Petit of the historic riverside town of La Charité-sur-Loire—its massive 11th-century church, Notre Dame, was one of the medieval world's biggest, its Benedictine priory one of the richest, Joan of Arc fought here in 1423—sent her as a teenager to work in Paris as a *plumassière*, fashioning feathers used on ladies' hats and boas. She sang prettily in the workshop to pass the time, as many did in those days. Her coworkers, even her enlightened employers, encouraged her to try her voice in public. Ferdinand came across her at a benefit show around 1887 when he was 19 and she 22. They began performing as partners in the same shows, fell in love, and eventually moved in together. Children followed: Ferdinand in 1888, Madeleine in 1890, and they finally married after the third, Reine, in 1893. The following three, Suzane, André, and Alice, died in infancy. Hélène unhappily began to lose her singing voice. She blamed it on the frequent pregnancies.

Her career would be ended not only by childbearing and its consequences, but also by economic pressures. France's growing economy attracted more and more workers from the provinces, sending Paris housing prices soaring. That was a problem for a couple of starry-eyed young entertainers with children. They decided to move out of the city to Mériel, a village of about 500 souls on the right bank of the slow-flowing Oise River 20 miles northwest of Paris. The rural site, with its rolling wheat fields, extensive woods, and soft northern light, was picturesque enough to have attracted many painters to nearby Auvers-sur-Oise. They included the likes of Cezanne, Pissarro, Corot, Daubigny, and of course Vincent van Gogh. But the region's aesthetic appeal was less important to Ferdinand than the fact that he could buy a house in Mériel on credit at 61 Grande Rue. An added advantage was its location next to a train station with direct service to Paris.

That was all-important to him, for if Hélène's career was, to her outspoken regret, now over, his was taking off. He might never be a famous popular singer like his idol Paulus, but he had landed the job of master of ceremonies at one of the biggest music halls in Paris, La Cigale. Located at 120 Boulevard de Rochechouart in the Montmartre entertainment district around Place Pigalle, La Cigale could accommodate up to 1,000

Ferdinand in the early days of his career. In pleasure-loving Belle Epoque Paris he was able to capitalize on the big demand for entertainers in cafes and cabarets (Collection du Musée Jean Gabin).

spectators and featured some of the leading show business names of the day, stars like the leggy singer and dancer Mistinguett and her consort Maurice Chevalier—who seems to have performed in all of them at one time or another—the internationally famous actress Yvonne Printemps, the saucy comedienne Arletty, and the dapper Max Linder, then just beginning his long career as a top entertainer. (La Cigale still exists as part of the Paris entertainment scene, its ornate auditorium and vestibule classed as a French historical monument.) The name Gabin appeared increasingly in favorable reviews. "Monsieur Gabin is always droll," wrote one, and critics generally found his brand of faux-naif playfulness between the show's main star turns funny and refreshingly different. The pay was good and family life was improving, with the three surviving children showing early promise of soon having their own lives and careers. That would relieve Hélène of her domestic chores and maybe even let her return to the stage from what she considered a life of provincial exile.

It was not to be. Late one September evening in 1903, Ferdinand returned home on the last train from Paris to find his wife in tears. At 38 she was, she told him, again pregnant. To say that the couple's seventh child would hardly be a happy event is an understatement. They considered it a disastrous end to their new hopes for an easier life. But apparently neither ever contemplated any alternative to accepting this new, unwanted responsibility. And so it was that a baby boy was born on May 17, 1904. Not in Mériel, but in a midwife's Paris apartment at 23 Boulevard de Rochechouart, where Ferdinand had taken Hélène for the birth. Appropriately enough, that was just down the street from La Cigale, and steps away from the Folies Bergère and the Moulin Rouge. (As an adult, Jean Gabin liked to recall that he was born, as he put it, "between Villette and Montmartre," which was important to his Paris working-class identity on and off the movie set—"despite my childhood in the country, I'm a Parisian peasant who wandered into movies.")[7] Many French children have been lovingly named Désiré. This one certainly would not be.

The father dutifully went to the *mairie*, or town hall, of the 9th arrondissement, declared the birth, and recorded the child's name in the official register: Jean Alexis Gabin Moncorgé. The French tradition was that personal names reflected family history. Boys were named for their father or his family, girls christened with names from the mother's side. Fantasy names were discouraged. (Thus when my son was born some years ago in Paris and I declared his name as Christopher, the clerk objected that it was supposed to be *Christophe*; he relented only when I argued that I was American and had the right to use the English form of the name.) So when the municipal clerk heard the unusual third name, which did not figure on the father's official identity papers, he paused and asked Ferdinand to repeat it. Tired and exasperated, he raised his voice: "Gabin! G-A-B-I-N!" Then he headed to a nearby bistro for a stiff if not celebratory drink.[8] Why had he slipped his unofficial stage name, a name with which, in this still–Catholic country he had not been baptized, and had no deep roots in the Moncorgé family, into Jean's identity at birth? Simple professional pride? A sly nudge to encourage his son to follow in his footsteps? That he never explained.

2

Good for Nothing

They took the baby back to Mériel, where he joined his older siblings, 16-year old Ferdinand (to avoid confusion with the two other Ferdinands in the family, they called him simply Bébé), 14-year-old Madeleine, and 11-year-old Reine. Jean lived there for his first 11 years. The village and the surrounding rural area would be central to his personality and his views on life, his referential Rosebud. There many of his lifelong interests, attitudes, and reflexes were formed, from cycling to boxing, locomotives to hunting. Above all, it was there that he conceived his tenacious dream of having his own farm, with land to cultivate and cattle to raise—a typically French ambition for that era which he eventually would realize, at first happily, then with heartbreak.

Although he lived most of his life in Paris and liked to speak Montmartre slang, a dialect almost as incomprehensible to most French as London cockney is to most British, the country village seemed to pull him back time and again—several of his films were shot in its vicinity. Until she died in 1970, he returned there often to visit his sister Madeleine, who lived in the Moncorgé house surrounded by a herd of cats and a flock of hens; she was too tenderhearted to kill the latter for dinner. It couldn't have been the fond memories of a loving family that he associated with the village. His mother Hélène, embittered and irritable over the definitive loss of her career and the unexpected new burden of childcare, showed him little affection. "I wanted something from her that never came," he later recalled, "but I didn't really have an unhappy childhood. I was never cold or hungry. I never lacked anything essential, except maybe a little more affection, or at least a little more attention from my father and mother. I don't remember ever having been kissed by them when I was a kid. In the Moncorgé family we didn't do a lot of kissing."[1]

Basically the young Jean raised himself in Mériel. It appears likely that he suffered all his life from emotional insecurity due to a lack of maternal affection. But he seems also to have made his peace with that and seen the other side of the coin. "If I've always been a fighter," he recalled as an adult, "it's a sign of my independence. My parents let me develop a great desire for freedom, rather than making me into a conformist yielding to the petty meanness of life and conventional morality."[2]

With his hair cropped short and often wearing a downsized version of his father's worn-out trousers or a long black smock his mother fashioned from his sisters' old dresses, he spent his days roaming the banks of the Oise River and exploring fields and woods, observing nature. "It seemed to me that this was my private domain, a sort of little kingdom that was all mine," he once reminisced. "I didn't play games or cowboys

With his mother, Hélène, at the house in Mériel, circa 1909. "We didn't do a lot of kissing" (Collection du Musée Jean Gabin).

and Indians the way I saw the other kids doing. Instead, I would spend hours in the woods looking for a nest or a burrow or the trace of a fox that I would follow as far as I could for hours." Often he would take off in the morning after breakfast and not return until evening. When he got home, his clothes torn by thorns and his face covered with scratches and bruises from the frequent fights with kids his age, his mother would give him a spanking and scream at him, "Where have you been, you little brat? You've been fighting again, you good-for-nothing. You'll end up on the scaffold."[3]

Heading for the woods on one of his excursions, Jean came across a large stone cross. It marked the spot where the Mériel resident Louis Lannes, Marquis de Montebello and descendent of Jean Lannes, one of Bonaparte's favorite field marshals, who fought in many major Napoleonic battles ("The bravest of all," the Emperor said of him), was struck and killed by lightning. Graven in the stone monument was the direful verse from Matthew 25:13: "Watch, therefore, for ye know neither the day nor the hour." That intimation of inevitable, unpredictable mortality struck some resonant chord within the child Moncorgé and seemed to encapsulate the existential anxiety that gnawed him all his adult life. Many of his friends heard him quote it verbatim. Even while basking in Hollywood at the age of 38, that childhood insight haunted him, as he told an enquiring journalist from *Photoplay*: "People forget that they are just temporary guests on this earth, they forget they will end up in a little box, and then everything will be finished.... And you don't know the day, the hour, or the minute when that will happen.... You busy yourself with little things—and all ends in that box. *Always*. That's the only thing you are absolutely sure [of] in this world."[4]

On another restless outing he decided to take his first trip by himself. During his time walking the banks of the Oise he had observed with interest the little ferry that shuttled between Mériel and Auvers-sur-Oise, to him that foreign land on the other side of the river. With a few centimes he pinched from his mother's shopping budget he bought a ticket and embarked. After exploring the town and running through the wheat fields that, unbeknownst to him, had inspired several of Van Gogh's paintings, he got back to the dock too late to catch the last boat to Mériel. When night fell with no sign of Jean, Hélène set out to find him. Distraught with fear of what might have happened to him, she eventually knocked on the door of the ferry captain. Not only did he remember the young man, he was willing to start up the boat and take her across to find him. Which she did, he preparing to bed down on the dock to await the morning boat. Result: another memorable bawling out and spanking.

When he was out roaming the countryside, he obviously wasn't where he should have been—in school. Sometimes he attended the elementary school classes taught by the mustachioed local *instituteur*, Monsieur Dervelloy, where one schoolmate was Fernand Braudel, who became the eminent French historian and creator of the important Annales School of researching and writing history. But he honored his studies mainly in the breach, the only classroom activities that interested him being starting the morning fire in the schoolhouse's pot-bellied stove, and filling the inkwells on each desk. "To me, school seemed like a prison that I had to get away from," he remembered. "I hated learning and that stayed with me a long time. They told me that if I didn't go to school I would never be a 'monsieur.' I sometimes saw 'messieurs' on the bus when my father took me to Paris. With their starched collars strangling their throats and their frock coats that made them resemble penguins, and their hats. I thought they looked *con*."[5] (That last

Father and son at the house in Mériel, circa 1909. They were seldom together, Ferdinand preferring to spend his time playing cards or betting on the horses in Paris (Collection du Musée Jean Gabin).

adjective is an impolite anatomical reference that the French, being a famously polite people, use all the time. We will translate it here as "ridiculous.")

Except for the rare occasions when Ferdinand took his son to Paris for the day, Jean had little contact with his father, who became "a sort of mysterious traveler" to him. A family photo shows Ferdinand standing before the front door of their house with an unsmiling five-year-old Jean beside him, holding what appears to be a pet cat. Ferdinand, natty in high-top shoes, pegged pants, stylish jacket and vest, and rakish fedora, looks every inch the showman as he peers casually at the camera. Because of his engagement at La Cigale, he came home late at night, slept all morning, and left again in the

On the bank of the *Oise*, circa 1911. Jean spent more time there and roaming the nearby woods than in school (Collection du Musée Jean Gabin).

Looking tough in Mériel despite the smock made from one of his sister's old dresses, circa 1912 (Collection du Musée Jean Gabin).

early afternoon when the boy was taking his nap, at school, or roaming the countryside. Ferdinand's job didn't require him to leave the house in the afternoon, but his leisure activities did. That included playing *belote* card games with his friends at a Paris bistro or going to the horseraces, and usually losing money on them, at the Longchamp or Auteuil racetracks. That at least had an upside for the boy, for while Hélène was bawling out Ferdinand for wasting food money, she left Jean alone.

In a typewritten, undated, ten-page document on yellowing, crumbling paper that I discovered in the files of the Jean Gabin Museum in Mériel, Gabin himself describes how his restless need of action gave rise to one of his most memorable childhood adventures. Internal evidence indicates that the text, entitled "*Confidences*," was written in 1950, possibly with some future biographer in mind. It recounts what he calls "my best escapade," which occurred when he was ten years old. In 1914, during the first days of World War I, French troops were moving toward the front that August. Little Mériel had a taste of the reality of that war, seemingly so far away, when a flamboyant light-infantry regiment of Zouaves marched through the village one morning, flags flying and trumpets blaring. Created in the 1830s following the French colonization of Algeria, Zouave regiments were a sort of Foreign Legion initially composed of Berber troops led by French officers. Their ranks were progressively Europeanized, but retained their reputation for ferocious fighting and their colorful uniforms with billowing red Turkish-style pants, tight jackets, and tasseled caps. "It was the Fourth Zouaves Regiment," he recounts. "The music, the red uniforms! I don't know exactly what urgent attraction that regiment suddenly had for me. But I fell into step with them. And for four days I followed those soldiers."[6] He tagged along and became the regiment mascot, happily sharing their field rations and bedding down with them in their bivouac just outside town. The adventure ended, inevitably, when an exasperated Hélène sent the gendarmes out to find him and bring him home.

Any woman would have had her hands full with a boy like that. Hélène especially so, because of her nervous, depressed mental state. In later life he would admit that maybe she wasn't entirely wrong about him after all. "I really was good for nothing," he told André Brunelin. "I mean, really nothing at all. An incredible mediocrity at everything." Especially when compared to his siblings. Elder brother Bébé was good at math and an overall brilliant student. Sister Madeleine was artistic, writing poetry, playing the piano and painting—one of her works, a copy of a Reubens *Descent from the Cross*, hangs today in Mériel's Saint Eloi church. His other sister, Reine, showed enough acting talent to share the stage briefly with her father.

The closest the rebel Jean actually came to a socially approved activity was serving as an altar boy at Saint Eloi. That had little to do with budding piety, and more with the fact that when they served at a marriage or baptism it was traditional for the groom or other participants to hand out sugar-coated almonds called *dragées* to the altar boys. Another tradition he respected was that on Good Friday the village children ran through the streets brandishing noisy wooden rattles. They made such a din that the townspeople gave them coins, candy and other goodies to make them stop—a form of trick or treat. At that he excelled.

One of his best friends was a youngster named Auguste Haring. His family owned a small farm outside town and Jean spent hours there, fascinated by how Auguste and his parents worked the land and took care of their animals. He occasionally lent a hand, milking and feeding the cows and cleaning out the stable. He also tended the chickens, ducks and rabbits. Instinctively he took to harvesting hay, handling horses, and guiding a horse-drawn plough through a field in a straight furrow. When not doing that, his next-favorite activity as he approached adolescence was train spotting. The track to Paris ran just behind the house and he could either watch the big locomotives rumble by from his bedroom window or, better, go stand on the embankment to get a better feel for their power. He especially liked the express trains that ignored Mériel and sped on by in a swirl of noise and dust and wind that fascinated him. His maternal grandfather, Louis Petit, had worked at the important Cail locomotive factory in La Charité. Jean peppered him with questions about how those big, beautiful, steam-snorting machines worked. The more he learned about them, the more he knew that he wanted to be a locomotive engineer. Many small boys want to drive trains, and Dr. Freud would no doubt have a theory to explain why. But in the case of Jean Gabin, it was an ambition that never quite left him—and that he would one day realize, thanks to a movie.

His mother psychologically unable to accept him, Jean came to rely on his affectionate big sister, Madeleine, 14 years his senior, as a surrogate. Given their difference in age, that began when he was very young. Their close relation continued after Madeleine married a professional boxer originally from Marseille, Jean Poësy. It was to them that he turned when things got rough at home. "It was with her and Jean Poësy that I found help, comfort, and understanding," he recalled to Brunelin. "Poësy, who was 16 years older than I, was a sort of big brother and the best of pals. I can say frankly that he is the only man I ever really loved in my life." The self-portrait that emerges is that of a boy starved for affection.

Poësy was Jean's kind of man, action-oriented and a lover of outdoor activities like hunting and fishing. He taught his young companion how to wet a line and carry a shotgun. He was a first-rate boxer, having beaten the British and European bantamweight champion, Digger Stanley, in a match at London's Covent Garden in 1912. He opened a training camp near Mériel for professionals and taught Jean the sport that he would practice for several years as an adolescent amateur—a stiff punch to his nose rearranged the cartilage and contributed to his later rugged screen profile. Jean's intense attachment to Poësy is seen in letters he sent him when the boxer was occasionally absent from the village. In one, revealing the result of playing hooky, with its almost illegible handwriting and spelling errors, he implores Poësy to come back soon from Marseille, where he opened another training camp. He eagerly promises to meet him at the train station, and signs it "Your Jean who will always love you." Came the war, and Poësy was mobilized as an army lieutenant. He fought in the bitter battles of the Argonne Forest in 1914, and the Somme in 1915. In the latter he was seriously wounded in September and had his left leg amputated. His family hid the news from Jean, then 11, until October 20, but when they did tell him, they avoided mentioning the amputation. He hastened to write a letter, touching in its naiveté and longing, to Poësy at the hospital:

> My Dear Poësy, I have learned that you were wounded and that you are at the hospital.... I hope you are doing well and that you are in good health. The big game hunting season has begun in Mériel, so I hope that when you come back to convalesce we will go hunting together and that we will bag lots of game. I think my letter will give you pleasure and will boost your morale. It is to be hoped that your wound is not too serious.... When you come back, I will ask to be with you, because you know how happy I will be to see you and to give you a big hug.... Can you start walking and washing yourself? The soup must be better in the hospital than in the trenches. Oh, if I had some money I would take the train and come to see you right now. I put all the money they give me in my piggy bank and don't spend a cent so I can buy you a good little treat when you come.... I end my letter hugging you with all my heart and with all the love I have for you. Your faithful and good pal, my brother.[7]

At the bottom of the page he drew a little vase full of flowers.

Needless to say, there would be no more tramping through the fields and woods with Poësy after they fitted him with a wooden leg. But there was another reason the rural life in Mériel was over for Jean: by late 1915 the front was moving ever closer. Cannon fire could be heard in the village. Ferdinand decided to take the family to Paris for greater safety. At first they lived with his sister-in-law, Louise, Jean's favorite aunt, while Ferdinand's brother, Marie-Auguste, was mobilized. Then he found a ground-floor apartment at 17 rue Custine in Montmartre, a short walk from La Cigale. Although the family would return briefly to Mériel once the Allies began to repel the Germans, Jean would now become a city boy, roaming the streets of Montmartre the way he had explored the fields of Mériel. Here he absorbed the working-class street smarts and slang that he would have for the rest of his life.

He dared hope at first that the move to Paris would mean he wouldn't have to attend school any more. Ferdinand put an end to that idea by quickly enrolling him in the local elementary school in nearby rue de Clignancourt. One classmate was Marcel Bleustein, who would later found the multinational Publicis advertising firm. As Bleustein later recalled the husky bully named Jean Moncorgé, "He was a force of nature and he slapped me around all the time."[8] Still, to everyone's surprise, Jean showed himself a more assiduous pupil, even passing the exam for the coveted elementary studies diploma that for most French youngsters in those days marked the end of formal schooling. That did not mean he suddenly began hitting the books. As he later explained, "Thanks to having learned to spot a partridge in flight or a fleeing hare in the fields, I could glance at a paper on the desk next to me and copy it. On exam day a buddy let me look over his shoulder and that's all it took to get my diploma."[9] Today one wall at the school bears a plaque commemorating the fact that such illustrious alumni as the former president Paul Doumer, the writer and member of the French Academy Jules Romains, and the actor Jean Gabin passed through its halls.

In early 1917 the war front stabilized sufficiently for Ferdinand to move the family back to Mériel. He hoped that Jean, having "successfully" completed his elementary schooling, would continue his studies. But, at 13, the restless boy thought only of leaving school to find a job and independence. As it happened, Ferdinand himself was unemployed, being between engagements, and found temporary work with the railway doing rails and ballast maintenance. To augment the skimpy family income he got Jean, underage but big for his years, hired on the same crew. It was hardly appropriate work for either of them; the father soon found another cabaret engagement and the son, thanks to his older brother Bébé, was hired as an office boy by the Paris electricity utility where he worked. That meant Jean had to catch the 6 a.m. train to Paris, and when he got there the job only amounted to cleaning offices and emptying wastebaskets. Still, it was his first real employment and he was proud of his first paychecks. But Ferdinand had other ideas for him.

It was, in fact, a serious misreading of Jean's rebellious personality, though on the face of it the idea certainly seemed a good one to Ferdinand. Somehow he used his relations to obtain a scholarship for his son at the prestigious Lycée Janson de Sailly in Paris' chic 16th arrondissement. The student Jean Moncorgé entered as a boarder in the fall of 1918, just as the war was drawing to an end. Most young men with any ambition would have jumped at the idea of attending what is still today considered one of the city's elite high schools. The trouble was, Jean was decidedly not one of the elite and had no desire to be one. His origins, which he bore proudly, were working class. His classmates were the offspring of professionals such as doctors, lawyers and high civil servants. They regularly attended *rallyes*, those super-snob Parisian parties organized by families of the *grande bourgeoisie* and aristocracy to help their progeny meet and, hopefully, marry, only young people of their own inbred kind—and certainly *not* pugnacious young men with broken noses and names like Moncorgé. His teachers were accustomed to dealing with such gilded youth and protective of the school's elitist reputation. They treated Jean, with his humble origins and uncouth manners, with all proper disdain and condescension. He occasionally revolted and used his fists in brawls with other students when it got to be too much for him, resulting in more sniffy scorn and disciplinary measures like refusing him permission to go out on weekends. It was an untenable situation.

His letters to Madeleine reveal the frustration and isolation he felt, the incomprehension he faced from Ferdinand. Neither could he count on any moral support, even though it would have been minimal, from Hélène, who died in her sleep that September. At one point he wrote his sister, "I'm bored stiff here. I told father that I was. I prefer not to remember his answer." Other letters concern his worries over getting the basic clothing he needed—shoes, socks, collars for his shirts—to avoid looking like a bumpkin. As the weeks wore on, the letters became increasingly desperate, like the one dated March 17, 1919:

> I have a headache all the time and now I've got a new cold.... I'm in an awful mood tonight and if I had a revolver handy I would blow my brains out because I'm so bored. I believe that I'm becoming more and more depressed. It's dreadful, another four months like this and I'll be dead! I saw my father Saturday night but he doesn't want to believe that I'm sick. But he'll see.... When I [words illegible] he'll be sorry maybe.... Come and visit me because you're the only one I can count on now. That will make me a little less bored. While waiting to see you, I hug you with all my heart.[10]

Jean Moncorgé wasn't made for school, and vice-versa. He stood the torment at Janson for five months, until the spring of 1919, before deciding that rebellion and defiance of his father was his only course. One night he packed up his few belongings, slipped out of the dormitory, and took the train back to Madeleine and Poësy in Mériel. Ferdinand was furious. He had pulled strings to get the scholarship to a prized school, and now he felt betrayed and humiliated. "You'll never be any good!" he bellowed when they met. "Do you hear? A good-for-nothing! I'm having nothing more to do with you!"[11] In a sense, Jean, at 15, was finally cut free to fend for himself. To *be* himself. But who was that?

The first thing was to show he could earn his living. He headed back to Paris and stayed with Aunt Louise in rue André del Sarte, in the familiar Montmartre neighborhood near where he had lived four years before. He took the first job he found, mixing cement for the new Gare de la Chapelle train station on the city's northern periphery. He was strong and big for his age, but this was hard labor and the pay was minimal. After a few months he quit and explored possibilities around Mériel. He found a spot as a laborer in a foundry not far away, in Beaumont-sur-Oise. That too was hard, dirty, menial work, and Jean's faithful Poësy saw that it was grinding him down prematurely. He found his nephew a job as a storekeeper in an automobile warehouse in Drancy, just north of Paris, where he himself now worked. There Jean made 12 francs a day, about $2.40. It was there that he acquired a lifelong taste for luxury cars—he owned a Buick and a Chrysler simultaneously when his career took off in the late 1930s, and drove only Mercedes after the war.

Bit by bit, father and son got back together. Ferdinand, perhaps trying to make up for being remiss in raising his son, now occasionally took him along with him to his favorite bistros and hosted him to a glass of *vin rouge* while he slapped down cards with his friends until 2 in the morning. There were also trips to play the horses at Longchamp and Auteuil. Some evenings, too, Jean accompanied him to his new gig at the Folies Bergère. There he had the run of the wings and dressing rooms and got his first taste of show business. Mostly, it disgusted him. Seeing half-naked showgirls change costumes between numbers wasn't bad, but what he found indecent was men putting on makeup just like women. Used as he was to the earthy reality of village life and countryside, he couldn't understand how anyone could take seriously something as obviously fake as the theater. The makeup, costumes, sets, lighting, artificial snow on stage—everything was phony, a hoax, in sum, "an enormous lie" as he put it. How could prancing around in a silly costume on stage compare with the manly work of driving a powerful steam locomotive at top speed? As he recalled later:

Jean after leaving home at 15, when his father declared he was good for nothing. His first jobs, hard menial labor, seemed to bear that out (Collection du Musée Jean Gabin).

> I detested my father's profession. What he did was incomprehensible to me. When I was little, I sometimes saw him in his room learning his lines. He tried one intonation, hesitated, and tried another one that still wasn't right. He also worked on his facial expressions. I had the feeling that he was suffering, and I said to myself that never, absolutely never, would I take up that profession. The effort he was making resembled what I went through when I was going over my schoolbooks. Learning a lesson of French history or the lines of a play seemed all the same to me. It was just as repellant. But one thing reassured me: I was certain that I would never be smart enough when I was grown up to know as much as my father did, and that I would never be able to do what he did because you had to know a lot.... I thought too that this profession of "lifetime student" was one he did to feed his family. So I had a sort of respect for him, and at the same time pity.[12]

Ferdinand, whose heart was in the right place despite years of neglect, was not ready to give up on his wayward son. He sat Jean down one day in 1922, and had a father-and-son talk. What would he really like to do, now that he was 18? When Jean answered stubbornly, "drive locomotives," Ferdinand checked his irritation and said that unfortunately he didn't have any connections in that field. But if he liked cars, he had a friend with an automobile garage in Paris and they could go see him about a job. Jean agreed that it could do no harm to check it out. But first, Ferdinand said, he had to run by the Folies to see a friend on the way. The friend turned out to be Pierre Fréjol, a former cabaret singer—and, since 1914, general manager of the Folies Bergère.

3

Becoming Gabin

The Folies manager, in on Ferdinand's ruse, hired the 18-year-old Jean Moncorgé on the spot. But agreeing to join Paris' most famous music hall of the day at 600 francs, about $120 a month, twice what he had been earning as a laborer, did not mean Jean had suddenly found a show business vocation. "I still hadn't changed my opinion about the stage," he said later, "and I'd decided that I would get out of there the first time something went wrong. But my reconciliation with my father was still too recent and fragile, and I didn't want to upset him. This way I was showing him I was willing to give it a try. When it didn't work out, he would finally have to admit that I wasn't cut out for this."[1]

His aversion to the theater must have been very strong indeed, for Jean was reluctant to take advantage of a career opportunity that any aspiring performer of the time would have killed for. The Folies Bergère, dating from 1869, was not only the first purpose-built Paris music hall, but also for many years the gold standard in France for popular entertainment. It was the French version of the great London music halls that began to appear in the Victorian 1850s. The English innovation, compared with traditional theaters, was led by the impresario Charles Morton, one of the first to use the expression "music hall." He created an open area with tables where the audience could have a drink and a meal while watching a revue composed of everything from class-act singers and dancers to clowns, trained dogs, performing seals, and the odd snake charmer.

The Folies and subsequent Paris establishments kept the English term music hall. (Despite the similarity, the name Folies is not akin to the English word "folly," but is said to derive from the Latin *foliae* and French *feuilles*, "leaves," the original, medieval site of the theater having been a garden with leafy shade trees where Parisians gathered for outings of singing and dancing; Bergère is name of an adjacent street.)[2] Besides professional singing and dancing, they served up a salmagundi of jugglers, tightrope walkers, acrobats and contortionists, elephants, strong men and wrestlers, and, on a lucky day, the great, the unique pétomane Joseph Pujol, all of which could be seen in a single kaleidoscopic show. The acerbic, erudite French writer J. K. Huysmans came away fascinated in 1879, calling it "ugly and superb … of an outrageous yet exquisite taste."[3]

Starting in 1907 it was the first to present nudes onstage; the novelist Colette, needing the money, was among them, scribbling novels in her dressing room between scenes. Much of the show was offstage. Charlie Chaplin, who appeared there in 1909 at the age of 20, later wrote, "No theater, I thought, ever exuded such glamor, with its gilt and plush, its mirrors and large chandeliers. In the thick-carpeted foyers and dress circle the world promenaded. Bejewelled Indian princes with pink turbans and French and Turkish officers with plumed helmets sipped cognac at liqueur bars."[4] Many gentleman patrons ignored the onstage activities entirely in favor of the heavily rouged and perfumed ladies available in the promenade area, of which Edouard Manet's famous painting, *Bar at the Folies Bergère*, gives some idea.

But the Folies was also famous for discovering talented new performers and showcasing them. Many became worldwide stars, like the ballerina Anna Pavlova and singers such as Yvonne Printemps and Yvette Guilbert. The debonair English playwright and actor Noël Coward was greatly impressed during a Paris visit in 1919 by what he called "the shock of seeing Paris music hall revues for the first time. I already had some idea of the power the French performers injected into their sad love songs, the hilarious low humor into the funny ones, their finesse in the witty ones and above all I had been bowled over by their glamor and the strength of their personalities."[5]

Of all the glamorous performers featured at the Folies, none were brighter than the duo of Mistinguett and Maurice Chevalier, who were to leave an indelible mark on early 20th-century showmanship. Mistinguett was born Jeanne-Florentine Bourgeois in 1875 in a working-class suburb of northern Paris. Her mother was a seamstress, her father refurbished old mattresses. Unlike Jean Moncorgé, she was fired with a burning ambition to get into show business, taking music and dancing lessons as soon as she could. Thanks to a chance encounter with an impresario, by the age of 18 she had her first contract at the Casino de Paris, warming up the audience. She went on to the Eldorado, and after ten years there was enough of a star to be known simply as La Miss. A perfectionist, her technique was impeccable, including how to descend gracefully a revue's inevitable grand staircase with several pounds of plumes on her head and a yards-long train of feathers behind, all with the requisite brilliant fixed smile.

In her extraordinarily long career of some 60 years she became the idol of Paris music hall revues. Her face was more wistful than beautiful, her voice unmusical, she was not an especially good dancer. What she did have that enthralled audiences was a dazzling pair of legs—rumor had it that she insured them for up to a million dollars—in a country where some shows imported English talent like the renowned Bluebell Girls to get the desired height for their chorus lines. That, along with a ferocious will to succeed and, like Jean, a *parigot* accent that Parisians identified with. The poet Jean Cocteau lauded her "implacable determination to shine with that light … which is the essence of stars."[6] But her greatest and most apt compliment came from the sculptor Auguste Rodin, who told her, "If I had to personify the Muse of music hall, without the peplum and the Greek profile, I would give her your legs."[7]

Her partner onstage and off, Chevalier, born in 1888, was the son of a house painter and a curtain maker. Like Jean, he knocked around at odd jobs, from acrobat to assembly line worker making thumbtacks. Evenings, he tried singing, dancing, and mime acts in cafes, eventually getting into music hall revues and becoming the partner and lover of one of France's biggest female stars, Fréhel. He ended their liaison in 1911 due to her self-destructive alcoholism and drug addiction, which was about the time when he caught Mistinguett's professional eye. Besides what she called his handsome little mug, she liked his unusual way of singing almost as if to himself, and his light-footed dancing. By then she was starring at the Folies Bergère, and she got him hired to do a comic dance number in which they knocked over all the furniture on stage. During one rehearsal, when the routine was to end the dance rolled up together in a rug, Chevalier remembered, "Miss was wrapped in my arms as we began to roll ourselves up into the rug. And suddenly my lips were pressed against hers, there in the dark and confining world of that carpet. Passionately, demandingly."[8] Their very public romance would last ten years, during which she polished the rough edges off his plebian manners and taught him how to tease and manipulate an audience.

This was the proud show business institution that Jean was hired to join in 1922. Naturally he was assigned only walk-on roles with nothing to say or do, parts that he called "lampposts in the distance."[9] That suited him fine. While the other beginners did everything they could to be noticed and get bigger parts, he stayed in his corner and did nothing more or less than what he was asked to do. Not only did he not mind being literally a spear-carrier, he actually liked it because it solved the eternal stage business problem of what to do with his hands.

Eventually he had to admit that this was considerably more pleasant than sand blasting in a foundry at half his present wages. Working evenings and Sunday matinees gave him plenty of time off for things like afternoons in the local bistro playing cards. He began to understand why his father had spent his life in this milieu. The people were friendly and helpful, the mores liberal and easy-going, and an added bonus were the battalions of pretty, available girls he could ask out and show off to his envious pals in Montmartre. All in all, not a bad job, but not one to be taken seriously, like driving locomotives. Still, as long as they didn't discover how untalented he was and fire him, it was an agreeable enough way to kill time while waiting to be called up for his obligatory military service.

Jean was underestimating himself as a performer. He turned out to have a good, clear, well-pitched singing voice, and as a dancer he had rhythm and supple grace. The others in the company appreciated his simple, unaffected manner and constant good humor—rare qualities in the often striving, backbiting world of the stage. He was quickly promoted to *boy* and singer in the chorus line, then to understudy for the male lead who played one of Napoleon's top marshals, Maurice de Saxe. Unlike the usual understudy, Jean did not pray that the lead would break a leg so he would have his chance to shine; his hope was that he would remain in obscurity and never be called to replace him.

One evening, however, the lead wanted to leave early and skip the finale, so he asked Jean to fill in. He knew the song well from having heard and practiced it dozens of times, but that night he panicked with a severe case of stage fright. The scene had him, resplendent in gaudy, 18th-century mock-marshal's uniform, blonde wig, and plumed kepi, standing on a little balcony. Below was a wagon full of naked virgins, peace offerings from a conquered town's notables. The music cued him, he opened his mouth to sing, and nothing came out. Attempting to control his case of *trac*, he unthinkingly took a step forward—off the balcony, plunging into the wagon full of giggling nudes. For a marshal of the Empire, the position was ridiculous. The audience loved it, everyone agreed that the act had never provoked such laughter, but management was not amused. He was not asked to replace anyone else for the duration of the revue. This, surely, confirmed Jean's conviction that he was not destined for a career on the boards.[10]

And yet, he appears to have had a change of heart. Instead of emphasizing the incident to Ferdinand as proof that there was no point in pursuing this line of work, as might be expected, he did the opposite. He never brought it up with his father, and when the revue ended after one year, and along with it his job, he immediately began to search for another engagement. Whether this was out of growing love of the métier or simply recognition that "acting the fool in public for a few francs," as his grandfather put it, was easy money, we can only conjecture. In any case, in April 1923 he landed a six-month contract at the handsome Théatre du Vaudeville on Boulevard des Capucines for walk-on parts. During the course of an evening he was successively an Egyptian guard, a sleeping-car conductor, a drunkard, and a pirate. If nothing else, he learned one of the basics of acting on stage: how to change costumes fast.

He now had begun to acquire a taste for his father's trade. Soon after that show closed, he signed for a minor part in an operetta called *La-Haut* at the Bouffes Parisiens, a famous mid–19th-century theater off Avenue de l'Opéra which had been created by the prolific composer and impresario Jacques Offenbach. The role had the advantage of being in an operetta rather than a music hall revue, giving him new professional experience. It featured two of the biggest names at the time. One was the comic Dranem, a precursor of the Charlie Chaplin character, who often performed with big shoes, wide pants, extra-tight jacket and funny little hat. The other, more important from Jean's viewpoint, was Chevalier, whom he idolized. "When Maurice Chevalier came on stage with his slim, athletic figure, his arms out to the audience and his smile, and sang his famous song *La-haut*, it was like the sun breaking out," he recalled. "And like idiots, we all tried to imitate him."[11] This contract was also important because his father sang in the show as the third male lead. It would be the first of only three times that father and son would appear on the same stage. That gave Jean the opportunity to observe him at close range and more fully appreciate, and admire, his hard work and professionalism.

When that show closed, the theater had already contracted for another operetta, *La Dame en Décolleté*, and engaged Jean for the brief part of bar tender in the first act. The part was insignificant—as in *La-haut*, he had only a few lines and no songs—but the job marked two turning points, one professional and one personal. First of all, management asked him to choose a stage name for the same reason that his father had eschewed Moncorgé. Jean talked it over with Ferdinand and tentatively suggested Gabin Junior. Ridiculous, replied the old pro. What would that look like on programs when he was 60? That had not occurred to Jean, who still had not quite digested the idea that he might remain all his life what he called, with some derision, a *saltimbanque*. The right stage name was after all obvious. Henceforth he will be Jean Gabin.

The operetta star. In 1923 he decided his stage name would be Jean Gabin (Collection du Musée Jean Gabin).

The other major event at this point in his life was his meeting with a young woman he noticed in the audience. Sitting there in a front-row seat every evening, she had mischievous black eyes, fetching dark bangs down her forehead, and fashionable spit curls on each cheek. As if to make her point that she came only to see him, she looked at him insistently and invariably left after the first act, when Gabin was no longer on stage. One night he overcame his basic shyness—he often described himself as *timide*, which can mean either shy or timid in English, but he was certainly not timid, especially with the ladies—left the theater after the first act, and accosted her. She was named Camille Basset, known as Gaby, and like him, she was trying to get a start in show business. Her mother, a young widow, had raised Gaby and her three sisters on what she could earn as a seamstress. She enrolled her as a teenage apprentice to learn the same trade.

Gaby had seen what the life of sewing other people's clothes was like, and wasn't having it. She was more interested in the shows at La Cigale, where Gabin's father had been master of ceremonies for so long, and where one of her girlfriends was a dancer. When a showgirl there fell sick, she boldly approached management and, sans dancing experience, proposed to fill in on the chorus line. The first night she tried the cancan she tripped and fell. Letting fly an explosive "*Oh merde!*" in frustration, she fled in tears to the wings while the audience burst into the biggest laugh of the evening. It was similar to Gabin's fiasco as Marshal de Saxe, with the difference that the director of La Cigale was smart enough to ask her to come back and do the same stunt every night. After the show closed she hit the *café chantant* circuit, singing and dancing for whatever fee she could pick up.[12]

The young Gabin had known any number of women. Not only were they attracted to him, but early on he appears to have had an imperative need of femininity in his life, and not only for the physical side. His numerous affairs, real and rumored, would be a continuing theme through the years. If we are to believe a story that he told a Hollywood movie magazine in 1942, he met his first love in Paris when he was 19. Josette, three years older than he, was a midinette, an office girl doubling as a café singer at night, "a brown-eyed madonna-face framed in pale gold hair." (Was it the lack of maternal affection that drew Gabin to older women? Speculation is easy, but the fact is that nearly all those with whom he had a serious relationship before the war were older, the singular exception being Michèle Morgan.) He wanted to marry her. He gave her a ring that stood for an informal engagement, telling her it was "for always." But one evening when he went to pick her up, she was gone. At the café where she sang they gave him an envelope containing the ring and a Dear Jean letter. It is difficult to evaluate the authenticity of the story, written as it is in the florid prose of 1940s Hollywood. It could have been generated by a studio press agent to feed the voracious, indiscriminate appetite of fanmags and promote the image of Gabin as the great French lover. In any case, he never denied it.[13]

What is certain is that for most of his stage and movie career he admitted freely that he often liked to, as he put it, court his leading ladies. Shortly before meeting Gaby he was rumored to have been squiring one Marthe Davelli, a former leading singer at the Opéra Comique then onstage with Gabin at the Bouffes Parisiennes. Connoisseurs of such things considered her one of the most beautiful women in town; she also was a fashion setter, one of the first to wear the designs of a new couturière named Coco Chanel. But Gaby Basset, at 22 two years older than he, was the first woman he would cohabit with. Possessing barely a few francs between them, planning to live, as the French say, on love and fresh water, they moved in together at a shabby Montmartre hotel in rue de Clignancourt, not far from his old school. As Gaby later described those days:

> The conveniences, as they say, were down the hall. We slept in an awful iron bed that made a racket every time we moved. We didn't have a cent and many times not much to eat, getting along on hard-boiled eggs. But we didn't care, at least at the beginning, because we were still very much in love. Jean was so handsome! Women liked him and there's no doubt that he knew it. With his face he didn't have to do much to attract them. He was sweet, not at all mean or cynical. He was a smooth talker, had a cocky sense of humor, and was fun to be around. Despite his shyness he was very forward with the

girls. I was mad about him. Those were hard times, but we got through them together and managed to have a lot of laughs. Still, there was a little problem between us. I really wanted to have a career, either as a singer or actress, whereas he didn't give a damn about that. He was just "passing through" show business, as he put it. "Can you see me clowning around on a stage all my life?" he said. "I'm a man. I could never get used to putting on makeup." He had his military service to do, and then he said he wanted to be a locomotive engineer. I never knew whether he really believed that when he said it.[14]

For the moment, it's clear that Gabin still had not fully resigned himself to a show business career. When the time came to answer the draft in 1924, he was assigned to a unit of navy fusiliers and sent to the port at Lorient, in Brittany. Disciplined obedience never having been his strong point, his superiors soon labeled him a *forte tête*, an insubordinate rebel. As if to prove they were right, one day he socked a non-com who gave him an order he didn't like, landing him in the brig and getting him a mandatory extension of three months more service time.[15]

He lived for his periods of leave, when he could race back to Paris and Gaby, whom he called Pépette, but those were too few and too short. Then he hit on the solution: married draftees benefited from longer and more frequent leaves. Neither he nor Gaby had thought marriage necessary, but here was a tangible advantage. They wed in early 1925 at the town hall of the 18th arrondissement behind the Sacré Coeur and just up the street from rue de Clignancourt. Ferdinand, probably glad that his son seemed ready to settle down with a young woman who appreciated the entertainment world, made them the gift of their rings and paid for the modest wedding banquet in a Montmartre bistro. Gaby's mother Josephine, who opposed her marriage to a man with so few prospects, refused to attend.[16]

4

Moulin Rouge

Jean returned to the naval base in Lorient and Gaby went to live in the Moncorgé house in Mériel. When he came there on leave she discovered a man different from the swaggering, slang-spouting city boy she had known. He showed her the green, tree-bordered Oise with its little ferry that he had taken on that memorable escapade. He took her walking on his favorite paths through the woods. He showed her the monumental stone cross where Marshal Lannes' descendent was struck by lightning, and where he had bivouacked with the Zouaves. On one outing he surprised her by stooping down in a field, scooping up a handful of soil and breathing in deeply its fragrance, exclaiming, "That smells so good!"[1] He promised her that one day they would have their own little farm.

In the last months of his service he was posted to sentry duty in Paris at the Naval Ministry on Place de la Concorde. Nice duty if you can get it. Gaby worried about all the pretty girls who seemed attracted to the building's main entrance where he stood guard; only half-jokingly she called him the Casanova of Clignancourt. They moved back into a Montmartre hotel, or rather a succession of scruffy hotels, for sometimes they were evicted for failure to pay the bill. When the hardboiled eggs ran out, they shared thin sandwiches. They also shared a bowl of *café au lait*, adding more milk when it was half-empty. The continuing hard times led Jean to swallow his pride and write Ferdinand what was obviously a difficult letter on April 9, 1925:

> Dear Father, I'm going to ask you for something, but don't get excited! Especially since I don't want to upset you while you are rehearsing…. Of course, it's money that I'm going to ask you for. But wait! If you can't manage it, too bad! If you can, all the better, that would help me out. Voilà! I know you have a lot of expenses this month, but I prefer to ask you rather than just anybody. I'm already embarrassed to ask it of you, and it would be worse with others. Now I'm going to get to the point. Could you LEND, NOT GIVE me, because I will pay you back little by little, of course, 300 francs? I can just imagine how you look right now!!! You know that it's not to have more fun. It would be separate from what you give me every week. It would be a service to me. As I say, if you can't, too bad. But above all, don't tell anybody, and when I come to see you at the theater, don't yell and bawl me out. That's all I ask. I'll come to see you and you'll give me your answer. No hard feelings, huh!… Your son, J. Gabin.[2]

The letter, with its awkwardly formal signature "J. Gabin," is surprising in its embarrassed diffidence on the part of a young man who usually let his feelings be known in no uncertain terms. It shows that relations between the son and his choleric father are still strained despite their reconciliation. It reveals that Ferdinand has been helping to support the young couple financially, giving them money every week. And if Jean asks him not to speak to anyone about the loan, it is likely because other members of the family were also helping finance him and he didn't want his father to know.

Ferdinand further helped the young couple by pulling his show business strings to get a part for Gaby in a new show at the Bouffes Parisiens with the titillating title *Trois Jeunes Filles Nues* (*Three Nude Young Girls*) in December 1925. One of the biggest successes of France's pre-war theater, running for 381 performances at the Bouffes before moving on to other theaters until 1941, it had a brief career in French on Broadway in 1929, and was made into a French film starring Annabella that same year. It again starred Dranem, who was then, in a different style, almost as popular as Maurice Chevalier, and Ferdinand as third male lead. Gaby gained her first professional recognition in the role of "the lobster woman," requiring her to carry around a fake lobster, which for some reason must have seemed hilarious in those days.[3]

Gabin was less inclined to merriment, being discharged from the navy in early 1926 after two years of service, with no job and none in view. The first tremors of the Great Depression were already being felt in France, an early taste of the economic, social, and political turmoil that was to roil the country in the 1930s. Again Ferdinand lent a hand, getting his son a part as an understudy in the musical. That was better than moping around in the cheap hotel room he and Gaby again shared, but he was once more relegated to the wings to watch others perform. Mentally he still had one foot in and one foot out of show business. He made a secret vow to himself. "In deciding to take up acting again, mainly due to the economic crisis," he recalled, "I gave myself five years, not one more, to succeed in this profession. I was determined to make a name for myself, to find my place in the sun, and not be a second-rate performer all my life. Otherwise I would hang it up and do something else."[4]

At first, his return to the stage was lucky. The actor for whom he was the understudy left the show in September 1926 for another engagement, again giving Gabin the opportunity to appear on stage with his father—and this time with his wife. The program lists him well up, above Gaby, and the photo shows him in handsome profile, hair fashionably slicked back.[5] He appreciated the irony of playing a young naval officer only months after having been a lowly swabbie. This was his first actual singing role in a musical and was considered a success. But the show closed at the Bouffes in early 1927. While Gaby went back to singing on the café and music hall circuit in the suburbs, he was again reduced to knocking on producers' doors and being told, "Don't call us, we'll call you."

Finding no roles in operettas, Gabin decided to try the same route as Gaby. He didn't have her driving ambition and self-confidence, but he made the rounds of music shops, chose a selection of popular scores and started practicing, imitating Chevalier. After a few auditions he got brief engagements in dingy Paris suburbs like Clichy and Asnières. "The theaters were seedy," he remembered, "the stages were swept by drafts that gave me colds, the curtains so full of dust they made me sneeze, the seats squeaked loudly whenever members of the audience moved."[6] All this for about $10 a night—when a fly-by-night impresario didn't take off with the box office receipts.

But he was overcoming his stage fright and shyness at being alone on stage. He was even beginning to enjoy holding an audience, bringing it along with each song, and drinking in the applause at the end. "It was a hard and magnificent school, better than any other," he told the journalist Merry Bromberger, who interviewed him for the newspaper *L'Intransigeant* in 1937. "I learned how to handle myself, to be real." Also at this time, 1927, he became a dues-paying member of the Confédération Général du Travail (CGT), the hard-line communist labor union that did what it was told by the French Communist Party—especially when to hold street demonstrations and go on strike to weaken the French government in particular or the capitalist system in general. His membership card, number 4,185, lists his profession as *artiste dramatique*. The back of the card reminds members it is their duty to read the newspaper *Le Peuple*, official organ of the CGT.[7] Judging by cards I have seen, he remained a member at least until 1951, when he was 47, but there is no indication that he ever actively participated in its events. Most likely, joining a labor union at the time was considered the thing to do in a country that had a high percentage of union membership; it may even have been a prerequisite for getting show business jobs. But his long-time adherence to the CGT in particular, when other labor union memberships were available, is consonant with his identification with the working class.

One evening in Clichy an impresario approached him after the show and asked if he would like to go on tour in Brazil, along with Gaby. With no other options, visions of a luxury cruise and a grand hotel in Rio dancing in his head, he accepted and they embarked on the Royal Mail Lines ship *Andes* for the seven-day crossing. The first disappointment for Gabin was that the ship was British. That meant English food, a gastronomic hell for him, and cup after cup of tea instead of his preferred red wine. The arrival in Rio was another disappointment, the hotel being a dump not much better than the one they had left in Montmartre. As they sang excerpts from France's most popular operettas, Gaby noticed one thing in particular in the theater: a fiery Brazilian chanteuse named Lolita Vasquez from a cabaret across the street came regularly, sat in the front row, and had eyes only for Gabin. It was a technique that Gaby knew only too well. She threw a jealous tantrum, he replied in kind about a suspicious bijou that a wealthy Brazilian admirer had given her, and they ended the evening in tears and tender reconciliation.

The tour over, they returned to Montmartre to blow their earnings on lavish dinners in the best bistros, and a fancy racing bike for him. He rode the bike everywhere, it eventually becoming an indelible part of his persona, like the accordion he learned to play, and stamping him as the typical proletarian Frenchman of that period. He was proud of his conditioning, as his friend and fellow actor Marcel Dalio, who would star with him years later in *La Grande Illusion*, recalled in his memoirs: "Jean Gabin made his grand entry in the brasserie after parking his bicycle at the door. He was a good-looking guy in a flat cap, with big light-colored eyes and a muscular body that he conscientiously kept in shape. Jean always got noticed wherever he went. We found him intelligent, but he didn't talk much."[8] His friends knew that Gabin always preferred slapping cards on a table to conversation. Even Gaby often wondered what was going on when he was silent for hours. Was he angry about something? No, he would reply, just mulling. She never could figure out about what.

Gabin was ready in early 1928 to continue, if need be, his career singing in drafty, dusty music halls when he heard that Jacques-Charles, one of the best-known producers of the day, was putting together a group of singers for a South American tour. He had mixed memories of his Brazil tour, but Jacques-Charles had a big reputation and this could lead to something. He went to the Moulin Rouge, where auditions for the group were being held, and joined a gaggle of about a hundred other candidates, most of whom he knew had more professional experience than he did. There were only ten spots to be filled. When his turn came he picked one of his favorite pieces, a Chevalier song of course, handed the score to the pianist, and launched into it. Dazzled by the footlights, he couldn't see who was sitting in the front row beside the producer. When he finished, the stage manager came up and asked him if he had another song. He did another Chevalier and sat down. The auditions over, he was about to leave when the stage manager told him La Miss, who had been sitting in the dark of the theater, wanted to speak to him. Wouldn't he, she asked, rather join her in her new revue at the Moulin Rouge than go to South America? He couldn't have hoped for a better break than to act with a star of her magnitude, but he summoned up the nerve to ask for 60 francs per night. She countered with 40 and they shook on it.[9]

But what was Mistinguett doing at that audition and why did she single him out? It seems likely that Ferdinand, who had been master of ceremonies at La Cigale when she performed there, knew La Miss. It's also likely that, knowing Gabin was going to audition, he suggested she check him out. As to why she chose him that day, it was likely because his selection of Chevalier songs and his imitation of his style touched her. She had been deeply in love with Chevalier, who had been wounded and imprisoned by the Germans early in World War I. She had done everything from working for French espionage to leaning on admirers like Italy's King Victor-Emmanuel III and Spanish King Alfonso XIII, to obtain his release from a POW camp in 1916.[10]

When Chevalier returned to France a broken man, taking to alcohol and drugs, she stood by him and commissioned the famous song *Mon Homme*, quickly translated into English and a worldwide hit, as a token of her support. Now though, their affair had ended years ago—he had married the French actress Yvonne Vallée and was beginning his film career in Hollywood with Paramount—and she was getting over him with an English dancer named Earl Leslie. She was on the point of dumping the handsome Leslie because of his wandering eye and alcoholism, and at 53 was emotionally vulnerable. With his echoes of Chevalier, Gabin attracted her, and not only professionally, despite the 28-year difference in their ages.[11]

At the apogee of her career, known as the music hall Sarah Bernhardt, she was now *directeur artistique* at the Moulin Rouge. No mean position, for the Moulin Rouge had long been a Paris entertainment institution to rival the Folies Bergère. Located in the heart of the city's 19th-century entertainment district, between Place de Clichy and Place Pigalle, its four rotating, illuminated red blades echoed the few remaining windmills atop the Montmartre monticule. Its grand opening in October 1889 competed for attention with the Eiffel Tower, completed that same year for the Paris Universal Exposition. One breathless account went,

> Last evening the Tout Paris inaugurated it, and the show was as much in the theater as on stage, with His Highnesses Prince Stanislas de Poniatowski and Troubetzkoï, the Count de la Rochefoucauld, Monsieur Hélie de Talleyrand-Périgord, and the fine fleur of the arts. Imagine the fine carriages coming from the elegant neighborhoods of Neuilly and Passy joyfully slumming with the natives of Montmartre and Rochechouart, hooligans in flat caps and young ladies with chignons.… Imagine too the collective delirium when the dance called the "naturalist quadrille" came on.… Never have we seen people have such fun. It's indescribable! You have to have lived it to believe it![12]

The naturalist quadrille referred to would come to be known, in demotic French, as *le french cancan*. It is believed to have evolved from the courtly quadrille for four couples as early as the 1840s. When it became the cancan, it was originally performed by both men and women, the high kicks being performed by the men.[13] Then in 1861 the enterprising Charles Morton introduced it in a spiced-up version at his Oxford Music Hall until the London authorities adjudged it immoral and banned it. It now included splits, physiologically limiting it to women. In the strait-laced Britain of the time, some considered it a challenge to social conventions, not to say a grievous danger to Victorian mores. At the Moulin Rouge, however, it was mainly a pretext for showing black stockings, a naughty bit of thigh, and cascades of frothy petticoats as shrieking girls did high kicks, cartwheels and splits to the frenzied rhythm of Offenbach's *Infernal Galop*.[14]

Besides the cancan, Mistinguett's revues featured up to 200 performers on stage, including dozens of bare-breasted showgirls.[15] Every evening she herself had up to 11 changes of costume, from waif to streetwalker to superstar descending the grand staircase in sumptuous if scanty furs and feathers.[16] In one spectacular tableau she gave the illusion of being trapped in a forest fire, complete with burning trees. She ruled her cast with an iron hand and a keen eye for detail. If one of the girls in the chorus line was an inch too short, she was replaced. If a dancer's shoes were scuffed, they had to be shined. If a spotlight went out during the performance, she would notice it and slip code words into her routine to signal the electrician to change the bulb at the next intermission. Before shows she would give the cast a little pep talk along the lines of "Look sharp tonight, girls, the king of Spain is in the audience." The cast griped about the discipline like army recruits, calling her Missolini behind her back, but respected her professionalism.[17]

Joining La Miss on April 18, 1928, for the premiere of her lavish new revue, *Paris qui Tourne*, launched Gabin on the most popular show running in Paris. When he signed to do it, he had the impression that he would be just one of the *boys* in the chorus. Instead, she gave him several numbers in which he sang and danced with her, letting him shine. Still in thrall to Chevalier, perhaps wanting to show him she could create his replacement just as she had created him, she initially wanted Gabin to sing and dance in top hat, white tie and tails à la Chevalier, but that manifestly was not his style. She converted him to a more convincing *mauvais garçon* in apache-style striped jersey, baggy checked pants and tight jacket. In one number, looking like a cheeky street urchin, he had his hand poised as if to tap her on the bottom.

That raised no Parisian eyebrows, but the show did create a scandal with the sketch called "Madame du Barry's Salon." In it Mistinguett, playing the mistress of Louis XV, avoids the revolutionary guillotine by suggestively raising her skirt to reveal the famous legs. Royalists protested vigorously and the police commissioner made her drop the number.[18] Gabin got some good press, though certain critics warned him he would do well to find his own style. "Monsieur Gabin," wrote one, "who has a real knack for show business, would do better to shake off the influence Maurice Chevalier has on him, as indeed he does on many of our young singers."[19] But now he felt better about his prospects of making a name for himself within the five years he had allotted. "The days of walk-on parts were over for me, thanks to La Miss, who knew how to make her partners stand out," he recalled. "At least, as long as they didn't put her in the shade. And I wasn't at that point yet."[20]

As for persistent rumors of an affair with Mistinguett, they were probably just that. She liked Gabin well enough, at least, to indulge his frequent requests for a raise. After a few weeks he knocked on her dressing room door and explained that it was hard to get along in Paris on 40 francs a day. She raised him to 60. After a while he knocked again and claimed a producer was putting together a South American tour where he could make more. She got the point and raised him to 100, commenting more or less good-naturedly,

"I don't think there's any danger you'll end up in the poor house." When they had a spat, she would call him a pig. That led to his giving her a piglet with a ribbon around its neck that she long kept at her country house in Bougival, west of Paris. Gabin was one of the few who had the right to use the familiar *tu* form of address and had his own pet name for her, Mick. Gaby was convinced she just liked to have him around. "Mistinguett had a soft spot for Jean," she once said. "She appreciated his talent and found him charming and funny, the way he could be with women. I believe they flirted a little, nothing more. Oddly enough, she was jealous, liking to be surrounded by men, but without their wives. We were the ones who should have been jealous, given the way she attracted our men and tried to have them to herself."[21]

After that show closed, Mistinguett went on to produce one at the Casino de Paris. Gabin stayed on at the Moulin Rouge to be second male lead in a new revue, *Allô, ici Paris*. It opened on January 18, 1929, with the 40-year old American singer and actress Elsie Janis as female lead. But she lacked the star power of La Miss and the show closed after a short run. It had the distinction of being the last Moulin Rouge revue for many years. In a sign of the changing times for entertainment, the owner suddenly announced to the cast rehearsing a new show that he had sold it to the film production and distribution company Pathé Natan. It would now become a movie theater.

For the Red Mill it meant that it would be a long time before *le French cancan* would be seen there again. For Jean Gabin it meant that he had done his last music hall revue.

5

First Films

Past now were the days when Jean Gabin had to run to auditions and keep his fingers crossed that he would get a part. Leading show business producers were beginning to see him as a valuable property. One was the versatile impresario and lyricist Albert Willemetz. Besides being a prominent figure in the entertainment business, Willemetz served as secretary to Prime Minister Georges Clemenceau during the First World War. Following that, he was the incredibly prolific author of dozens of musicals. As it happened, Willemetz had also written *Trois Jeunes Filles Nues*, and liked what he saw of Gabin's performance.

In March 1929, having become manager of the Bouffes Parisiens, he asked Jean to take the comic male lead in his new musical, *Flossie*, due to open in May. It would be a one-year contract at 3,000 francs, about $600, per month. It was the juiciest proposal Gabin had ever had, but now he was sure enough of himself to reply by letter on March 27 in coolly professional terms pinning down every contractual advantage: it would be for one year, starting May 1; he would be paid 3,000 francs beginning on that date; he would be the comic male lead and his name in the playbill would be printed in letters appropriate to that and on a single line.[1]

All that agreed upon, *Flossie* opened at the Bouffes Parisiens on May 9 for a run of 327 performances. Gabin played opposite Jacqueline Francell, the top operetta singer of the day, who had the title role. Both the public and the critics loved it—it would go on to other theaters for seven years—and praised Gabin for his ability as a comic. (Ironically, the actor who would be associated mainly with tragic roles during his early film career was at first typecast as a comedian.) One critic went so far as to declare, "Monsieur Gabin has many fine qualities, including a quiet authority and humor. He reminds one of Sacha Guitry." Given Guitry's immense standing at the time as a stage actor, that was high praise indeed.[2]

The astute Albert Willemetz knew a bankable talent when he saw one. Six months after the opening, he signed Gabin to a three-year contract at the Bouffes to start September 1930. Jean was happy with the deal, but some dreams die hard. At 25 he still considered the stage no more than a means to the end he had set himself as a boy in Mériel. As he remembered his attitude at the time:

> It was the jackpot. I figured that three years with that salary would get me to the end of 1932. I would then be nearly 30, and in only a few more years I could stop being an entertainer. If I was careful and put aside a little of all that dough, I would probably be able to buy myself a little farm in Normandy, and I would be through with the theater.... I'd dropped the idea of becoming a locomotive engineer.

That was kid's stuff, but I thought more than ever about having some land with cattle on it. And I had every reason to believe that with this contract with old man Willemetz I was on my way to getting it.[3]

Life was good. After earning his living singing in *Flossie*, Gabin had plenty of time for keeping in shape. He played soccer with an actors' sports club and tried his hand at tennis, which he quickly dropped as being too dainty and bourgeois for his taste. (Similarly, he tried golf in middle age and quit after a few futile swings, calling it "a game for idiots." In both cases, the basic problem was simply that such rich men's games didn't fit with his working-class self-image.)[4] In 1920s France, biking was the consuming national pastime. Gabin could reel off the names of all the winners of that weeks-long mid-summer ritual, the Tour de France—he was enough of an expert to be a guest commentator on French state radio during one Tour—and, in winter, the six-day races at Paris' enclosed Vélodrome d'Hiver with its inclined wooden track.

For him it wasn't only a spectator sport. His custom-made racing bike was built to his specifications at a small workshop in suburban Neuilly. He was inseparable from it even during the war and his exile in the U.S. Now he was going out virtually every morning for a round in the Bois de Boulogne with friends like Alfred Letourneur, the professional cyclist known in America as the Red Devil because of the red jerseys he always wore, who set a world speed record of 108 miles per hour. (He was the subject, jersey and all, of Edward Hopper's 1937 painting, *French Six-day Bicycle Rider*.) On one vacation

Gabin (left) was inseparable from his racing bike. Here he was cycling through France with his friend Alfred Letourneur, a professional cyclist, circa 1930 (Collection du Musée Jean Gabin).

jaunt, Gabin and friends did a mini Tour de France of nearly 1,200 miles through the Loire Valley, Brittany, and Normandy.

He also had time to experiment with acting in silent films when Gaumont, the world's first studio, founded in 1895 by Léon Gaumont, invited him to try two short subjects in 1930. Gabin and Raymond Dandy, who had been together at the Moulin Rouge, did two eminently forgettable subjects, *L'Heritage de Lilette* and *Les Lions*. The result left Gabin unimpressed. For one thing, his blond hair looked grey on the screen. For another, silent films deprived him of what had been one of his main attributes until then, his voice. Most of all, he was horrified by the way the camera treated his face. "The only thing I saw on the screen was my nose," he remembered. "I knew it was big, like all the Moncorgés, and it had been broken when I was boxing. But this! When I saw *that* in the middle of my face, I said to myself that movies weren't for me, even if they did become, as the producers promised, talking and singing."[5] So when the big German film studio UFA offered him a contract shortly thereafter to star in one of their first talkies, a musical entitled *The Three from the Filling Station* with the English leading lady Lilian Harvey, he turned it down. He had been discouraged by his appearance in the shorts, he didn't want to go to their Berlin studios for the shoot, and, perhaps most important, he had personal reasons for staying in Paris.

The fact was that Gabin's head was again turned by his leading lady. Jacqueline Francell was the attractive daughter of a leading tenor at the Paris Opera, Fernand Francell, and herself a first-rate singer. Before starting a career in operetta with *Flossie*, she had sung Mozart's *The Magic Flute* and *The Marriage of Figaro* in Paris. She would go on to do a few other operettas and also a dozen films, including one in Hollywood with Maurice Chevalier, *The Way to Love*, in 1933. True to form, Gabin began courting her, fell in love, and began an affair. It didn't take long for the worldly-wise Gaby to get wind of it and have a showdown with him. This was serious, he told her. She said in that case they should get a divorce. As it was, they had not been spending a lot of time together, she being much in demand as a cabaret singer and comedienne. They decided to divorce by mutual consent in early 1930. As she recalled it:

> With a tender, sad little smile, he said, "So there we are, Pépette, we're separating for good?" I was really hurt, but I hid it. "I'll never forget you, you know," he said. And that was true all the way to the end. Every chance he had, he got me a part in his films. I was so happy to get back together with him on a movie that I sometimes complained when I thought it had been too long since I heard from him. Later, when he was settled down, he introduced me to his wife Dominique, and when his children, of whom he was so proud, were born, he asked me over to see them. After our separation, he continued to involve himself in my life. Sometimes abusively. One day, when he was bicycle racing in the Bois de Boulogne with Albert Préjean and several cycling professionals, he learned that one of them, Jean Cugniot, was my fiancé. He made a point of beating him in the race, and then came over to me and made a scene. Jean was always like that, all of a piece, and a little jealous of what had belonged to him. With time, at least in my case, he got over it.[6]

Immediately after *Flossie* closed, he opened as second male lead in the operetta *Arsène Lupin Banquier* at the Bouffes Parisiens on May 7, 1930, with Francell again the leading lady. Also in the cast was Gabin père. This marked the last time father and son would appear together on stage—and the first time Jean's name would be higher in the playbill than Ferdinand, who chose to use the name Joseph Gabin to avoid confusion, leading some to wonder whether Gabin was beginning to eclipse his father as an entertainer.

It was to be a case of lucky in work, unlucky in love. He had decided to separate from Gaby because he believed he had begun something serious with Jacqueline Francell. But now, when he decided to make his move and proposed, she turned him down, yielding to opposition from her family. Although he did eventually have three marriages, it was one of the paradoxes of Jean Gabin's private life that Francell would be the first of several women who rejected marriage with him. This for a man whom women reputedly found irresistible, who in fact had many well-documented affairs, and was sold to the American public as the Great French Lover.

Good troupers, they nonetheless continued to act together in the operetta until it closed on December 7, 1930. But Gabin's professional luck held. One day that autumn he received an intriguing letter from Pathé Natan. Founded in 1896 by Charles, Émile, Théophile and Jacques Pathé, it was by then the largest film equipment and production company in the world. It was also an important producer of phonograph records, and the inventor of the newsreel (and in the U.S., producer of the famous 1914 serial *The Perils of Pauline*). It had recently been acquired by the dynamic Franco-Romanian actor and director Bernard Natan, and the letter invited Gabin to drop by their studios in the Paris suburb of Joinville le Pont. When he did, they explained that, with the industry now pivoting toward talkies, they were looking for actors who could sing and dance in their musicals. Would he like to audition with them? He agreed more out of courtesy than conviction, and returned a few days later for the tryout. Although he affected a casual indifference to motion pictures at this time, he surely was aware that Pathé, the first to industrialize filmmaking and a leader in world film distribution long before Hollywood, represented the big time.

The professional culture shock was greater than he expected. The movie set was to him an impersonal, incomprehensible machine where technique counted for all and the actor seemed to be a mere cog. He tripped over cables, moved awkwardly out of shot, turned his back to the camera, spoke his lines inaudibly to the microphone on a boom above his head. The director, cameraman and soundman all barked confusing commands at the same time. Trying to concentrate on staying within his marks, projecting his voice upward, and facing the camera, he was stiff and artificial. He was relieved when the director called "cut" and he could head back to the Bouffes Parisiens with its comfortable stage where he had only to please the public, not a camera and a gang of technicians.[7]

Two days later he received another letter from Pathé Natan, this one asking him to come back. The meeting was in the office of Bernard Natan himself. Gabin went, expecting a polite explanation that they were sorry, but it hadn't worked out. No matter, he had a solid contract with Willemetz for some time to come to do operettas. Maybe they would even pay him a pittance for his pains. But no, they wanted him to sign a contract for a film that paid 500 francs a day. It was to be a 20-day shoot, meaning the total would be more than twice what he was making doing operettas. Incredulous, he asked whether they had actually seen the audition. It was fine, they replied, just sign here. "Without quite understanding what was happening, I signed and left with a small advance on my contract. But I half-expected them to come running after me to ask that I give it back because there had been a misunderstanding."[8] He might well have been dazed by this turn of events, for suddenly it was raining money. Gabin was now double dipping, acting on the Pathé set all day for the shoot, and showing up in the evening for the operetta.

Filming of the providentially named *Chacun sa Chance/Everybody Gets His Chance* began that fall. It was a Franco-German production shot in both languages with actors from both countries, as was the frequent practice in those days to spread costs and max-imize box office. Gabin was delighted to find that he was playing opposite Gaby Basset, who had signed with Pathé Natan for three years. Also in the cast was Jean Sablon, who would soon after quit cinema to concentrate on his successful singing career in France and the U.S.

In this bit of fluff Gabin played a simple department store salesman who somehow is mistaken for a baron who happens to be in prison. Being an ersatz noble naturally improves his chances of winning the heart of the salesgirl in the chocolate shop across the street. He and Gaby frolicked and sang in the high-pitched voices then in fashion, and danced a bit awkwardly—"when he moved, it was like a bear in a cage," wrote one critic.[9] Doubtless they felt inhibited by the constraints of filming. But when it was released on December 19, 1930, most reviewers liked it. "Jean Gabin makes an excellent start in talking films.... There seems to be no doubt about his movie career," said one. Wrote another, "Jean Gabin comes across as an excellent talkie actor, perfectly at ease, whimsical without going too far, with a good voice for the microphone … reminiscent of Maurice Chevalier."[10]

Before the film was released, Gabin wrote a letter to Ferdinand on December 10, 1930, giving him all the latest news. It casts an instructive light on how he felt about his new situation, about himself, and his evolving relationship with Ferdinand.

He said he hadn't seen the finished film yet, so he didn't know whether he was any good in it, but he thought Gaby had done well. With some shy pride and self-astonishment, he explained that he had already signed to do another film, a musical that Willemetz had written especially for him. Not only that, but Henri Varna, manager of the Casino de Paris, was promising him a lucrative three-year contract to do revues, including one with Mistinguett. He felt his moment was finally coming. Varna promised him that, Chevalier's latest Paris show before he headed back to America having been a flop, he would now be the number one music hall entertainer in Paris. "But no more promises," he vowed, "I want acts.... I'm not a little boy any more. You know I'm shy, and when a shy guy goes into action, look out!" He showed a new determination to succeed, even if acting was still only a means to an end. "I only ask God for one thing, and that's enough good health to work hard, because you have to work hard when you want to succeed, and I *want* [his emphasis] to become somebody. I'm 26, at 40 I want to quit."

The letter's last lines are touching in their solicitousness for his father, then 62, with his promise to be there for him if ever he needed it:

> But I've bored you enough about me. How about you? Be careful, don't catch cold, and just be patient about getting through the rest of your career. If things go as I hope, when you get back [from touring the provinces] you can tell them to go to hell and you can go take it easy in Mériel with my sister, and get out of this rotten profession. It will be your turn. Again, no kidding, if ever you don't feel well on tour, drop it and don't worry about it, I'm here now. Goodbye old father, I hug you affectionately with all the love I have for you. Your good-for-nothing son who's doing pretty well all the same![11]

He was indeed doing well. Movie contracts started coming fast now. He would do six films in 1931 alone, by 1933 he had done 15. He was being noticed not only by studios eager for new talent. He was also attracting the attention of some first-rate directors like Jean Grémillon, who would work with him in two films. "Jean Gabin had a very special personality," Grémillon later recalled. "His acting—he was so natural that he didn't seem to be 'acting,' but we know how hard it is to look that natural—had a simplicity and effective-ness that were entirely new at a time when many great theater actors tended to exaggerate

With his ex-wife Gaby Basset in his first feature-length film, *Chacun sa Chance*, 1930. Reviewers predicted a successful movie career for him (Collection du Musée Jean Gabin).

their expressions or voices, despite the fact that the camera amplified them mercilessly."[12]

As they left the theater where a Gabin film was playing, Grémillon's friend and fellow director, the great René Clair, said, "I wouldn't be surprised if we hear more about him. Better make a note of his name."[13]

One of his first glamor shots when starting in movies with Pathé in the early 1930s (Collection du Musée Jean Gabin).

6

Rising Star

Synchronized sound had been technically possible for some time, but there was little economic incentive to produce talkies. The public was satisfied with silent films. When box office began to decline in the late 1920s, however, the studios decided it was time for something new; Warner Bros. released the first successful feature-length talkie, *The Jazz Singer*, in 1927. This was shaking up the motion picture industry and the acting profession itself as producers urgently sought performers with potential to do talkies. Both in America and Europe, they first concentrated on musicals to show off the new technique, then evolved toward drama.

Thus Gabin was unwittingly following the then-normal career path from singing and dancing to non-musical roles. He had that in common, for example, with James Cagney, to whom he is often compared. Like Gabin, Cagney spent years as a song and dance man in vaudeville before Hollywood typecast him as a tough guy. As Colin Crisp writes in *The Classic French Cinema, 1930–1960*, "In its heyday, the Boulevard, music hall, vaudeville, and the *caf'conc* circuit provided a vital source of talent for the classic French cinema.... Nearly all the early 1930s stars had initially been singers. At the very least, the ability to carry a tune was an essential career requirement. Gabin, Fernandel, Tino Rossi, and Maurice Chevalier all came from the music hall, as did Arletty, Josephine Baker, Garat, and others.... To sing was to be a folk hero at the time."[1]

A proletarian folk hero is exactly what Gabin was shortly to become at a fraught time in France when heroes of any kind were sorely needed. It was an era of rising populism. French movie magazines seized on him as "the people's star," "the proletarian star," "the man of the people."[2] His music hall background would also position him for this role because of the new demands of sound film, demands that disrupted the careers of many established actors and actresses. As the film historian Alan Williams observes, "Some careers went into eclipse, others suddenly blossomed. Ivan Mosjoukine, not surprisingly, had a strong Russian accent which hindered the intelligibility of his dialogue. His career quickly faded, as did those of most of his compatriots. Even native speakers with trained voices could find themselves in trouble."[3] (Gabin himself would have similar difficulty during his brief Hollywood career.) Then there was the "stagey" performance of theater actors, whose grand gestures and voice projection technique often looked wildly exaggerated on film. Those who couldn't adapt their acting style to the new medium often found themselves at a career dead end.

Jean Gabin's ability to make the transition—much to his own surprise—meant he would not sign a contract with Henri Varna to do more revues at the Casino de Paris or any other music hall. In fact, he would not step on a stage again, other than a sound stage, for 19 years. He remained convinced that he was not cut out for making movies, that he would soon tire of the whole charade and walk away from it, or that, on the contrary, the studios would get sick, as he put it, of "seeing my mug." But when producer Adolphe Osso, who had worked for Paramount in the U.S. and then headed the studio's French company before starting his own, Osso Films, proposed a contract for *Mephisto* (1930), Gabin quickly signed for a five-week shoot at 40,000 francs, about $8,000. The film was a turbid, four-episode affair complete with a wealthy American husband stabbed and his Swedish bride kidnapped on their wedding night by a mysterious masked man known as Mephisto, who wants a secret formula for poison gas invented by the bride's father. Amid all the melodramatic intrigue, Gabin gets to sing a droll song entitled *Vive les grosses dames* (*Hurray for Fat Women*), presumably for comic relief. He was the male lead in his first police inspector role; he would later play that many times, especially in the *Maigret* series, but would not return to it for 24 years.

He was now signing contracts hand over fist, indiscriminately accepting every role that came his way. His career plan? It hadn't changed since he was ten years old. As he put it to the French press covering his new status as a movie actor, "Another one or two years like this and I'll hang it up. I'll retire to the country with a nice little farm of my own."[4] Acting was merely a means to a greater end, not to be taken seriously. In his skeptically detached view of his film career he was unknowingly echoing Gary Cooper, whom he admired. "Movie acting is a pretty silly business for a man," Cooper once observed, "because it takes less training, less ability and less brains to be successful in it than any other business I can think of."[5]

It was in this period of the early 1930s that Gabin developed his persona. His third film, *Paris Béguin/The Darling of Paris* (1931), was the first in which he played the tough guy with a soft heart who comes to a bad end. It was the role he would make his own all during the decade. In this film he was Bob, a burglar who breaks into the apartment of a music hall star, played by the Belgian actress and singer Jane Marnac, intent on stealing her jewels. She surprises him in the act and, this being France, they end up spending the night together. When he is arrested the next day for a murder he didn't commit, she generously provides an alibi. Bob's girlfriend gets wind of this and jealously hires two hit men to kill him, making him the victim of circumstances beyond his control.

A significant aspect of this film is that one of the hit men was a bit player named Fernandel. He, like Gabin, previously had been mainly used in comic parts and they considered each other rivals. As time went on they would become lifelong friends, acting in several films together and creating their own production company. After two more movies—he would act in a total of six in 1931, done practically as fast as he could change makeup—Gabin was confident enough to feel that, as he put it later, "I'd become an actor."[6]

The Gabin persona of the good-hearted loser disappointed in love was taken a step further in *Pour un Soir/For a Night* (1931). Here he is a French navy sailor on leave in the Mediterranean ports of Toulon and Saint Tropez, where he meets a fickle nightclub singer (Colette Darfeuil) felicitously if improbably named Stella Maris. He falls in love with her, but she considers it just another brief fling. Crushed by her infidelity, he returns to his ship at Toulon, only to kill a nightclub pimp during a drunken brawl. Overcome with lovelorn grief, the gendarmes on his case, he dives into the sea and drowns. The film, directed by the silent movie actor Jean Godard, is marred by awkward transitions, amateurish camera work, interminable musical and dance routines, and theatrical overacting and makeup—Gabin's eyes are so mascaraed that he's practically unrecognizable at times. Today it comes across almost as a caricature of the transition from silent to talking films. It is important for Gabin's career, however, as the first of several violent murder/suicide roles he would play as the protagonist with a tragic destiny.

Of this series of films, the most important in some respects was a Franco-German number called *Gloria* (1931). Shot in both French and German versions in Berlin at the Neubabelsberg studios and directed by Yvan Noé (for the French version) and Hans Behrendt (for the German), it has Gabin in the second male lead as an aviation mechanic who accompanies his pilot on a risky transatlantic flight. The melodrama, with its crude special effects, was of little interest, but Gabin's acting attracted the attention of a budding young movie critic named Marcel Carné, who would become one of Gabin's favorite directors. "The big revelation of this film," Carné wrote, "is again Jean Gabin, amazingly natural and true.… With *Gloria* he reaches the level of one of our most believable actors."[7]

The film was also significant on the personal level because it marked the start of a two-year affair with the beauteous German star Brigitte Helm, who had played the female lead in Fritz Lang's famous 1927 expressionist silent film about urban dystopia, *Metropolis*. True to form, Gabin was again courting his leading lady. They would do two other films together in 1933, *L'Etoile de Valencia/The Star of Valencia* (1933) and *Adieu les Beaux Jours/ Happy Days in Aranjuez* (1933). Helm, née Brigitte Eva Gisela Schittenhelm, who incurred Nazi wrath for marrying a Jew, would go on to do more than 30 films before retiring from movies in 1935 and moving to Switzerland. She was the first of several blue-eyed blondes for whom Gabin seemed to have a predilection, including Michèle Morgan, Marlene Dietrich and his eventual third wife, Dominique. Although they did not have an affair, he was also very taken with the blonde Brigitte Bardot, whom he declared one of the most beautiful women he had ever seen. (Small movie world: in 1936 Paramount released a remake of *Happy Days* called *Desire* with Gary Cooper in Gabin's role and a certain Marlene Dietrich in Helm's.)[8]

He was fast becoming a succès d'estime among the critics. In *La Belle Marinière/The Beautiful Sailor Shirt* (1932) he was the ill-fated skipper of a river barge who jumps overboard to save a girl trying to commit suicide and marries her, only to see her leave with his best friend. It was one of his favorite early films because being on the river reminded him of Mériel and the Oise. He also liked the fact that this role let him escape typecasting as a gangster. In any case, it had reviewers pulling out all the stops. "He gets prodigious effects with just a simple movement of his eyebrows, shrugging his shoulders, tapping his fingers on the table," wrote one. "Touching and poignant," wrote another. "With a look in his blue eyes, he communicates a wealth of reflections on love, on fidelity, on guilty impulses, and the quest for happiness."[9] (Critics and audiences alike always had trouble deciding what color Gabin's eyes were. Opinion was divided between blue and green, with French speakers able to beg the question by simply calling them *clairs*, or pale. Like most light-colored eyes, they probably changed color with the ambient light. Several official documents I have seen in the archives of the Musée Jean Gabin, including a French passport issued in 1955, list them as green.)

Gabin always conceded the important part luck played in his career, claiming that his success was 80 percent due to it and only 20 percent to talent.[10] It is certainly true that his early films fortunately coincided with the accelerating technical progress of black and white film. Besides synchronized sound that allowed him to use his voice and singing to best effect, there were important advances in lighting, panchromatic film emulsions, and travelling shots, all making him look better, as did montage, reframing, and especially, close-ups that emphasized his expressive eyes with their flickering emotions—the most important part of acting, said Cicero.[11] Though his face was chiseled and masculine, he wasn't conventionally handsome and couldn't count on that to make him a star. His big nose and thin lips, for example, compared poorly with Charles Boyer's smooth good looks. Neither was he tall, at five feet eight inches. He claimed that he needed beautiful female leads to make him look better, even when he turned his back to the camera. But what he did have, as the French say, was *une gueule*, a look you didn't forget.

As far as we know, he never read Shakespeare, but he would have agreed with Hamlet's instructions to the players not to saw the air too much with the hand. He instinctively understood that, contrary to acting on stage, cinema required a more economical style. This sober, even minimalist approach was similar to that of his American coeval Henry Fonda, and in the 1930s was considered the "modern" technique. Jean Renoir, who loved to work with him, said, "Gabin was at his best when he didn't have to strain his voice. This immense actor could achieve the most impressive results with the simplest means. I devised scenes especially for him that could simply be murmured. We never imagined that this style was going to conquer the world and that murmuring actors were going to be legion. The results of that style are not always good. Gabin, with only a slight twitch of his impassive face, can express the most intense feelings. Another actor would have to scream to get the same result."[12]

Many French actors agreed with Renoir on this point, often acknowledging their debt to Gabin for the way he improved their technique. Michèle Morgan was one. "The great thing about working with Jean Gabin was that I learned so much from him," she told a French television interviewer in 1956. "I was lucky to do several films with him at the start of my career, and at least half of everything I learned about acting came from him. When you're playing a scene with him he speaks his lines in such a natural, realistic manner that it's not even like he's acting. And when you're in a dialogue with him, you're almost obliged to adopt the same tone. You're not acting any more. I learned to listen during a dialogue, too. For me it was an immense step forward in dramatic technique."[13]

Gabin himself was restrained in explaining his famous restraint. He never suffered fools or phonies gladly, and expected critics and reviewers to understand his acting style without his spelling it out by the numbers. His blunt frankness often resembled that of Spencer Tracy, who, once being asked what the most important thing was about acting, snapped back, "Learning the blasted lines."[14] Gabin's understated style, his contempt for self-dramatizing sham was evident throughout his life and career—what you saw was what you got. As he explained it, when he deigned to, his method was nothing like The Method of Actors Studio:

> I soon learned that with the mug I had, I was better off doing as little as possible in front of the camera because it exaggerated every movement like a magnifying glass. So I avoided expressing my characters' feelings by expressions that were too heavy because I knew that, with my rugged face, even when it was well lit, it would look like too much on the screen. After a few films, I came to understand that the less my features moved the more natural I looked, and my feelings were simply suggested. For example, if during a close-up somebody stuck a revolver in my face, I knew I didn't have to express too much fear, because it would be obvious to the spectator I must have been afraid.... I never really paid attention to technique, it just came like that. The critics said I played parts from the inside. That made me laugh because I never did understand what 'acting from the inside' meant. I acted with my

gut. I sweated blood to try to make my characters seem true and natural. But I never had the impression that it came from "inside my head." I preferred to think I was just doing my job, that's all. And it's never been easy. Sometimes, to get rid of a journalist asking me questions about that, I would reply that I never thought through my characters, all I had to do was get in front of the camera and it worked effortlessly. The idiot hurried to write that down. He must have known nothing about this profession to think I'd told the truth. So what good would it have done to tell him it wasn't that simple? He wouldn't have understood anyway. Besides, I don't like talking about my little tricks of the trade, because that seems pretentious and I imagine nobody cares. The only thing that counts is the result: you're either good or bad.[15]

In sum, he was a natural who worked hard at it.

It was in this period of the early 1930s that Gabin began incarnating virtually every professional and socio-economic category in France. It was a range of roles that over the next 40 years would make him the actor the French people most identified with. In the 15 films he did from 1930 to 1933, he played a salesman, police commissioner, burglar, proprietor of a radio shop, petty thug, sailor, movie house projectionist, aircraft mechanic, soldier, barge captain, racing car driver, engineer, and football player. There would be many more to come, but during this period of his ascension to stardom he established two main personas that would mark him indelibly: the street-smart working stiff quick to anger, and the moody, romantic *séducteur* of beautiful women.

With his slangy vocabulary, trademark working-class cap cocked over an ear, and inevitable cheap Gauloise cigarette dangling from his lips, he was the archetypal man of the people, the one who danced the night away at the local *bal populaire* and tried, usually successfully, to pick up the prettiest girl. His well-known love of cycling, boxing and hunting further anchored his status with a touch of regular-guy virility. As director Julien Duvivier once put it, Gabin was "the type every Frenchman enjoys drinking a glass of red wine with."[16]

It was this rough-hewn quality, paradoxically, that made him believable as a lover. "He was a seducer we could identify with," Didier Goux, a prominent contemporary French writer and critic, told me. "He didn't have that impossible handsomeness of Hollywood stars of the same era. Even while he was obviously attractive to women, he remained the guy in a cap pulling on a cigarette butt with his hands in his pockets."[17] Françoise Arnoul, a versatile actress who did some 60 films, including playing Nini, the laundress-turned-dancer in *French Cancan* (1955) with Gabin, and no slouch at screen seduction herself, told me, "The French recognized themselves in him because he loved everything that makes France, France: the soil, eating well, drinking good wine, seduction, women, l'amour, all the things that you associate with this country."[18]

His own love life took another turn in the autumn of 1933 at a chic dinner party in the prosperous Paris suburb of Sannois. On the rebound from his affair with Brigitte Helm, he met a statuesque, red-haired beauty with exotic slanting eyes named Jeanne Mauchain, stage name Doriane. Known as Dodo to friends and several wealthy admirers for whom she served as desirable arm candy, she was originally from poverty-stricken Brittany. Ambitious and determined, she had made her way in the world of show business thanks to inherent shrewdness and sharp elbows. When she met Gabin she was a star nude dancer in a revue at the Casino de Paris. "She was an extremely intelligent woman," thought Marcel Carné, "who had a great deal of influence over Gabin, even advising him which films to do and which to avoid. Tall, slim, and with a strong character, her mind was as impressive as her body."[19] Gabin, still in thrall to older women—Doriane was four years his senior—was impressed enough to marry her on November 23, one month after their meeting.

She was what the French call *une femme de tête*, headstrong and willful. She promptly set about making over Gabin. He, who until then never cared about luxury and had for years lived a nomadic life going from one Paris apartment to another or even sleeping at his Aunt Louise's home, now moved into an elegant apartment in a quietly chic street in Passy, on the fashionable west side of Paris. Doriane furnished it with antiques, wood paneling, taffeta, and flowers. She also became in effect his agent, handling publicity, interviews and contracts. Extremely possessive, she wanted to keep his acting career as separate as possible from their private life.

"Once he's out of the studio for the day, movies are finished and we never talk about his work," was the way she put it to one interviewer. "He is an extremely simple person, sometimes even taciturn, and embarrassed by the demands made on him due to his celebrity. He has broken off once and for all with all those obligations and is determined not to let movies take over his life." The journalist interrupted to note skeptically that the Gabin she described must be an exceptional case. "I couldn't stand to be married to someone whose goal in life is to be a star heart and soul," she continued, "it would be too demoralizing to share the life of someone like that. He is completely indifferent to everything concerning his life as an actor.... He lives a normal, healthy life and wants nothing to do with agents, journalists, or photographers, or anything else touching on his life his life as an actor."[20]

In other words, keep away from him. It must quickly have become stifling for a man like Gabin, who prized his freedom. Still, he recognized that she contributed largely to making him what he was. He would regain his freedom after a while, but even after their divorce she would be a vindictive thorn in his side for years.

While it lasted, however, the mutual *coup de foudre* must have been strong indeed. Even Ferdinand's death on November 20, only three days before their wedding, could not delay the ceremony. Ferdinand had died alone in his apartment in Montmartre's rue Custine, apparently from inhaling toxic fumes from a coal-fired heating stove. He and Gabin had long since reconciled and the son's affection could be seen in the letter quoted earlier. In return, Ferdinand was inordinately proud of his son's success. He repeated to anyone who would listen, "You know, I'm the father of Jean Gabin!"

His pride in the rising young star was amply justified, most recently by the critical reception of a new film called *Du Haut en Bas/High and Low* (1933). This was a touching comedy about the quarrels, loves and losses of the quirky inhabitants of an ordinary apartment building. It was directed by the great G. W. Pabst, renowned for previously having discovered Greta Garbo, and for *The Threepenny Opera* (1931) with Lotte Lenya. The impressive cast included the young Peter Lorre and Michel Simon as well as Gabin in the role of a good-hearted, overalls-wearing, working-class guy. He was in love with both football and a pretty chambermaid played by Janine Crispin, who went on to a long career in French films and television, including the movie version of *Lady Chatterly's Lover* (1955). "Jean Gabin has now achieved worldwide fame," gushed a movie magazine. "This young actor is following in the footsteps of other great screen stars, possessing as he does a force and strength of projecting character that audiences everywhere appreciate.... He gives his characters a moving, realistic presence; they are emphatically male, but their bursts of violence are always tempered by a certain subtlety."[21] When Ferdinand's daughter Reine found his body in the apartment, he was sitting slumped in an armchair.

On his lap was a copy of the October 26, 1933, popular movie magazine *Pour Vous*, a full-page photo of his son on its cover.

Gabin's next leading lady was the first black woman ever to star in a major motion picture, the American Josephine Baker. In *Zouzou/Zou Zou* (1934), Gabin was clearly upstaged by her radiant vitality, mugging, dancing, and singing. She justifiably got top billing. But judging by the pleasure he visibly took joining the fun with his own singing and dancing—always a smooth ballroom dancer, as many of his lady friends attested, he does a graceful waltz with love interest Yvette Lebon—he was pleased with his part. Audiences agreed: it was the most popular Gabin film until that time. In Baker he had a partner to whom he related easily because she came from the same working-class and music hall background.

Baker had electrified the Paris of the interwar period. Her performances there began when she starred with an all-black American dance troupe in the *Revue Nègre* at the Thèâtre des Champs Elysées in 1925. Then came her wicked *Danse Sauvage* at the Folies Bergère, which she did topless in a mini-skirt of artificial bananas. In 1931 she sang her famous *J'ai Deux Amours*, the anthem of every American who ever lived in Paris, and our name is legion. Carlo Rim, the French screenwriter who did the *Zouzou* script with Albert Willemetz, described her androgynous form as "built like a boy, with long, slim legs, square shoulders, a flat chest, and concave stomach. Her head has the perfect shape of an egg, and when she smiles, her lips let you discover the whitest teeth you ever saw."[22]

The film was a showcase for Baker. She made the most of it and was perfectly in character, possibly because it recalled her poor childhood in Saint Louis when she yearned for a

With Josephine Baker in *Zouzou*, 1934. The first major film with a black woman as female lead, it was Gabin's most popular until that time (Collection du Musée Jean Gabin).

show business career. In this fanciful romp Zouzou and Jean (Gabin) are two orphans brought up by a circus manager as brother and sister. They perform as children in a circus act, she later becoming a laundress and he joining the navy before working as an electrician in a music hall. She of course falls in love with him, while he treats her as his sister. He manages to get her an audition at his music hall, she wins the part in a big production, he's falsely accused of a murder, she proves he didn't do it, he falls for her best friend, and so on.

Gabin's performance was natural and understated, as was now normal for him. He was so convincing in his sailor's uniform that one day off the set when they were filming in the Mediterranean port of Toulon, he was picked up by a navy shore patrol who thought he had jumped ship.[23] She and Gabin got along famously on and off the set. "I've always liked Jean Gabin," she said. "He speaks so naturally that it's hard to tell if he's acting or not. When he growled, 'With a body like that, you've got no worries,' I wasn't sure whether he was speaking one of Mr. Willemetz's lines to Zouzou, or trying to encourage his co-star, Josephine."[24]

7

Breakthrough

Gabin's next film in 1934 was *Maria Chapdelaine*. His first under the direction of Julien Duvivier, it was based on the 1913 international bestseller of the same name by the French writer Louis Hémon. In this one he plays a hearty, simple Canadian trapper named François Paradis who meets and falls for Maria, a pretty village girl played by the distinguished Comédie Française actress Madeleine Renaud. She has two other suitors, but promises to wait for him until he returns from his next trapping season. After he gets lost and dies in a snowstorm—a typically tragic end for a Gabin character of this period—she does her familial duty in an act of abnegation and marries a local boy.

The screenplay was mainly a vehicle for grandiose views of Canadian scenery around Péribonka, in the wilds 175 miles north of Quebec City, where the film was shot. It also praised Franco-Canadian friendship on the 400th anniversary of Jacques Cartier's exploration of the Saint Lawrence River, and described the provincial folkways of Quebeckers, in what Voltaire scornfully had dismissed in the 18th century as "a few acres of snow."[1] It's said that the movie's depiction of wholesome, traditional family life in the country, the satisfactions of hard manual labor, and dedication to duty was so uplifting that Adolf Hitler asked to see it and praised its morality.[2] Two other movie versions of the book were done in 1950 and 1983, as well as a Quebec television series in 1985. It won Duvivier the Grand Prix du Cinéma Français as the best French film that year, the first time it was awarded.

From Gabin's point of view the film is notable mainly for the opportunity it afforded him to get acquainted with Julien Duvivier. It was on the ship taking them to Canada that they formed their productive friendship. Their mutual appreciation led to doing five other films, including some of Gabin's most important roles, more than he did with any other director. Duvivier's jaundiced opinion of mankind and his pessimistic view of the ultimate futility of most human endeavor made him one of the major precursors of what would be called film noir—Graham Greene, in one of his pieces of film criticism, thought that "his mood is violent, and belongs to the underside of the stone."[3] During an extraordinarily long and varied career from 1919 to 1967, he was one of France's most prolific directors with more than 60 films to his credit, including five done in Hollywood. He was also one of the most admired. Jean Renoir said, "If I were an architect and I was going to build a monument to the cinema, I would put a statue of Duvivier above the entrance."[4]

In their shipboard conversations Duvivier explained many basic aspects of cinema technique which Gabin, in his headlong rush to do as many films as possible, had neglected.

Particularly important for him was how different lenses affected the way an actor would be framed, and thus how he should move on the set as a consequence.[5] Thereafter he was able to work more closely with his directors on setting up shots in ways that were flattering to him, advice that they did not always welcome. Gabin considered Duvivier one of only two directors who contributed substantially to his development as an actor in the 1930s. "They were Duvivier and Renoir," he told *Le Figaro Littéraire* in 1964. "Duvivier is the great clockmaker of the profession. He takes the palm for handling the camera with precision, for rigorous timing, and exactitude in the smallest details. Renoir, on the contrary, showed me the occasional advantages of improvisation and imagination."[6] It says much for Gabin's innate cinematic savvy that, unschooled as he was, he was drawn instinctively to some of France's greatest directors of the 1930s.

Other than that, Gabin remembered the film principally for the opportunity to discover Canada. It was an eye opener for him, who never liked leaving France and did so as little as possible. "It was a magnificent trip," he recalled. "I've often been disappointed by trips abroad, for example when I saw New York. Other countries, too, didn't measure up to my expectations. Canada and Brazil are the only ones that did, Canada even more so because they speak French there. Even the redskins speak 'frança,' as they call it. I went looking for them and met 'savages,' as they are known there, dressed just like you and me."[7]

His predilection for a country where they speak French was of course typical to the point of stereotype of the average Frenchman, often impermeable to foreign cultures, then as now—I have known French persons who struggled to utter a correct sentence in English after years in the U.S. His aversion to foreign countries in general, and a seemingly congenital blockage about the English language in particular, were traits he would keep all his life, even during and after his time in Hollywood. Among other things, that meant his directors would have a hard time convincing him to leave his haunts in Paris and Normandy to shoot on location—he was notoriously reluctant even to venture south of the Loire River.

In the 1930s, however, Germany's superior movie industry meant he had no choice but to cross the Rhine frequently for shoots in what were then the most advanced film production facilities in Europe. It was also necessary because French producers often lacked the means of their ambitions and had to seek co-financing deals with their German counterparts. Such films usually were shot in both French and German, with actors of the respective nationalities playing the lead parts. Gabin wasn't the only French cinema figure made uncomfortable by that state of affairs. The big UFA (Universum Film Atkien Gesellschaft) studios at Neubabelsberg were foreign, in every sense of the word, to the temperament and work habits of French directors and actors. As Marcel Carné described them, "The atmosphere in the German studios, gigantic and impersonal, the Prussian discipline that reigned there, the feeling that they worked without enthusiasm, displeased me enormously and, worse, made me feel really uneasy."[8] From 1933 to 1939, Gabin would overcome his inborn French distaste for the *schleus*, or Krauts, as he always called them, to do at least four films for UFA.

In *Variétés*, a Franco-German film shot in Berlin and released in 1935, he would act the part of still another profession. Here he was one of a team of three circus acrobats doing breakneck numbers on a flying trapeze. One of the three being Anne, played by Annabella, née Suzanne Charpentier (she took her stage name from the poem *Annabelle Lee* by Edgar Allan Poe),[9] then France's top box office draw and highest-paid female star, the contentious love triangle is inevitable. Georges (Gabin) loves her as does Pierre (Fernand Gravey), a dicey situation when one of the rivals has to be caught by the other when he leaves the trapeze. The three underwent ten weeks of training on the trapeze and were doubled for the more perilous sequences, but accidents did happen. Annabella was a curious choice for her part, as she tended to suffer from vertigo; she sprained an ankle and had to sit out the shoot for several days. Physically, Gabin was in excellent shape, as usual, but faltered once and nearly failed to catch Gravey during a practice session. Overall it was an unattractive part for him because he played the heavy, made an unsuccessful attempt to kill his rival, and lost the girl before finally giving up on the circus, none of which burnished his image. But the role had its compensations, notably in the form of a generous fee of 350,000 francs, about $70,000, his biggest until then.[10]

If that part was unattractive, his next one was positively embarrassing. Julien Duvivier had decided he wanted to do a great historical film recounting the last week of the life of Jesus Christ. Duvivier had been a devout Catholic and was one of France's most intensely serious directors. Like Jean Renoir, he clearly loved the world that died in the First World War, which, if not characterized by sincere religious faith, at least had the good manners to go through the motions. He loathed the crassly commercial one that followed it. In 1923 he did a silent film, *Credo*, imbued with his fervent Catholic faith, about the pilgrimage center of Lourdes in southwestern France, where thousands of the ailing and elderly go every year in hope of a cure. The simplistic, predictable script tells of a positivist, atheistic scientist whose daughter has an incurable disease, makes the pilgrimage, and is miraculously restored. The film, supported by the French Catholic hierarchy, drew vigorous condemnation by the Communist Party as Papist propaganda, but was hugely successful, and lucrative.[11]

For his Biblical epic about the Passion entitled *Golgotha/Behold the Man* (1935), Duvivier wanted Gabin to take the part of Pontius Pilate. Robert Le Vigan, usually cast in supporting roles, would be Jesus, and the shoot would be in Algeria with thousands of extras playing the jeering crowd shouting that he should be crucified. Gabin rightly considered the part too much of a stretch from his budding screen persona and said so. He hated the idea of cutting his hair short while wearing a Roman skirt and buskins—he never did get the hang of walking in them, stumbling several times at dramatic moments during the shoot and breaking up everyone on the set. Duvivier asked that he do it as a favor, so they cut a deal.[12] Probably at the suggestion of his wife Doriane, Gabin had read a novel, *La Bandéra*, a few years before, and was convinced it would make a good film. "I read and re-read, I don't know how many times, Pierre Mac Orlan's novel," he said, "and when I met Julien Duvivier he understood immediately what a good film it could be. With time, [its protagonist] Pierre Gilieth had become a friend to me, a brother, I could see him."[13] He had persuaded Duvivier to join him in purchasing the movie rights. He agreed to play Pilate if Duvivier would direct *La Bandéra* as Gabin's next film.

He got the bargain, but still felt ridiculous in the role of Pilate. Anticipating the incredulous sarcasm he was sure it would provoke in sophisticated cinema circles, he made an unusual declaration to the press justifying his decision. It is particularly interesting because it shows how aware he was already of his screen persona and what his audiences expected of him. He was, in effect, making excuses for taking a part that he and they both considered unworthy of him, and warning them not to be disappointed. "I imagine that my decision to play the role of Pontius Pilate in Julien Duvivier's next production, *Golgotha*, will surprise many people," he began. "What, Jean Gabin, who has played laborer, bargeman, trapper, sailor, engineer, each time likeable and each time so much part of the people, in the role of prefect of Judea? What audacity! Why not? Above all … it must be understood that *Golgotha* won't be a Biblical production like those of the Americans or Germans…. It will show, as realistically as possible, the events that led the population to demand and obtain the death of a man, with all the stupidity, injustice and horror typical of such events."[14] He distanced himself from the subject's religious aspects, promising to play Pilate simply as a Roman civil servant, a man of the people and a soldier who had come up through the ranks, doing his job. And he couldn't resist the temptation to add a naughty punch line, an allusion to Pilate's exculpatory hand washing after Jesus is sentenced to death: "I'll do my best, I won't wash my hands of it."[15] Despite the big, costly production and the Catholic Church's support—interestingly, Duvivier later admitted that he had lost the faith even before the first take—the film flopped.[16] But for Gabin, his next film proved that it was worth the sacrifice.

La Bandéra/Escape from Yesterday (1935, U.S. release 1939) would be his breakthrough movie, the one that showed he was a serious actor with charisma, gravitas, and surprising depth. It established him beyond question as a new star to be reckoned with. It was also the start of an extraordinary six-year streak of 12 movies, including ten acknowledged classics still shown in film festivals the world over. As the film academic Ginette Vincendeau, who teaches the history of cinema at London's King's College, writes, "It was neither the best French movie of 1935, nor the best Duvivier, nor the best Gabin of the time. But it is the film in which the ingredients of the Gabin myth first gelled…. The historical 'moment' of *La Bandéra* made possible the conjunction of the star's image with a certain number of social, political and cultural discourses external to the film."[17]

It was based on the book of the same name by the French novelist and songwriter Pierre Mac Orlan, real name Pierre Dumarchey. Like Gabin, he had had an unconventional youth, having knocked around at odd jobs and traveled widely in his 20s, hung out with a bohemian crowd in Montmartre, singing his own songs in nightclubs, and done a number of pornographic novels under pseudonyms like Sadie Blackeyes and Chevalier X. Before *Bandéra* he had written *Le Quai des Brumes* in 1927, which coincidentally would also be turned into a legendary Gabin film. He was closely implicated in the adaptation of his novel, working on it with Duvivier and the prolific Belgian screenwriter Charles Spaak, father of the actress Catherine Spaak and brother of a Belgian prime minister. Mac Orlan also went on location to follow the shoot in Spanish Morocco. He liked the result, as he explained just before the film was released: "Julien Duvivier, Spaak, and I collaborated on a script that was clear, exact, and nonetheless very close to the book as I wrote it. Having followed hour by hour the location shots, I find that the film is the way I would have shot it."[18]

As the film starts, Pierre Gilieth (Gabin) has killed a man in Paris and is on the run. Ending up in Barcelona, his wallet stolen in a louche cabaret, he is without money or ID papers. He joins the Spanish Foreign Legion in desperation and his battalion, or *bandera*, is sent to fight the native resistance led by Abdel Krim in the Protectorate of Spanish Morocco in the desolate Rif Mountains—an historical fact of the 1920s on which the novel was based. He is tailed by a fellow Legion recruit named Lucas (Robert Le Vigan), in reality a French investigator intent on claiming the 50,000-franc bounty on Gilieth's head. Pierre meets an Arab prostitute, Aischa la Slaoui (Annabella, who actually got top billing above Gabin, playing a glamorized version of the book's fat old whore) in a brothel and marries her. Before leaving on a suicide mission to save a besieged Legion fortress in the Rif, he confronts Lucas and says he will kill him and then commit suicide if Lucas denounces him to the police. They both end up in the fortress as the last two men standing and, in a scene of virile camaraderie, are reconciled.

A suddenly heroic Gilieth—"Since I have to die, I prefer to die honorably"—is killed just as reinforcements arrive, driving home Duvivier's pet themes of the need to transcend the absurdity of existence and redemption through sacrifice. The extent to which Jean identified with his part is clear in an interview he gave to the French movie magazine *Cinémonde* in September 1935: "Gilieth is a crook, but a likeable

Gabin as a member of the Spanish Foreign Legion in *La Bandéra*, his breakthrough, 1935. It was the first film in which he did his trademark angry explosion (Collection du Musée Jean Gabin).

crook because he does the honorable thing at the end and his crime at the beginning is almost forced on him. If I had nothing to eat, I too might become a killer like him to keep from starving to death. Then if the money I got from that crime was stolen, it would seem normal to me to try to disappear into the Legion, like a sort of temporary suicide."[19]

Duvivier, meticulous and demanding as ever, was determined to avoid studio settings and use real backgrounds as far as possible.[20] In that, he was following to the letter Mac Orlan's desire for the same realism he had achieved in his novel. "In a film like this," the writer explained, "there had to be great authenticity to create that dramatic atmosphere of desperate and sentimental violence."[21] He obtained the cooperation of the Spanish Foreign Legion, modeled on the French Foreign Legion and used for the same purpose: to fight colonial campaigns and other unpopular wars with anonymous foreigners who wouldn't be missed back home when killed. The film was initially dedicated to General Francisco Franco, who authorized the shoot in Spanish Morocco and was himself a high-ranked former Legion officer. (The dedication was withdrawn when his fascist tendencies, including war on the Republicans, made him a political pariah in the West.)[22] That cooperation enabled Duvivier to use the 1,500 troops of the Fifth Bandera as extras, even though the story is about the Third and Fourth battalions.

He moved the cast and production unit to Ceuta, on the Moroccan coast. They spent hours every day riding by truck to the battalion's post at Dar Riffen, where for three weeks Gabin and the others shared the troops' lives from six in the morning until eight at night. "At Dar Riffen we lived like the Legionnaires," Gabin said just after filming was completed. "Of course, we slept at a hotel in Ceuta. But the rest of the time we were with the soldiers. We ate with them at their mess, and while it was picturesque, it wasn't exactly fun."[23] Ironically, the greatest risk he took wasn't fighting fake Arab rebels, but taking a plane back to Paris after the shoot was over. After takeoff from a stopover in Barcelona, the aircraft had an emergency and barely managed to return to the airport, nearly plunging into the Mediterranean. A shaken Gabin—despite his numerous tough-guy roles, he always admitted that he lacked physical courage—vowed then and there never again to take a plane. As far as anyone knows, he never did, even favoring trains for transcontinental travel in the U.S.[24]

During one barroom brawl sequence when he attacks Lucas, he does a slow burn and explodes in uncontrollable rage. It was the first time he used this bit of business—wide eyes glaring, lips drawn back tightly against clinched teeth. He would perform it so often in subsequent films that it became a virtual trademark, a sequence audiences came to expect in a Gabin movie. Some reviewers even suspected his contracts required that the screenplay include at least one such scene, a rumor he denied, not entirely convincingly. He did however confess to drinking heavily before the film's drunk scenes, as he did in several other movies when the part called for him to appear inebriated and/or out of control. "I very conscientiously got drunk to play those scenes," he wrote in a biographical note in 1950. "You either have a professional conscience or you don't. I never hesitated to get plastered to get into the skin of the character I was playing."[25]

The socio-political atmosphere in France made the movie's timing perfect. This was the height of France's colonial empire in Africa and Asia, and in *Bandéra* the public saw Gabin not as a working stiff but as a French colonial soldier, albeit in a Spanish setting. This too emphasized Gabin's Frenchness, his embodiment of the national identity. France's so-called *cinéma colonial* of the period was heavily politicized and glorified patriotism and the empire. It included a number of films such as this one, and several other of Gabin's movies like *L'Imposteur*, *Le Messager*, and *Pépé le Moko*, where he personifies the Frenchman deliberately contrasted with non–French and non-white peoples.[26]

Often such pictures in the 1930s were frankly jingoistic and capitalized on the audience's reflexive affection for the French Foreign Legion (motto: Legio Patria Nostra, the Legion is our Fatherland). Its legendary bravery and sacrifice were celebrated in films like *Un de la Légion* (1936), *S.O.S. Sahara* (1938), and *Le Chemin de l'Honneur* (1939). French attitudes at the time, however we might judge them today, looked on explicit racism as normal, and the country's films were not squeamish about reflecting this. When natives attack the colonial outpost where Gilieth seeks a redemptive death on the field of honor, they are identified as *salopards*, or bastards, while his Arab mistress is necessarily, in the popular view, a prostitute.[27] Gabin's roles in colonial cinema even contributed to making him "the pinnacle of the French male ideal," as the film historian Colleen Kennedy-Karpat calls him in her study of 1930s French cinema.[28] Interestingly, the Hungarian-British writer Arthur Koestler said he was thinking of Jean Gabin in this particular role when he joined the French Foreign Legion as a refugee from Nazism.[29]

The depressed, apprehensive French, bled white by the recent war, feeling the pinch of the Great Depression, very much needed a male ideal. In a sharp essay preceding the release of *Bandéra*, the influential writer Jean Fayard, winner of the prestigious Goncourt literary award and editor-in-chief of the prominent Fayard publishing house, said France needed a stimulating shot of virile motion pictures. "Virility has undergone a serious crisis," he wrote. "Possibly out of a reaction against the barbaric excesses of the hundred-percent male, we have adopted a feminine sensibility ... we have gone overboard in an excess of delicacy and refinement. The 'artistic' and 'intellectual' milieux have naturally been the most affected by this trend."[30]

Not Gabin. Writes the movie historian Edward Baron Turk:

> The mystique of Jean Gabin is best appreciated within the context of masculine image. Like Marlon Brando in the 1950s, the pre-war Gabin gave shape to feelings of anger and frustration among his audience. Like the star of *On the Waterfront*, he projected suppressed power through hesitant, inarticulate,

almost incoherent speech and through explosive violence. Like Brando, Gabin's acting style contrasted with the polish and finesse of many of his contemporaries—for example, Charles Boyer and Pierre Brasseur. And like Brando, Gabin exuded raw sexual magnetism of a kind that was new to the screen. But where Brando's striving for naturalism betrayed his debt to the Actors' Studio, Gabin was perceived as simply playing himself.[31]

The critics loved *Bandéra*, making it a box office and critical success. Jean Fayard was delighted that "la Bandéra spares us the maudlin tears of the usual melodrama. Here we have men, Legionnaires, living a tough life in a tough climate."[32] "A fine, solid work that is skillfully put together right down to the smallest details," wrote Alexandre Arnoux in the prestigious magazine *Les Nouvelles Littéraires*. "It is simple, direct, picturesque and human. It's certain to be a success with all classes of movigoers."[33] And French audiences loved Gabin in this role with which, in their unhappy straits of the interwar years, they could immediately identify: the tough guy with a soft heart, the romantic outsider, the proletarian loner who was the helpless victim of forces beyond his control, unlucky in love and ineluctably headed for a tragic destiny. This was how he would be typecast for years to come. It was a role he would play so successfully in his laconic, understated, but often explosive style, that the movies featuring it would come to be considered some of the great works of cinema.

But those implacable forces were not entirely external and due to an unjust, uncaring society. They were often portrayed as being, to a large extent, within him, which is a pretty fair definition of the tragic hero. André Bazin, long the high priest of French film criticism and theory beginning in the 1940s, co-founder in the 1950s of the ur-film magazine *Cahiers du Cinéma*, noted, "It is nearly always in a moment of anger that Gabin calls down his misfortune, setting the fateful trap that inevitably leads to his death." He considered that "it is always the same story—his own, and one which must inevitably end unhappily, like the story of Oedipus or Phaedra. Gabin is the tragic hero of contemporary cinema. With every new Gabin film the cinema rewinds the infernal machine of his destiny."[34] Thus Gabin's typical persona at this time in his career had an Aristotelian personality flaw, giving his films a distinctly tragic view of the human condition, as opposed to the upbeat Hollywood tradition of the happy ending.

Thanks to this film Gabin could now write his own ticket. "*La Bandéra* will be the fondest memory of my career for a long time to come," he said in a magazine article. "It was the first time I did a film I had chosen myself, and it was very satisfying. Maybe there'll be other chances to do that, but they won't be as exciting as the first time."[35] Years later, when both he and the world had changed for the worse, the time would come when he would again be at the mercy of the market, strapped for money, accepting whatever roles he could get, and doing movies that many critics considered unworthy of him. But for now he was riding high. He could and would be choosy about his movies, directors, and screenwriters, even if that meant making a few financial sacrifices while waiting for the right opportunities. He could afford it. He was on a roll and the French motion picture world was becoming aware of it.

Filmmakers would also have to get used to his demands, which more often than not turned out to be to their benefit. When talking over a script with screenwriters like Charles Spaak, who did the scripts for eight of his films, he would often ask them to write scenes "like in life" that he could act naturally. He also frequently saw the movie potential in subjects that others initially missed, like *La Grande Illusion*. In other cases he risked his own money to co-produce one he believed in, such as *Bandéra* and *La Belle Equipe*.

Charles Spaak once mock-complained that "when Gabin isn't on the set, he spends most of his time explaining why he doesn't want the parts we're proposing.... He only likes screenplays that are developed with interior rigor, that are completely faithful to the characters.... That's why I like Gabin not only for the films he has done, but also for all those he has kept us from doing."[36] As Gabin himself later described his approach to acting at the time:

> I was looking to do the right films, only those with screenplays I could believe in, and with writers and directors I admired. I worked hard at that, and I worked hard during the shoot at trying to keep producers from ruining things with their ridiculous demands. I always supported my directors and screenwriters. I was well paid when I did a film, but sometimes I was willing to sacrifice some of my fee to incite a producer to take on a movie like, for example, *La Belle Equipe*. I turned down some high-paying contracts for mediocre films I didn't feel like doing. I could really have lined my pockets if I hadn't decided to work only with people like Duvivier, Renoir, Carné or Grémillon. Now the films I did with them have become classics, some say masterpieces, and they are shown again and again in cinematheques and university film courses the world over.... We didn't know then that we were making films that would be talked about decades later. We just tried to do our job as well as possible, films that the public wanted. Sometimes we failed. That just made it a little harder to sell the next idea to producers.... As to what makes a good movie, I've always said you need three things: first, a good story, second, a good story, and third, a good story. They'll never convince me that cinema can be anything else.[37]

From 1936 to 1939, Gabin ran up an uncommon streak of nine exceptional films. All were with the best French directors of the day: two with Duvivier, three with Renoir, two with Grémillon, and two with Carné. Some of his success during this period was due to luck, but mainly it was thanks to careful calculation. As the Australian film analyst Colin Crisp notes, "It is instructive to observe how attentive Jean Gabin was to the construction of his mythic persona, never accepting a role unless it contained those aspects of his past roles which had begun to emerge as mythic—the underprivileged origins, the social and legal marginality overlaying a fundamental goodness, the outburst of frustration with the constraints of his existence, the fatality that this attracts in the form of a tragic death."[38]

Yet when he was asked on the cusp of that phase whether he had any big plans for the future, his reply revealed some residual ambiguity but also a new professional ambition and a maturing taste for acting. Even his tenacious dream of having a farm and living on the land was receding as he finally accepted that movies would be his life for some time to come. "Not for the moment," he replied. "Still, I know that deep down, there is one, but it's a very big project, or rather a desire, for later on: retiring to the country and getting back to the outdoor life of my early years, the varied and active life of the farm. Later, much later, because my acting career is not yet over. I have, I hope, many films to do. I'm not going to quit this profession just when I'm really beginning to like it. I went on the stage reluctantly, I did my first movies unenthusiastically, without any hope of making it. But now, *voilà*, I'm hooked."[39]

8

Politics and Poetics

Thus began the great creative period of what came to be known as the Gabin myth. Composed in equal parts of despair, bewilderment, the thwarted quest for love, and the frustrated hope of escape to a new life, it started with *Bandéra*. The films of this period continued until France collapsed under the German onslaught of the Second World War, taking the country's motion picture industry down with it as most of its best talent fled. The myth would take another form years after the war when Gabin reached deep into himself to find a new persona.

Not only were top French producers and directors now seeking him out, Hollywood too would soon be offering him attractive contracts. To some extent this was due not only to Gabin's deliberate career development, but also to the mass audience that the cinema had by then created. As André Malraux philosophized about the new phenomenon of motion picture stardom, "A star is a person with that necessary minimum of talent whose face expresses, symbolizes, embodies a collective instinct.... So true is this that stars recognize more or less vaguely the myths that they embody, and demand scenarios capable of perpetuating them."[1] Malraux's definition seems made to order for Jean Gabin as he increasingly became aware that he embodied something like "a collective instinct."

That Gabin was able to vault to celebrity this quickly despite prewar French cinema's lack of an organized star system is a tribute not only to his acting ability and intrinsic charisma, but also to his canny understanding of what made a star. Within a remarkably short time he became the biggest movie celebrity in France despite there being no professional publicity machine to fabricate stars. Agents handled details of contracts, but did little to feed the press with the constant flow of interviews and personal tidbits that celebrity thrives on. Nor were there many fan clubs, or even a systematic way of handling fan mail addressed to him. What Gabin and his wife-cum-agent Doriane instinctively understood was that this was the dawn of the age of mass entertainment. Mass man could not often afford the legitimate theater, but he could afford to spend a few francs for a Saturday night movie for himself and his family, which became a leisure institution. When he did, he wanted his money's worth, and there was no better way than to pick a film with his favorite actor. Illustrated movie magazines proliferated, movie reviews, infrequent during the silent era, became a fixture in the daily press, and it was all focused on the actor, whose name on the marquee meant profit or loss at the box office in a way not seen since.

Directors usually followed Gabin's suggestions. They nearly always included reviewing and eventually altering dialogue and screenplays to make the plot more believable,

the lines more natural when he delivered them. He explained his technique to an interviewer who asked him if, in the final analysis, he didn't actually direct his films himself.
"No, but I don't like to be the prisoner of a script," he replied. "When it's finished, I like
to look it over and exchange my impressions with the director. The words have to come
out of the eyes, because movies are visual. If you don't really think what you're saying, it
won't be in your eyes. And to really think it, you have to be able to say it easily. So I
always try to make the dialogue my own. I would be completely unable to play classical
roles, like Molière or tragedies. That would be catastrophic."[2] Jean Renoir didn't mind
admitting that Gabin's method often improved the films he was directing. As he once
recalled, "I had written two pages of beautiful literature. It was fantastic. I was so proud
of myself. Finally Gabin told me, 'Jean, your two pages of beautiful poetry are just trash
and we can't say it.' Which was true."[3]

    With stardom came the spoils. If his dream of owning land had receded, it hadn't
disappeared. Now he had the means to possess that little farm and enjoy it. In the mid–
1930s he bought the first of what during his lifetime would be three country homes, each
progressively larger. It was a small property in the village of Berchères-sur-Vesgre, in a
pleasant Norman region about 45 miles due west of Paris. It had everything he had
dreamed of since leaving Mériel: a bit of farmland, a small orchard, and a vegetable garden, with the little Vesgre River and the wooded Valley of the Chevreuse nearby. Between
films he would head there with Doriane to tend his vegetable garden, raise a few chickens,
and relax with her beside the rustic fireplace.
    In an article for a film magazine, he waxed poetic about the life of the country gen-
tleman: "Ah, the long walks across plowed fields, the joy of trampling the rich, heavy soil
that sticks to the soles of your boots, a shotgun under your arm and the hunting dog
running ahead. You're thinking of nothing, and suddenly the dog sniffs the air, a fleeting
form flashes by, and you fire instinctively." This was invariably followed by copious, bibulous meals with fellow hunters at a familiar country inn where the owner-chef knows his
customers personally and does the cooking himself. Then comes "that delicious moment
when everyone is telling tall tales and big lies, and there's one last stiff drink after the
coffee."[4]
    His time in Berchères lasted only briefly, however. Probably spurred by the ambitious
Doriane, still in the process of making him over, he soon spotted another, more attractive
and prestigious property only a few miles away. The manor house in the picturesque village of Sainte Gemme Moronval, known as the Chateau de Sainte Gemme, was not only
the largest and most handsome residence in the area. It would also, Gabin thought, be
the perfect place to create a Norman stud farm. That too was an old dream that had stuck
with him ever since his father had taken him to the races at Longchamp and Auteuil
years before.
    Sainte Gemme Moronval had played a significant role in the country's past, having
been for centuries a place of royal residency. King Jean the Second, known to faithful
subjects as The Good, possessed a royal castle there. Here it was that he wed his second
wife, Jeanne d'Auvergne on February 9, 1350, after his first, Bonne de Luxembourg, died
of the Black Death that ravaged Europe in the mid–14th century. The village featured
adjacent rolling fields, a small lake, and the meandering Eure River that runs through it
on its way to join the Seine. It had changed hands several times during the Hundred
Years War, during which the occupying English troops largely destroyed the chateau.

While they were at it, *les Biftecks*, as the French called them, also altered the village name to the more Anglophonic Saint James, before the French charged back and restored the French version for good.[5]

The three-story brick building with white shutters sat on the bank of the Eure, which is a comfortable 20 yards wide at that point. It was not actually a chateau, but more in the typical severe style of an imposing Norman manor of the local bourgeoisie. It had a tree-planted lawn running down to the river, and outbuildings including a boathouse for storing canoes. Here Gabin and Doriane lived well indeed amid antique furnishings such as Louis XV chairs and Louis XVI tables. According to an impressive list of belongings I have seen that Gabin once filed with an insurance claim, his Sainte Gemme estate contained fine silverware worth, at the time, $2,521, and clothing that included no fewer than 40 suits, ten dozen shirts, 200 ties, 20 cashmere sweaters, and 60 pairs of socks. There were also some 1,000 books worth $4,200, many of them original editions. Under Doriane's tutelage, the uncouth kid from Mériel was developing some very expensive tastes.[6]

Paradoxically so. For the actor who would come to represent so many aspects of 20th-century France was now, in the quality of his personal life, out of sync with his country. While he was happily going from strength to strength on the screen and in his bank account, the real France was in the throes of economic depression, political chaos—it had 34 revolving-door governments between November 1918 and June 1940—and collective panic at the idea of impending war with Germany. France in the 1930s was a sick, traumatized society, morally depleted and physically weakened by the wholesale slaughter of the recent four-year war that saw 1.4 million Frenchmen, or 3.5 percent of the total population, killed, and another 1 million mutilated for life.[7] To be sure, many were wildly partying away the final *années folles* of the interwar years in cabarets, dance halls, and masked balls, but the merrymaking often smacked of desperation. The poet Paul Valéry summed up the zeitgeist: "Never has humanity joined so much power and so much disarray, so much anxiety and so many playthings, so much knowledge and so much uncertainty."[8]

The country was suffering through what the historian Eugen Weber called the Hollow Years. "The absence of young and, some contend, of the best and brightest, cut down on the Marne, on the Somme, at Verdun," he writes, "accounts for the pacifism, the defensiveness, timidity, indecisiveness, shortage of breath and of initiative that aggravated earlier tendencies to mediocracy and gerontocracy.... France was not an underdeveloped country, but a developed one in an advanced state of decay.... The crisis of the 1930s was as much economic as diplomatic, as much institutional as economic, as much about public morality, confidence, and self-confidence as it was about economic interests, employment, or the balance of payments."[9] The dark joke making the rounds of Paris salons was that France was governed by decrepit 75-year-old men because all the decrepit 80-year-olds were dead.[10]

Thus when Hitler defiantly violated the botched Treaty of Versailles and remilitarized the Rhineland in March 1936, a paralyzed France looked on passively. The French wanted very much to believe their government's official line that their army was invincible and the 200-mile-long Maginot line would protect them. They clung to the September 1938 promise by British Prime Minister Neville Chamberlain and French Premier Edouard Daladier that the Munich Agreement meant "peace for our time." The army chief of staff General Maurice Gamelin declared confidently, "We will slice through Germany like a knife through butter."[11] But in reality they knew better. Just as Jean Gabin had achieved his breakthrough film and was beginning to reap the professional and financial benefits of stardom, the police and local authorities were distributing posters and brochures with instructions on what to do in the event of aerial bombardment. As early as 1935, the U.S. ambassador to Paris, William Bullitt, cabled Washington that the French "now regard [war] as inevitable."[12]

Seldom known for their phlegmatic calm, steady nerves, or grace under pressure, the French were succumbing to another of their periodic bouts of collective hysteria. Among the intellectual class, timorous pacifism to the point of capitulation was the order of the day. "Anything, Hitler rather than war!" wrote Roger Martin du Gard, winner of the Nobel Prize for Literature in 1937.[13] Other well-known French writers gave voice to the pervasive feeling of despair. Jean-Paul Sartre published his nihilistic *La Nausée*, while the novelist Jean Giono, a veteran of the trenches of WW I, declared he would rather be a live German than a dead Frenchman.[14] The American writer Julien Green, who was born in Paris and spent his adult life there, asked his diary, "I wonder when and how we shall escape from this hideous age." He noted that the only thing anyone talked about was war. "In salons, in cafes, that is all one hears with the same tone of horror," he wrote. "Some expect it in two months, others less pessimistic grant us another year of peace."[15] Sartre's feminist companion and fellow existentialist Simone de Beauvoir, unable to believe in either the socialist-communist chimera or democratic capitalism, threw up her hands: "Was there nowhere on earth where we could cling to hope?"[16]

If the country's political situation was bad, the state of its economy was worse. Britain and Germany felt the effects of the Great Depression earlier, but France could not long escape contagion. From 1929 to 1935, unemployment quadrupled as the business climate deteriorated, with bankruptcies and company failures rising sharply. Industrial production fell, and with it exports, meaning that by 1936 France was exporting only half what it had in 1928. Those who still had jobs faced partial unemployment as companies shortened working hours—in one Paris suburb unemployment doubled between 1930 and 1932, rising another 60 percent by 1935. During the same period agricultural prices fell by half, so farmers could only sell their produce at a loss; that left farmhands and day laborers virtually without income. Getting enough to eat was a real problem for many families. Gallows humor had it that the unemployment situation was improving as those out of work starved to death. The franc was such a sacred cow that the government feared to follow other countries like the U.S. and Britain in letting it float to a lower level, making French goods too expensive on the world market. That in turn hit the country's important income from tourism as foreigners found France too expensive for vacations. On the French Riviera 18 big hotels closed in Menton in the 1930s, 22 in Nice.[17]

In some countries hit by the Depression, such as Britain and Canada, the unemployed expressed their desperation by marching on the capital. These events came to be known as hunger marches, and were often supported by the Communist International, or Comintern, as part of its "anti-fascist" strategy.[18] In France too it was active, especially after Hitler outlawed the German Communist Party in 1933 and many of its members fled to Paris. But since 1789 peaceful demonstrations had never been the French way of expressing displeasure with government policies. With right-wing factions like Action Française, Croix de Feu, and Mouvement Franciste facing off against left-wing movements including the French Communist Party (PCF), its faithful CGT labor union, and the French Section of the Worker's International (SFIO) and their followers, conflict was inevitable.

Adding to the volatile mix was the financial scandal sparked by Alexandre Stavisky. A slick embezzler and con man with useful contacts among government ministers, he had floated millions of francs of worthless bonds backed by nothing more than a pawnshop in the Basque country town of Bayonne, causing many ordinary investors to lose heavily. When police killed the fleeing Stavisky (the official line was that he had committed suicide), the affair fired the public imagination and the right accused the Socialist Prime Minister Daladier of having protected him. Violence began on February 6, 1934, when right-wing demonstrators massed on Place de la Concorde to protest against Daladier's new government. Fearing a coup d'état, the government ordered police to fire on the crowd, killing 15 and injuring 1,435. Daladier resigned the next day and his government fell. It was France's worst night of political violence since the Commune of 1871, the first time since the collapse of the Second Empire that a government fell due to street violence.[19]

With the economy sputtering and social conflict continuing, the left won the legislative elections of May 1936. The Socialist Léon Blum formed a coalition government including ministers from the Socialist, Radical-Socialist, and Communist parties, and called it the *Front Populaire*. By the time it took office on June 6, thousands of factories were closed as France was paralyzed by a general strike. To the tune of *The Internationale*, Socialist and Communist youth organizations competed for leadership of the left with flag-waving, fist-raising demonstrations that struck some observers as strangely similar to the decade's Nazi gatherings at Nuremburg.[20] Government negotiations with employers' representatives resulted in the so-called Matignon Accords, which instituted collective bargaining, a 40-hour workweek, and two weeks of paid vacation.

There was celebratory dancing in shipyards, factory workers hanged their bosses in effigy, intellectuals held verbose conferences and meetings to discuss the meaning of it all. A young journalist named Françoise Giroud, who later created the highly successful women's magazine *Elle* and had a prominent center-right political career in the 1970s, went to hear the Communist Party chief Maurice Thorez harangue the faithful. "He was captivating," she reported, deadpan. "Jean Gabin plus the dialectic."[21] With the extra income from the negotiated accords, workers could buy the new wireless radios and hand-cranked phonographs coming on the market. Families took off on their first vacations, many on third-class railway tickets, others on bicycles, whose sales jumped by one-third.[22]

Bliss was it in that dawn to be a French worker, but hopes that a new era for humanity had begun were dashed in March 1938 as the Popular Front coalition fell apart due to quarrelling factions. The retread Daladier returned as head of government. Determined to end continuing labor unrest and put France back to work, he severely put down an attempted general strike by tear-gassing the demonstrators on November 30, 1938. It was the end of populist utopianism as France hurtled helplessly toward war.[23]

French filmmakers treated this tumult directly or indirectly several times. Most fervent was Jean Renoir, an active fellow traveler of the Communist Party if not an actual cardholder. His two 1936 productions, *La Vie est à Nous/The People of France* and *Le Crime de Monsieur Lange/The Crime of Monsieur Lange*, were pure propaganda, the former being produced by and for the party.[24] In *La Vie*, he mixed documentary footage of soup lines and actual speeches by party leaders like Thorez with fictional stories about grossly caricatured, heartless bosses, the 200 wealthy, bloodsucking families accused of controlling France's finances, and rich young men taking target practice at workmen-like dummies.

In *Monsieur Lange*, the employees of a publishing house take over the company and shoot the owner dead, with the heroic murderer safely escaping to Belgium with his worker girlfriend. But much better films were to come. The 1930s were a period of great cinematic creativity in France, which produced more than 1,300 movies during the decade, regaining its reputation as a world center of filmmaking.[25]

Best of the films directly inspired by the Popular Front period was *La Belle Equipe/ They Were Five* (1936, U.S. release 1938). Based on an original screenplay by Charles Spaak and Julien Duvivier written during the strikes, it couldn't have been made without the active moral and financial support of Jean Gabin, who immediately saw its potential as his vehicle. He also liked that Duvivier, his director on the successful *Bandéra*, and with whom he had developed a good working relationship since *Maria Chapdelaine*, would be doing *La Belle Equipe*. Producers, however, necessarily being employers and capitalists, were hesitant about financing a work with a strong populist tone. Besides, as one put it, "nobody's interested in movies about the working class, especially the working class."[26] Finally they were reassured by the presence of Gabin, newly one of France's top box office draws, as well as his willingness to reduce his fee to help financing. They also calculated that the script's tragic ending was hardly likely to send fired-up audiences out in the street to start a revolution.

At the outset the storyline expresses perfectly the temper of the times. Five jobless construction workers named Jean (Gabin), Charles, Raymond, Jacques and Mario pool their meager capital to buy a lottery ticket. When they win big, they can't decide whether to blow their 100,000 francs on champagne, cigars and vacation travel, or somehow to invest it. Gabin convinces them to hang together and try a cooperative effort—echoing the collectivist ideal then preached by the Popular Front.

They find a dilapidated old building on the banks of the Marne River and decide to turn it into a *guinguette*, a restaurant where their working class comrades could bring their wives and girlfriends on a Sunday outing for eating, dancing, and boating on the river. It would be a workers' paradise, a utopian dream where, as one character puts it, "all the citizens are presidents." They happily set about the renovation, with Duvivier including evocative footage of lush summer foliage, the sun shimmering on the river, and boaters on the Marne similar to 19th-century Impressionist paintings.

But ominous events start to mar the project: Jacques decides to leave for Canada, Raymond falls from the roof and is killed while dancing a drunken jig, a gendarme tells Mario, an illegal immigrant, that he will have to leave France. Worse, Jean and Charles compete for the same woman, Gina, played by a provocative, manipulative Viviane Romance in a lacy negligee. The restaurant opens with Jean and Charles the only remaining members of the original group. Gabin in his best cabaret mode sings a charming ditty, *Quand on s'promène au bord de l'eau* (*Strolling Beside the Water*), everyone dances, goes canoeing, and has a grand time. Then comes the inevitable moment of Gabinesque tragedy: Jean finds Charles and Gina together in her room, and shoots him in a fit of jealous anger as the camera does a tight close-up of his glaring eyes. As a gendarme leads him away, Gabin murmurs dreamily, "It was a beautiful idea. A beautiful idea that we had…. Too beautiful, certainly, to succeed." A prophetic epitaph for the Popular Front's promise of worker camaraderie and solidarity.

The screenplay was literate, solid, and coherent, Gabin incarnated the typical working class guy as he swaggered around, cloth cap atilt, cementing his status as the proletarian hero, *un homme du people*. His incarnation of France's mood was later praised by

Left to right: **Raymond Aimos, Gabin, and Charles Vanel in** *La Belle Equipe,* **1936. The film was seen as a metaphor for France's short-lived Popular Front movement (Collection du Musée Jean Gabin).**

the *New York Times* film critic David Kehr, who noted that Gabin "took on the doom-laden passivity of a dispirited nation moving inexorably toward war."[27] The film itself appeared to many to be a metaphor for France's brief Popular Front movement. The other actors, particularly the felicitously named Romance, were flawless in their roles. Gabin's song became a hit of the day, hummed all over France. Duvivier's direction was brilliant, certainly one of the high points of his career. As he himself explained with his usual disenchanted view of human endeavor, "It's a fairly pessimistic film because it tends to prove the inanity of trying to do anything at the present time."[28]

But the Front and the hopes it gave rise to had another two years to run. The nervous producers worried that the public wasn't ready to pay for disillusionment. Fearing they would never recoup their investment, they asked Duvivier to give it a happy ending. Probably thinking it would never be used, he complied reluctantly but professionally with a brief scene where Jean breaks up with Gina. He and Charles talk things over man to man and decide sensibly, "There are things between us which are worth more than a woman." Camaraderie among workers wins out and the cooperative is saved.

The dithering producers hit upon a way of making up their minds about which ending to release: they would show both versions in a suburban Paris theater, with the members of the audience voting for their preference. The happy ending predictably won and was duly chosen as the official version released in September 1936. Even so, it was never commercially successful, possibly because the contrived, tacked-on ending was so obviously phony, ringing false with the story that had gone before. The French public wouldn't see the original film with its tragic denouement until many years later, though foreign audiences often saw the original.

Gabin, who had made a financial sacrifice to do this one, was extremely disappointed. "We all believed in *La Belle Equipe*, and I more than anyone else," he recalled. "We thought that the story of workers who got together in a cooperative was something people would want to see. After all, we were right in the middle of the Popular Front. Everybody was talking about a brighter future. But by the time we came out, it was already clear that that was a false hope. We got it completely wrong, and that was a bitter pill to swallow."[29]

He shouldn't have been surprised. Its optimistic, cheerful opening, with jobless workers popping champagne corks to celebrate their good luck, simply sets audiences up for the tragedy that follows. Despite the artificial, revised ending, *Equipe* in both versions is in fact a bleak film in which all of the characters' hopes—male friendship, a successful business project, escape from poverty and a miserable existence, love of a good woman—are disappointed, leaving a dazed, demoralized Jean to wonder how such "a beautiful idea" could fail so utterly. One by one, the bright wings of Popular Front butterfly dreams are cruelly torn off by Duvivier's screenplay, while the film's terse, noir tone typical of *réalisme poétique* emphasizes the film's joyless ending. Not exactly a formula for success with mass audiences looking to be distracted from the decade's anxiety.

Gabin's next film, *Les Bas Fonds/The Lower Depths* (1936, U.S. release 1937), was another early example of poetic realism, even if Jean Renoir did, unfortunately to my mind, give it some comic scenes and an upbeat ending distorting Maxime Gorky's grim tragedy of 1902 about life among Russian society's outcasts. Alexey Maximovich Peshkov, pen name Gorky, was after all an uncompromising rebel, champion of the underclass, and the idol of Czarist Russia's restless young generation protesting against the country's establishment of landowning nobility and Philistine bourgeoisie. His romanticized portrayal of tramps and glorification of the worker as superior to the middle class appealed to Renoir as an enthusiastic communist sympathizer. That comes through in his film. But Gorky's powerful message is diluted by Renoir's mixed motives and early confusion about how to treat the Russian play as a French movie, due in good part to pressure from his comrades in the Stalinist-lining French Communist Party. Though not officially a Party member, Renoir was at the very least a traveling companion and susceptible of influence by the comrades, as his *La Vie est à Nous* clearly shows.[30]

Before becoming a star, Gabin had wanted to work with Renoir for some years, but Renoir took no notice of him until *Bandéra*. "He thought his career could be helped by an appearance in a different sort of role," Renoir recalled. "He had seen some of my films and liked them, so he let it be known through his agent that he would be interested in a role in *Les Bas Fonds*."[31] If Gabin felt he needed Renoir to boost his career at this point, Renoir, who had not yet achieved recognition—or financial success—as a major director, also needed Gabin. His early films often looked amateurish and makeshift, and revealed technical awkwardness, while critics found his free-wheeling composition and montage confusing. Their collaboration in this film marked the start of a long friendship—interrupted by Renoir's years in Hollywood, when Jean disapproved of the director's taking American citizenship—with Gabin giving him the pet name of *Le Gros* (Big Guy). When he began making serious money in the 1930s, one of Gabin's first purchases of fine art was a painting by Renoir's Impressionist father, Pierre-Auguste.

It was a case of opposites attracting. Renoir, the son of a world-famous painter, had a university education and spoke cultivated French. Gabin was up from nowhere, didn't make it through secondary school, and got by on street smarts while speaking Montmartre slang. But if Gabin was no intellectual, he was a very close and astute observer of human nature and the ways of the world. Both he and Renoir were French through and through, loving the *terroir* and traditional French values, and greatly enjoying good food and drink. Moreover, Renoir was an actor's director, genuinely liking and supporting them. "If Duvivier taught me the elements of cinema technique, Jean Renoir helped me understand the acting profession," Gabin told André Brunelin. "It might seem surprising, but he made me like actors. Movie actors are doing a high-wire act without a net, and when we're shooting, even the toughest and most professional among us is fragile. Any little thing can ruin the take."[32]

Renoir, who spoke of Gabin's "profound honesty" as an actor, understood that. He also appreciated what he called Gabin's sixth sense for the camera: "He doesn't act in front of the camera, he just exists, and that makes a marvelous impression on the film.... He's the only one like that I know in France."[33] The two related to each other intuitively. "Renoir couldn't fool me with his little tricks," Gabin once said. "When he arrived on the set, he often pretended there was some little detail that bothered him and had to be changed. I knew that meant he hadn't quite figured out his *mise en scene* and needed more time to think about it."[34]

Renoir had a proposition from a Russian émigré producer in Paris, Alexandre Kamenka, to do a French version of *Les Bas Fonds* with a script by another émigré, Eugene Zamiatin. As he mulled what to do with this amid the atmosphere of mixed despair and hope that was the France of the Popular Front, Renoir suggested to Gabin that maybe he could play the lead role of Pépel, a petty thief. Their original idea was to do a purely French version of the play, set in recognizably suburban Paris, with French-name characters. That, initially, was the only approach that interested Gabin, who didn't feel he could play a Russian credibly. Renoir called on Charles Spaak to rework Zamiatin's screenplay along those lines.

The production was ready to roll, when suddenly everything came to a halt. Renoir's communist affiliation came at a price: the French Communist Party, which was putting up part of the film's financing, was calling in the IOU. Possibly on orders from their bosses in Moscow, high FCP officials let it be known that they didn't like Gorky's masterpiece being turned into a purely French movie. It was fine that for him the film symbolized the weakness and corruption of the aristocracy and the coming victory of the proletariat, but they insisted that it be set in the Moscow of pre-revolutionary Czarist times, the better to contrast Gorky's lost souls with the New Soviet Man.[35]

Renoir dutifully complied, adding samovars and other Russian trinkets to the set, giving the cast Gorky's original names, and referring to kopeks in the dialogue instead of francs. Gabin, now deeply involved in the project, went along, though not out of political conviction. Although he did play the proletarian role many times, was the archetypal working-class character of the 1930s, and, as mentioned earlier, was a dues-paying member of France's communist labor union, he was never overtly a political animal. Renoir took him along to a few Party meetings and rallies, but Gabin kept his distance. He was distrustful of any kind of mass movement.

Shot in the overheated Popular Front atmosphere of August to October 1936 in the Éclair studios in Epinay-sur-Seine, the film has the thief Pépel (Gabin) living in a Moscow flophouse along with a handful of raffish derelicts. The hostel is owned by the slum land-lord Kostylev and his wife Vassilissa, who loves Pépel. He, however, is enamored of Vas-silissa's sister Natacha, a pure soul amid the world's corruption. Pépel breaks into the mansion of The Baron, played by the distinguished actor and director Louis Jouvet, then 17 years his senior and a more established star than Gabin. Pépel is surprised in the attempted burglary by The Baron, who informs him that he has lost everything at the casino. They become friends and the broke baron joins him in the flophouse. Kostylev and his wife beat Natacha to get her to marry a louche police inspector, hoping to gain some advantage. Pépel intervenes, Kostylev is killed, and Pépel is sent to jail. When he gets out, he and Natacha leave for a better life together in a Chaplinesque ending, complete with the couple walking happily along a road and carrying a knapsack on a stick.

Some critics objected to Renoir's injecting comic elements and a happy ending into a world-famous tragedy and setting it in a sort of imaginary land. André Bazin seemed to be of two minds, saying Renoir came perilously close to making a comic film of Gorky's tragedy. "He even refuses to allow Jean Gabin to die at the end.... This improbable game of hide-and-seek between vaudeville and tragedy, realism and parody, Gorki and Renoir, produces a work which is at the very least fascinating."[36] But with its innovative poetic realist treatment, including dramatic lighting—the scene where Gabin hesitates for a long moment, his face dramatically lit from below, before blowing out a lamp is an excellent example—and unusual camera angles, it was impressive enough to win the film the first Louis Delluc prize as the best French film of the year. After its release in the U.S. the following year, America's National Board of Review judged it one of the top ten foreign films of 1937. Jean Renoir's direction was itself recognized when the Socialist premier Léon Blum made Renoir a knight of the Legion of Honor. But perhaps the film's most memorable achievement was sealing the Renoir-Gabin working relationship, which would produce several cinema classics.

9

Prewar Classics (Part One)

Jean Gabin personified *réalisme poétique*. Taken together, his films over the next four years form a textbook example of this forerunner of film noir. They pervade the memorable 1930s productions of the Golden Age of French cinema. They are the classics reviewed in film studies courses and featured in many film festivals. They prefigured both the dark American crime films of the 1940s and '50s and the gritty films of Italian neorealism. Gabin would be one of the first major actors who understood this new way of dramatizing a story on film. Working repeatedly with directors he knew, liked, and felt comfortable with, he made it his own. For years he was identified with it.

The basis of poetic realism was the manipulation of light and shadow to create sinister moods with ominous shadows, crepuscular sets, and unsettling camera angles. Self-consciously modernist, it derived to some degree from the Expressionist school of painting. That went as far back as Norwegian Edvard Munch's 1893 *The Scream*, and German artists of the Die Brucke and Der Blaue Reiter schools before the First World War. It was there in seminal form in the German Expressionist films of the early 1920s like Robert Weiner's *The Cabinet of Dr. Caligari*, F. W. Murnau's nightmarish *Nosferatu*, and Fritz Lang's dystopian view of city life, *Metropolis*.

The claustrophobic, fatalistic mood of such German films and their suggestion of hopelessness later correlated all too well with the anxious atmosphere in 1930s France that directors like Marcel Carné and Julien Duvivier sought to depict. In the 1940s and early '50s, it was used by directors of the Italian Neorealist school such as Michelangelo Antonioni, Vittorio De Sica, and Luchino Visconti as the way to portray the hard living conditions and moral decay of Italy's postwar period. At the same time, it was adopted by American directors, but generally as a way to tell crime stories and without the profound societal overtones of the Europeans.

American film noir, as it became known—film historians oddly adopting a term used by French critics to describe American hard-boiled films, but not their own poetic realism—featured voice-over narrators and more violence than the European precursors to tell crime stories. John Huston's *The Maltese Falcon*, Billy Wilder's *Double Indemnity*, and Howard Hawks' *The Big Sleep* were early examples of the noir cycle whose origins can be traced, in good part, to poetic realism. (Noir style of course continued to express alienation in later films like *Blade Runner*, *Chinatown*, *Reservoir Dogs*, and many others.) The main difference between the American and French approaches is described by Dudley Andrew in his scholarly *Mists of Regret: Culture and Sensibility in Classic French Film*: "American cinema has always invested in maximum shock effects, in bursts of song, violence, eros, or language," he writes. "Poetic realism diffuses such energy in a warm mist of style that mutes the sound and brightness of every effect, even as it washes over us and seeps down to the roots of feeling.... Poetic realism is properly identified as French."[1]

It was certainly very French in its habitual violation of the Hollywood formula of the happy ending. It was as if the tragic endings of the French films of this era were in fact the "poetic" part of poetic realism, along with the tenebrous mood of the lighting and sets. André Bazin noted the paradox of ending so many of Jean Gabin's films in tragedy, even suicide, when "the commercial law of the happy ending ... forces so many producers to tack on artificial finales." Wouldn't it be more normal, he wondered, for one of cinema's most popular and well-loved actors to end up "happily married with lots of children?" Then he asks, rhetorically, "But can you see Gabin as a family man? No, it is impossible."[2] (It would become possible when Gabin adopted a different persona in his second career.)

Impossible because tragedy at this time in his career was Gabin's shtick. As luck would have it, poetic realism matched that perfectly. Due to his past roles in which he inevitably came to a bad end, as well as to the roles to come, he became the cinematic symbol of the human condition. If André Bazin compared him Oedipus, it was because his characters at this time were the archetypal victim of fate, both manipulated by outside forces and trapped by interior conflicts that lead to his doom. It is perhaps not too much to say that this was an era in which French cinema, despite its commercial constraints as entertainment, took seriously its role as a new art form—French critics like to call motion pictures "the seventh art"—and made a coherent effort to attain the heights of the great tragedies of antiquity. In ten major films Gabin did in the 1930s, his character dies a violent death five times (shot twice, suicide three times), and murders someone seven times. As for the love that he seeks as a haven in a corrupt, callous world, eight of his screen attempts to form a couple end in disaster, worst of all when he kills his mistresses to end his torment. As Bazin observed, "Gabin was the only French actor and almost the only actor worldwide (Chaplin excepted) whom the public expected to finish badly."[3]

Technically, too, poetic realism's use of light favored him. Starting with *Bandéra*, directors insistently highlighted his rugged face in every film, especially with shafts of light across his eyes—in one scene in *Pépé le Moko* there is so much light in his eyes that he suffered slight burns.[4] Gabin was lucky in this regard that some of Europe's best film technicians fled the Continent's growing anti–Semitic regimes in the 1930s. Some went to Hollywood, while others gravitated to the Paris studios. The prolific German cinematographer Curt Courant had worked on more than 100 silent and early sound era movies before, as a Jew, he was forced to leave Germany in 1933. He easily found work with both British and French studios, doing films with directors like Fritz Lang and Alfred Hitchcock. Thoroughly familiar with Expressionist style, he heavily influenced French camera technique. In several of Gabin's movies he used his typical soft-focus and highly contrasty shots, often creating special effects during the filming itself, then new to French camerawork.

Another influential refugee was the Budapest-born production designer Alexandre Trauner. Versatile and highly innovative, he worked in architecture and design before doing the sets for several of Gabin's movies directed by Marcel Carné, sometimes creating the illusion of whole city streets and buildings to fit a film's mood. Gabin quickly adapted to the techniques of poetic realism and used them to his—and his films'—advantage. As the director Raymond Rouleau put it after doing *Le Messager* with Gabin in 1937: "Sometimes during the shoot I would be disconcerted when I saw him acting certain scenes too subtly when I thought they required a stronger, more emphatic approach. But when we saw the rushes and final editing I realized that Gabin had done exactly what was right for that scene. I saw that no actor had a surer instinct for the camera, just as birds or Lindberg have a strong sense of orientation."[5]

Pépé le Moko (1937, U.S. release 1941), Gabin's fifth film with Julien Duvivier, prompted the usually demanding film critic Graham Greene to gush in his review that it was "one of the most exciting and moving films I can remember seeing ... a film which is really trying to translate into dramatic terms the irrelevances, the grotesque wit, the absurd, passionate tangle of associations which make up the mind. Perhaps there have been pictures as exciting on the 'thriller' level as this before ... but I cannot remember one which has succeeded so admirably in raising the thriller to a poetic level."[6]

The film has been compared by some to Howard Hawks' 1932 gangster movie *Scarface*, with its retelling of the Al Capone story.[7] But although there is a police sweep early in the film, Duvivier is reaching for much more than a cops and robbers action movie, and Gabin's Pépé—the only film of the 1930s in which he plays a gangster—has far more psychological depth than Paul Muni's Tony Camonte, as shafts of light show his suffering face nostalgic for Paris, his pale eyes dreaming of escape from the sheltering, claustrophobic Casbah. The film is in fact a *Casablanca* for grownups. Without the gin-fueled sappy overtones, Rick's two-bit philosophizing, the obligatory anti–Nazi propaganda, or an airplane improbably carrying the heroine to freedom and married happiness, it delves relentlessly into the problems of human evil, passion, and unquenchable longing. Gabin's alternating euphoria and despair are palpable.

Pépé, whose surname le Moko is underworld slang for someone from Toulon, is a big-time criminal who has been hiding out in the Arab-ruled Casbah quartier of Algiers for two years, following a big heist in Toulon. As the film opens, police officials from France have come over to the colony to ask the local cops why they still have not arrested him. But Pépé is revered in the Casbah as a *caïd*, a mob chief protected by his gang and the quarter's swarming, multi-racial, anti–French population who alert him as soon as a policeman sets foot in its labyrinthine streets. He is living with a gypsy girl, Inès, played with savage passion by Line Noro, but is bored by both her and his stifling confinement. An Algerian detective in fez and baggy Turkish trousers, the oleaginous Inspector Slimane (Lucas Gridoux), knows that the only way to get Pépé is to lure him out of the Casbah. He follows his prey closely and even establishes a relationship with him based on mutual respect among pros.

When a classy kept woman, Gaby, coolly played by Mireille Balin, arrives from Paris in Algiers with her sugar daddy, she goes slumming in the Casbah and meets Pépé. She is fascinated by him as a famous bad boy, he is professionally attracted by her ostentatious jewelry and the mere fact that she embodies his dreamed-of Paris and freedom. In a scene for the anthologies, they talk of places they love in Paris and recite the names of Metro stations like an incantation; the finest compliment he can think of is that she smells like the Metro, but in first class. She will unwittingly be Slimane's perfect lure. Pépé yields to temptation and races out of the Casbah to meet Gaby, but Inès, trying to keep him, alerts Slimane, who arrests him just as Gaby's ship is sailing back to France. As he watches it leave, and with it his hopes of a new life, he pulls a knife and commits suicide.

Unlike *Bandéra*, where Duvivier insisted on shooting on location for greater authenticity, he shot Pépé at the Pathé studios in the Paris suburb of Joinville except for one

Gabin (center) with Mireille Balin and Lucas Gridoux in *Pépé le Moko*, 1936. Balin was one of the many leading ladies whom Gabin courted (Collection du Musée Jean Gabin).

week of exteriors in Algiers. Still, the sets by Jacques Krauss evoke the Casbah's interlocking houses and steep, teeming streets—small shops, cafes, layabouts, stray cats and all—well enough to give goose pimples of recognition to those of us who have lived in Algiers. Gabin's acting is more self-assured than ever as he easily projects the authority of a gang chief who will brook no backchat, slaps punks around, and orders the murder of an informer. At the same time his moody vulnerability and throbbing nostalgia establish more than ever his tough-guy-soft-heart persona.

Always scrupulous about his wardrobe for a film, Gabin often composed it himself to support the image he wanted to project: the cloth cap for proletarian roles, a spectacular Spahi cape for *Gueule d'Amour*, just the right kind of battered fedora as a police commissioner, sharp suits for his parts as a businessman or mob chief. In *Pépé* it approaches the point of fetishism. The camera lingers several times on his two-tone, pimp-style shoes, while his black shirt, yellow tie, and neck scarf make him the very image of the dandy gangster. (The way he crossed the scarf instead of tying it sparked a new fashion among the pimps in Paris' Place Pigalle. So convincing was the image that after the film was released, Gabin was approached by Paris prostitutes asking to work for him. "I should have accepted," he joked. "I would certainly have made as much money and with less effort.")[8] At one point in the film he coquettishly calls attention to the fact that he is wearing clothes from his personal wardrobe: during a café scene he leans back on the bar, his

suit jacket opens, and the "JG" monogram on his shirt is clearly visible in a
sort of sartorial wink at the audience.

Pépé was an instant success at the
box office and with critics, who began
to compare him to Spencer Tracy and
James Cagney, "but Jean Gabin sur-
passes them both in ability and force,"
concluded one.[9] "Here the Gabin myth
is definitively created.... Gabin, the
pre-war Gabin, is all here, with his soft
heart and sudden outbursts," reflected
the critic and director Jean-Claude
Missiaen some years later, "his physical
presence and instinctive reactions, his
world of a ruined life and failed escape,
where the femme fatale passes like an
unattainable dream."[10]

Pépé le Moko, the dandy of the Casbah, 1936. The
way he wore the neck scarf was quickly imitated by
Paris pimps (Collection du Musée Jean Gabin).

At the time of its U.S. release in 1941 and for years thereafter, American reviewers
raved. *The New York Herald Tribune* called it "an outstanding screen achievement. It
ranks with the few masterpieces of the screen," while *Time* said, "It deserves a gold star
on any list." Pauline Kael, the eminent, longtime, often contrarian film critic of *The New
Yorker*, later summed it up as "superb entertainment. A classic romantic melodrama of
the '30s, and one of the most compelling of all the fatalistic French screen romances."[11]
When *Pépé* returned to a Los Angeles art cinema in 2002, the critic Kenneth Turan wrote,
"Fearless, humane, an intensely masculine and unflappably charismatic presence who
was completely natural on the screen, Gabin is a star for whom there is no exact American
equivalent. Often cast as a doomed man, the actor combines characteristics of Gary
Cooper and Jimmy Cagney and comes up with an immaculately dressed gangster who
makes women faint."[12]

Hollywood loved *Pépé*. Loved it so much in fact that it did not one but two remakes.
Warners bought the rights to it, but instead of importing it they asked the producer Walter Wanger to do a shot-by-shot remake to cut production costs, using as much of the
original footage of exteriors and interior scene-setting as possible. Wanger, apparently
afraid of the competition, promptly tried to have every print of the original destroyed,
but fortunately failed to do so.[13] To further reduce competition, the U.S. release of
Duvivier's film was delayed nearly four years to give Wanger's *Algiers* (1938) time to hit
American screens.

But his first task was to get the script past the Breen Office, which was upset by the
original's exotic sensuality and moral ambiguity, so dangerous to chaste American audiences. "In its present form," Joseph Breen wrote to the producer, "you will understand
that it is not acceptable from the standpoint of the Production Code by reason of the
definite suggestion that your two leading female characters are both kept women.... The
dialogue should be changed, so as to get away from the suggestion that Inès is Pépé's mistress."[14] It was also unacceptable that Pépé commit suicide, so he had to be shot at the
end trying to escape the police.

Wanger had Charles Boyer on a two-year contract and persuaded him to play Pépé, with Hedy Lamarr as Gaby, even though the smooth, sophisticated Boyer obviously lacked Gabin's proletarian authenticity—it's hard to imagine him knowing the names of the Paris Metro by heart. Boyer was understandably nervous about reprising Gabin's role, and agreed only on the condition of having the right to choose the director. He chose John Cromwell, but that didn't keep the result from being an insipid, emasculated, bowdlerized version of the original. "An actor never likes to copy another's style," he complained, "and here I was copying Jean Gabin, one of the best.... [Cromwell] would run a scene from the original and insist we do it exactly that way—terrible, a perfectly terrible way to work."[15] Not only that, but Boyer never actually said the line "Come with me to the Casbah," which followed and mocked him for the rest of his career like a bad parody, becoming the vocal model for the romantic skunk Pépé le Pew and an amorous tomcat in Tom and Jerry cartoons. As Bosley Crowther later summed up charitably in *The New York Times*, "It [the original] is a raw-edged, frank exposition of a basically evil story, whereas Mr. Wanger's version was a romantic and necessarily cautious re-telling of the same."[16]

As for *Casbah* (1948), the remake of the remake, the less said the better. Made by singer Tony Martin's production company, this misbegotten semi-musical has him trying to imitate both Jean Gabin *and* Charles Boyer, with Marta Toren as Gaby and Yvonne de Carlo as Inès. Peter Lorre's considerable talent is wasted as Inspector Slimane. Martin croons "For Every Man There's a Woman" in a make-believe Casbah, but the film was still a critical and box office failure, losing some $200,000.

No one believed in Jean Renoir's idea for a movie based on the First World War experiences of a friend of his, a French fighter pilot who had been shot down seven times, captured by the Germans, and escaped seven times. Renoir wrote up a rough story outline in 1934 and began pitching it to potential producers. It turned out to be a hard sell. Nobody wanted any more war stories, said some. It didn't have enough love interest, the only female role being a German peasant woman, objected others. Not commercial enough, was the consensus, producers of the day being convinced that the typical movie audience had the intelligence of a 12-year-old. "I touted that manuscript around for three years, visiting the offices of all the producers, French and foreign, conventional or avant-garde," he tells us in his autobiography, *My Life and My Films*. "Without Jean Gabin's help, none of them would have taken a chance on the film. He accompanied me on many of my tries. Finally we found a financier who, impressed by Jean Gabin's strong confidence in it, agreed to do the film."[17]

La Grande Illusion/Grand Illusion (1937, U.S. release 1938) came to be considered one of the masterpieces of French cinema, winning awards from the New York Film Critics Circle and the National Board of Review as the best foreign film of 1938. It was the first foreign language movie nominated for the Academy Award for Best Picture in 1939. Franklin D. Roosevelt declared, "Every democrat in the world should see this film,"[18] Orson Welles said if he had only one film in the world to save, it would be this.[19] Writing 60 years after its initial release, Janet Maslin, the durable movie reviewer for *The New York Times*, still found it "one of the most haunting of all war films ... an oasis of subtlety, moral intelligence and deep emotion."[20]

Not everyone liked it. Renoir made the film, he said, "because I am a pacifist."[21] Governments trying to mobilize their publics for Europe's next war called it cowardly, defeatist, even treasonable. A hit with the French public when released, it was banned by the government in 1939 as pacifist, even if audiences did rise to sing the Marseillaise, sometimes with arms raised in a Fascist salute, during certain sequences. Italy banned it as well, and Belgium, ironically by Premier Paul-Henri Spaak, brother of the screenwriter who worked on the script. Joseph Goebbels, Hitler's propaganda minister, is said to have liked it personally, but had it banned in Germany and the negative seized; he whimsically branded Renoir Cinematographic Enemy Number One and declared that Von Stroheim's portrayal was a caricature: "No German officer is like that." The publisher Jean Fayard tartly replied, "Too bad for them."[22]

Arguably Renoir's most famous film, its well-known story begins with Lieutenant Maréchal (Gabin) and Captain de Boeldieu (Pierre Fresnay) being shot down by Captain von Rauffenstein (Erich von Stroheim) over German territory during a reconnaissance flight. Taken to a POW camp for officers, Maréchal and de Boeldieu get to know each other better and their class differences become apparent. Besides its pacifism, the film's main theme in this time of the Popular Front and its lyrical glorification of the Common Man, is that even as the Old World of aristocracy was coming to an end, aristocrats of different countries still had more in common with each other, sharing a civilized code of honor, than with their own compatriots of the working class. Renoir, who loved the Middle Ages, distrusted the Renaissance, and detested the industrial age, which he saw as dehumanizing, later explained the spirit in which he made the film: "In some respects that world war was still a war of respectable people, of well-bred people. I almost dare say, of gentlemen. That does not excuse it. Good manners, even chivalry, do not excuse a massacre."[23]

In one of the most telling sequences, Maréchal, played with his usual earthy nonchalance by Gabin, who wears his officer's uniform (actually Renoir's old uniform from his service in the First World War) casually, tries to break the class barrier. "We've been together for weeks, and we still say 'vous' to each other," he tells de Boeldieu. To which the haughty aristocrat explains condescendingly, "I said 'vous' to my mother, and I say 'vous' to my wife." Maréchal sighs, "Decidedly, everything separates us." With von Rauffenstein, however, de Boeldieu reminisces, in cultivated English, about equestrian competitions in Britain and other worldly matters. The German commandant reflects on the end of their class: "Whatever happens in this war, it means the end of the von Rauffensteins and the de Boeldieus." The Frenchman replies, "We won't be needed any more." Later, as part of an escape plan, de Boeldieu, in an act of noble sacrifice, climbs up to the roof of the prison to distract the guards. Von Rauffenstein pleads with him, in English, to come down, then reluctantly shoots him.

Maréchal and another prisoner, the Jewish Rosenthal (Marcel Dalio) escape. They head for Switzerland, suffering cold and hunger. Rosenthal sprains an ankle, slowing them down, and they have a bitter argument when Maréchal's proletarian anti–Semitism comes out before they finally reconcile. They come upon a farm and enter, hoping for food and shelter. The owner, Elsa (Dita Parlo), a woman whose husband and brothers have been killed in the war, is unafraid of the Frenchmen, another message by Renoir of class solidarity. She shelters and feeds them until they can travel again, with Maréchal and she having a romantic interlude before he leaves with Rosenthal. They make it to the Swiss border as a German patrol intercepts them. As one of them raises his rifle to shoot, his superior stops him, saying they're in Switzerland now, and good for them.

The film's title, seemingly bitter and ironic, is ambiguous. As Renoir explained, he wanted it to be open to interpretation by the audience. "We must also allow the audience to create, to be an author," he said. "*Grand Illusion*? That means this and this and this."[24]

Gabin (left) with Erich von Stroheim in *La Grande Illusion*, 1937. Unhappy about what he considered von Stroheim's upstaging of him, Gabin snubbed the film's premiere (Collection du Musée Jean Gabin).

There are only two references to the title in the film itself. A French soldier says bitterly, "what an illusion," when another says the war will be over before they can escape from the POW camp. At the end, Maréchal and Rosenthal hope this will be the last war, *la der de der*, but you can tell they don't believe it.

Gabin's role as the working-class mechanic who becomes an officer through flight training lets him play his usual proletarian character, uneasy with aristocratic attitudes but a man with innate gallantry, a survivor in any circumstance. He is unmistakably the ordinary Frenchman as his telling little touches throughout the film show: carelessly wearing his officer's kepi cocked over one ear as if he were wearing a cloth cap back home in Montmartre; listening to the popular song *Frou-Frou* on a phonograph in the opening scene and singing along with it, rolling his r's like a true proletarian; standing beside de Boeldieu, who yawns with aristocratic discretion, and then doing his own impolite yawn with wide mouth uncovered; and expressing typically French working class anti–Semitism during his escape with Rosenthal.

Insisting that the mise en scène include a small spotlight trained on his eyes to emphasize them, he goes through an emotional range from volatile anger and despair in prison, to tenderness in scenes with Elsa. One day after a particularly dramatic scene, Renoir, in admiration, asked Gabin what he had been thinking of during the shoot. "Of that big steak I was going to down as soon as it was over," he replied.[25] Pauline Kael thought he did a fine, subtle job: "With Gabin you're not aware of any performance; with von Stroheim and Fresnay, you are."[26]

Renoir's virtual infatuation with von Stroheim meant he nearly stole the show from Gabin. When Louis Jouvet wasn't available to play von Rauffenstein, the producers hired von Stroheim. He was Renoir's movie idol, his silent films like *Greed* in 1924 being one of the things that made him want to be a filmmaker. Worried that his role as camp commandant would be upstaged by Gabin and Fresnay, Renoir rewrote it to give him much more importance, and let von Stroheim make his uniform more flamboyant than the head of a POW camp would normally wear. (The idea of playing the role in a neck brace, emphasizing the stiff, aristocratic character of the commandant, was von Stroheim's.)[27]

The result was that, although he got top billing, the story didn't seem to be so much about Gabin's Maréchal. Thematically, too, the proletarian vs. aristocrat tension between him and Fresnay was overshadowed in the final screenplay by the relations between de Boeldieu and von Rauffenstein. Convinced after seeing a private screening that he had been upstaged by both von Stroheim, whom he disliked anyway for what he considered his fussy overacting, and Fresnay, Gabin snubbed the premiere at Paris' grand Marivaux cinema, where it was shown continuously from 10 a.m. until 2 the next morning, and for many weeks, setting an attendance record. "All anybody remembers is the Kraut," he summed up.[28]

Gabin did *Gueule d'Amour/Lady Killer* (1937) for two main reasons: to play opposite Mireille Balin again, with whom he had had a romantic relation since they did *Pépé le*

With Mireille Balin again in *Gueule d'Amour*, 1937, the only film in which Gabin wept. He later considered the part a career mistake (Collection du Musée Jean Gabin).

Moko, and to get away from his typecast image of the "Gabin myth" tough guy by taking a role where he suffers more openly at the hands of a fickle woman. Neither reason was well advised. His liaison with Balin, then one of France's most beautiful actresses, led to nothing and didn't help his already difficult marriage with Doriane.

In this role Gabin plays Lucien, a handsome noncom in a regiment of Spahis—light cavalry made up of recruits from the French North African colonies in Morocco, Algeria, and Tunisia, and known for their dashing uniforms complete with long, billowing cape—in the South of France. As he parades by on his charger he turns the heads of all the girls in the little town of Orange, but falls for a faithless courtesan from Paris he happens to meet while on leave in Cannes. After she toys with him and makes clear she will not leave her sugar daddy, he kills her and ends up weeping helplessly in the arms of a friend.

He later considered the part a career mistake. Although the movie was enough of a museum piece to be featured in the Classics Section at the 2016 Cannes Film Festival, he was embarrassed by forgoing his usual understated style to display that much emotion on the screen—the first and only time he wept in a movie. His son Mathias recounts that when Gabin watched it with distaste on television in the family living room in the 1970s, his only remark at the end was a laconic "I've done better."[29]

10

Prewar Classics (Part Two)

He would do much better in *Le Quai des Brumes/Port of Shadows* (1938, U.S. release 1939), his first of three exceptional films with Marcel Carné. It was Carné's first big hit. It won the Louis Delluc Prize as the best French film, the Grand Prix National du Cinéma Français, and in the 1970s was declared by movie industry professionals one of the ten best French films in the history of talking movies. It also had the distinction of being the breakthrough film of an 18-year-old kid who would be Gabin's leading lady, and much more, Michèle Morgan, née Simone Renée Roussel. A perfect example of poetic realism, "it was, for its times, a sort of revolutionary film," Carné recalled in his memoirs, "coming at a moment when movie screens were full of comedies, musical and otherwise, sunny and full of busy extras. And I come along with a half-empty nightclub, fog, and dark, damp cobblestones."[1]

Ironically, this most French of films was almost German. Probably because Doriane had spotted its movie potential, Gabin had in 1935 bought an option on the screen rights to Pierre Mac Orlan's 1927 novel about underworld shenanigans in Le Lapin Agile, an actual Montmartre cabaret frequented by artists and poets. He was still under contract to the Potsdam-based UFA production company, so he pitched the idea to them, insisting that Carné be the director and that poet and screenwriter Jacques Prévert do a treatment of the novel. It was sent to UFA for approval in 1938, but German censors, under Propaganda Minister Joseph Goebbels, found the story "plutocratic, decadent and negative," mainly because it centered on a French army deserter.[2] When Carné and Prévert refused to alter the screenplay, UFA released Gabin from his contract. This then relieved the monolingual, German-allergic Carné from shooting the film in UFA's studios at Neubabelsberg, which he feared would be "heavy, ponderous and theatrical."[3]

They found a new producer in the person of the Russian-born Gregor Rabinovitch, changed the locale from Montmartre to Le Havre, and had only one more obstacle to clear, the French censors. Nervous about offending the army or demoralizing the public on the eve of what appeared to be coming war, they demanded that the word "deserter" never be pronounced in the film, and that the soldier, after changing into civvies, respectfully fold his uniform and place it on a table rather than contemptuously throwing it on the floor as the script called for.[4] Carné complied, but, in the weird, anxious France of the late 1930s, he still had to pay a price for directing the "demoralizing" *Le Quai des Brumes*: in 1939 he was sent to dig ditches at the Maginot Line as punishment for showing a French army deserter, even if the taboo word wasn't uttered in the film.[5]

Once again playing a character named Jean, Gabin is AWOL from a colonial regiment

French cinema's dream couple in *Le Quai des Brumes*, 1938. An example of poetic realism, it was the 18-year-old Michèle Morgan's first important part (Collection du Musée Jean Gabin).

in French-ruled Indochina. In the film's first minutes he describes graphically what it is like to shoot a man and watch him die. Now he seeks refuge in the dark, dismal, wintry Channel port of Le Havre in an attempt to, as he explains, "clear the fog in my brain"; today he would be diagnosed with posttraumatic stress disorder. He pitches up in a shabby waterside hangout, home to various down-and-outers including a comely waif in a rakish black beret and transparent raincoat—an outfit suggested by Coco Chanel—named Nelly (Michèle Morgan), herself seeking haven from her louche guardian Zabel (Michel Simon). Lucien (Pierre Brasseur), a smalltime local gang leader, insults Nelly and gets convincingly slapped around by Jean in one of his de rigueur movie outbursts. He is making plans to leave for Venezuela on a cargo ship and start a new life, but this is complicated when he and Nelly fall in love.

Prévert's moving dialogue gives them what I find some of the most memorable romantic lines in cinema. "A man and a woman simply don't understand each other," he says gruffly. "They don't speak the same language. They don't even share the same words." Nelly replies, "Maybe they can't understand each other, but they can love each other." Later, standing behind a line of trailers at a country fair, he delivers the deceptively simple words that became a cult phrase in France and followed them both the rest of their lives: "You've got beautiful eyes, you know." To which she replies urgently, "Kiss me." The romance is short lived, but lasts long enough to change Jean from a scoffer who mocks the idea of love as "that little guy with his wings and arrows" to a smitten man who murmurs, "I only have to look at you, or hear your voice … and I feel like crying."

Lucien, still smarting from the humiliation of being slapped in front of his henchmen, spots Jean in the street and shoots him. He dies in Nelly's arms on the wet cobblestones as the parting ship that was to be his escape blasts its whistle. As in the tragic vision of ancient drama, there is no hope for anyone at the end, stirring us to something like cathartic pity and terror even in the friendly confines of a neighborhood movie theater. Of such simplicity, in the hands of a screenwriter like Prévert, a director like Carné, and actors like Gabin and Morgan, are classic films made.

Much of the film's effect depends on Gabin's projection of rugged, undomesticated masculinity. He always prefers action to philosophizing. "Oh *merde*! I've had enough!" he shouts in a reaction to one character's effete prattle. "You spout words! Words! One leads to another and you have pretty phrases. I can't stand pretty phrases. You get it?" Pierre Mac Orlan loved Gabin's acting in the film, calling him "an artist who knows how to solve all problems through simplicity: he is calm, very attentive, well balanced. He looks like an international-class goalkeeper in front of the posts."[6]

The shoot began in January 1938. The cast suffered from Le Havre's damp, penetrating cold, but that and the short, dark days were perfect for the poetic realist atmosphere Carné sought. When the expected fog failed to materialize, the set designer, Alexandre Trauner, replaced it with artificial fog created by burning coal tar in big sheet metal barrels. That produced the desired effect, but at the end of every day the cast and technicians were covered with soot. This first of four films in which Gabin and Morgan played the leads was the beginning of what the press called "French cinema's ideal couple" and "the dream couple," preceding Bogart and Bacall by nearly a decade. That made good copy, but was premature by more than a year, since they actually did not start their affair until they did their third film. "Neither I nor Jean did anything to fuel that lie," Morgan says in her memoirs, "but even today people, even in show business, think it was true. Some legends die hard."[7]

Not that Gabin didn't seriously court his leading lady, as was his wont. To start with, there was the famous kiss. She recalled:

> I still remember that day very well. I hardly knew Jean Gabin, had met him only a couple of days before the shoot. He was a great teaser and I was very young and took everything very seriously. He had teased me a lot on the set, saying things like "You're very young, a kid like you doesn't know how to kiss." I didn't know what to reply, being very shy, and still am, I'm embarrassed to tell this anecdote. He had teased me so much that I was trembling and didn't know where to look. We started the scene and kissed, and he gave me a real kiss. Thank God I had plenty of makeup on, because I turned red as a tomato. But it was charming and we had a good laugh after.[8]

But the budding relationship was no laughing matter for Gabin. One evening before the scene where he slaps Lucien, Pierre Brasseur drank too much during a dinner with the rest of the cast and made some flirty remarks to Morgan. Gabin gave him a sharp look, but chose not to make a public scene. When they shot the scene where he slaps Brasseur, he put so much jealous force into it that Brasseur staggered, went pale, and clenched his fists. Carné cried, "Cut! Absolutely superb." Gabin had his vengeance, Carné his scene, and Brasseur was lauded for showing such realistic emotion.

Then there was Morgan's 18th birthday in February. After a month of shooting, Gabin surprised her that evening with an armful of roses—his standard tactic when wooing—then took her out for dinner and dancing. She had had her first impression of him when Carné was casting the film: "The astonishing blond hair, not the pale, Nordic sort, but the warm color of a wheat field in the sun," she remembered. "His blue eyes beneath golden lashes. As to the way he dressed, what a surprise! A very 'golf-style' elegance made up of English cashmere, a conservative Prince of Wales suit, club tie, and flower in the buttonhole. A smell of after shave and lavender."[9] Gabin's dresser for most of his career, Micheline Bonnet, had warned Morgan sotto voce during the shoot, "When Monsieur Gabin looks at women like that, they go gaga."[10] But Morgan, 15 years younger than Gabin, wasn't ready to go gaga just yet. As the evening drew to a close, he walked her back to their hotel and asked, "Shall we continue?"

Looking for an excuse, she said they'd better turn in because she had a scene the next day.

> "I'm not talking about tomorrow, but right now," he insisted, "What about it?" "See you tomorrow, Jean, I'll never forget this evening."
>
> As they parted, all he said was, "You're really a funny kid."
>
> She long wondered what made her say "goodbye" instead of "come in."[11]

When Monsieur Gabin looks at women like that... (Collection du Musée Jean Gabin).

Morgan, who was already being labeled by the French press as the most beautiful pair of eyes in the movies, and praised by André Gide for her "natural and strange grace," was not a young woman to act on amorous impulse. She usually put her own interests and career first and didn't hesitate to dump any man who didn't fit into her calculations, as Gabin was to learn.[12] As she later explained her mixed feelings that evening:

> I was in love with him, certainly. I was 18 that night and Jean was 33. He was married and, on my side, I had a fiancé whom I was leaving. In fact, none of that made me stop Jean at the door of my room, but rather it was, I think, fear of complicating our lives and the job we were doing together. Maybe too, the feeling that Jean and I were worth more than a fleeting little affair. But in the moments following, when I found myself alone in my room, I regretted not simply having said, "Come in." Jean wouldn't have been my first love affair, and in the morning everything would probably have seemed both marvelous and simpler, even if at the same time, everything would already have been over between us. That night could have been nothing but the affectionate ending to a charming evening that had brought us together an instant. Nothing more. I knew that he liked to court and seduce women, that he was romantic and tender, just the opposite of the characters he played most of the time. What he liked mainly was having an affair, and I could have been his affair of the moment that night in Le Havre. Maybe he saw in my eyes that it was possible, and since I was only 18, I was an easy conquest. And yet, it didn't happen. Probably it was just too simple.[13]

When premiered at Paris' Marivaux cinema in May 1938, the film set a French box office record, even bettering *La Grande Illusion*. Well received by the entertainment press, it was booed by France's spitefully partisan political papers of both the left and right for purely ideological reasons, while Catholic organizations condemned it as "a profoundly demoralizing story ... with a clearly offensive atmosphere."[14] Jean Renoir, ever faithful to his Communist Party friends, sniped that it was "a fascist film," much to the anger of Carné and Prévert, the latter offering to punch Renoir in the face.[15] Two years later, the collaborationist, not to say fascist, Vichy government, searching for scapegoats to excuse France's shameful capitulation to Germany, banned it "on moral grounds," implying that "effete" and "decadent" films like that were responsible.[16]

Port of Shadows was better received in non-ideological America. Otis Ferguson, the trenchant film critic for *The New Republic*, particularly praised Gabin for his "projection of strength in immobility" and his "command of the illusion that crossing a room even to get to the men's room has its meaning." Gabin had, he said, "that perfect eloquence of the thing as perceived, marked down, and brought across to all who have an interest in and hope for the processes of life, as lived."[17] In later years, the Film Society of New York said in its notes to a 2002 retrospective of Gabin's films that it was "one of the high points of French poetic realism," and thought his acting with Morgan "made losing one's life for love look positively inviting."[18] Pauline Kael liked Gabin as "the hopelessly rebellious hero, the decent man trapped by society," and praised the film itself as "a breath of fresh air to American filmgoers saturated with empty optimism."[19] The National Review Board awarded it the title of Best Foreign Film. In prewar France it won Carné the Prix Louis Delluc for best director; it was nominated for best foreign film at the Venice Film Festival, with a Golden Lion going to Carné for his direction.

As Michèle Morgan noted in the careful planning of her love life, Gabin had indeed been married to Doriane for five years. That may have deterred Morgan, but it didn't dampen his habitual appetite for romantic adventure with his leading ladies, for example his lengthy affair with Mireille Balin, which began during *Pépé le Moko* and continued through *Gueule d'Amour*. Doriane, who also had affairs, was broad-minded about it in the French manner of the day. Asked by a journalist whether she was ever jealous, she replied, "You have to deal with it. I don't think his female admirers are dangerous, but his beautiful leading ladies are more attractive. They are all young, pretty, and brilliant. Working with them creates an intimate atmosphere and the artistic relationship creates a sort of amorous friendship that is full of charm. Maybe I'm going to surprise you, but I understand that sometimes an actor, a man gifted with an extreme sensitivity, occasionally needs to renew his sentimental side, to respond again to the call of adventure. How can you avoid that? And how can you not admit it?"[20]

Gabin was also momentarily tempted by the adventure of taking his talent to Hollywood. As France's most popular movie star with a growing international reputation, he was being approached continually by fly-by-night producers brandishing lucrative contracts. He often signed them in good faith, only to see the project languish in limbo as one producer flipped it to another on the strength of Gabin's name, pocketing a nice profit.

Tired of being used like that, he met in Paris with Louis B. Meyer of MGM, then Hollywood's most prestigious studio, who very much wanted to add Gabin to his stable of stars. During several meetings, Meyer flattered him alternatively as the European Clark Gable one day or the Gallic Spencer Tracy the next. He told Gabin he could do two films per year for him and still do one in France. As *The New York Times* reported the story on May 22, 1938, "When Louis B. Meyer was in Paris, he approached Gabin and almost signed him to a contract. But this Frenchman, it seems, enjoys his freedom too much to part with it. He reserves the right to select or reject his own scenarios and even picks his own director. 'At such times,' he said, 'Hollywood seems like a veritable paradise. But I am not yet ready to sacrifice my independence for Hollywood's glamor and gold.'"[21]

Gabin was too rooted in France and too attached to working with directors like Duvivier, Carné, and Renoir, and screenwriters like Spaak and Prévert, to leave for Hollywood. Besides, he was enjoying his new country house in Sainte Gemme Moronval. As he told a French magazine, "I told [Meyer] no. I'm not interested in America. First of all, you eat badly there. And I'm French; this is where I belong, this is where my public is. Besides, I'm too pigheaded to adapt to the Americans. Unless circumstances keep me from realizing my projects here, I'm not about to change my mind." Did that mean he was happy with his life as it was? "To be really happy, you have to be satisfied with yourself," he replied. "I never have been. God forbid I ever shall be."[22]

Only three years later, circumstances would change his mind, and his life. But right now, one of his most interesting projects involved realizing his childhood dream of being a locomotive engineer. The idea of doing a railroad film had been germinating for some time. As he told a French magazine, "I've never realized my dream, but I've never forgotten it. It's just been transformed, that's all. Right now I'm hoping for the pleasure of doing a big film about trains. I'm doing some reading to find the right story. I'm sure I will find it and be able to share my love of trains."[23]

Director Jean Grémillon, with whom he had done *Gueule d'Amour*, worked up a script with screenwriter Pierre Bost called *Train d'Enfer* (*Hell Train*), but it fell through. The producers of *Pépé le Moko*, Robert and Raymond Hakim, anxious to do another profitable movie with Gabin, bought the project and had the novelist Roger Martin du Gard do a treatment. When that didn't work out, they got the idea of making a film based on Emile Zola's *La Bête Humaine*, a somber novel filled with murder, rape, and suicide, whose action takes place along the Paris-Le Havre railway line. Gabin asked them to pitch the idea to Renoir, with whom he wanted to do another film.

Renoir took it on and reworked the screenplay. In its tone, his very free adaptation bears very little resemblance to Zola's clear-eyed portrait of working class frustration and despair of betterment. Zola himself wrote in 1889, "I wanted to express this idea: the caveman remains within the man of our 19th century; there is something in us from this far-off ancestor."[24] In other words, man is condemned to suffer for the sins of his forebears. Renoir, on the other hand, preached the progressive ideals of French communism and the Popular Front: through worker solidarity man could take control of his destiny and improve his lot—just the opposite of Zola's theme. Thus his screenplay is full of the daily camaraderie of railroad men, from shaking hands every time they meet, to sharing frugal meals and mutual support. In one sequence Gabin, the engineer, and his fireman symbolically combine their meager rations to compose a complete meal.

In *La Bête Humaine/The Human Beast* (1938) Gabin is Jacques Lantier, engineer on *La Lison*, the name he has given steam locomotive 238, which makes the Paris-Le Havre run. "When you love someone, you don't call them by a number," he explains at one point, and he seems to love the giant machine, with its elbowing rods and wheels taller than a man, more than any woman. In fact, a hereditary mental illness, due to ancestral alcoholism, has given him a compulsion to kill any woman he desires. One of them is Severine, played by a pouty, feline, manipulative Simone Simon, wife of the deputy stationmaster, Roubaud, at Le Havre. (True to form, Gabin started a brief affair with Simon, whom he had known in his music hall days; she had had an unremarkable five-film career in Hollywood

Gabin finally becomes a locomotive engineer, *La Bête Humaine*, 1938. He practiced driving trains for two months, happily realizing a childhood dream (Hakim productions/Paris Film/Collection Screen Prod/Photononstop).

before returning to France at the producers' request to make *Bête*.) Roubaud learns that she is the mistress of her godfather, Grandmorin. He makes her meet Grandmorin with him in the Paris-Le Havre train so he can kill him. Lantier sees them exiting the train compartment after the murder, but at her request he says nothing to the police.

She becomes his mistress—at their first meeting he is so moved that he can only stare at her speechless, giving Simon the memorable line "Don't look at me like that, you'll wear your eyes out"—and goads him to kill Roubaud so they can be together. In the film's best noir sequence, shot in the dark, grimy, desolate rail yard at night, they hide in wait for Roubaud to make his rounds. Lantier grabs a crowbar and is about to strike from behind, when his better nature stops him in the act. Severine taunts him and breaks off their relation. He visits her apartment and again prepares to kill her husband, but succumbs to his compulsion and stabs her instead. He returns to the yard and starts *La Lison* on its run to Paris. Overcome by remorse and the knowledge that he can never live a normal life, he jumps to his death from the speeding train.

Gabin was obviously very much at home in this role of an ordinary railroad worker. Partly that was due to his instinctive feel and visible affection for the working class, its manners and values. It was also due to his extensive preparation, which included weeks prowling the rail yards in Paris and Le Havre with the full cooperation of the SNCF, the French national railways. At Le Havre, the company made available several miles of track and a locomotive that he and Julien Carette, who played his coal-shoveling fireman, could practice on until they had it down pat how to open and close the steam valves, control speed and braking, shovel coal, and replenish water for the boiler, communicating by sign language in the noisy cab. As Gabin wrote in autobiographical notes he put together in 1950, now in the archives of the Jean Gabin Museum, "I was madly happy, because the dream I'd had as a kid, driving a locomotive, was actually happening. For two months, between Paris and Le Havre, I was given training in how to be a locomotive engineer, and I can't say enough how great railroad men are. You can't help feeling great respect for their devotion and professional conscience. The day when I drove a locomotive for the first time was certainly the happiest day of my life."[25]

He must not have done it too badly—but the story that he actually drove the train on a real run, full of unwitting passengers, from Le Havre to Paris, is not true—for after the film was released the CGT railway workers' union presented him with an honorary oil can and an engineer's diploma, the only one he ever received besides his elementary school certificate. The role also suited him because it offered him several sequences in which he is either moody and reflective, with a shaft of poetic realist light across his eyes, or exploding in sudden, uncontrollable outbursts. The scene where Gabin and Simon hide at night in the menacing shadows of a Stygian rail yard waiting to kill Roubaud is Renoir's best poetic realist sequence, followed by the one where Gabin, having just stabbed the woman he loves due to an uncontrollable compulsion, accidentally glimpses his own hopelessly perplexed expression in a mirror.

As Renoir summed up Gabin's achievement in *Bête* in his presentation of the film in a movie magazine, "To be tragic in the classic sense of the word, while wearing a worker's cap and a mechanic's coveralls and talking like the man in the street, that's the tour de force that Jean Gabin has achieved in acting the part of Jacques Lantier."[26] The French film historian Claude Gauteur put it in a broader perspective: "The amazing thing about Gabin is that, without much formal education, and without drama training at places like the Comédie Française, he became one of the foremost tragedians of his day."[27]

Planning murder with Simone Simon in the railroad yard in *La Bête Humaine,* **1938 (Collection du Musée Jean Gabin).**

Shooting began in the summer of 1938. Renoir's insistence on authenticity meant so much footage was shot of railway operations that the film is a veritable paean to locomotives and the men who make them go. A good part of that footage was highly dangerous, but Renoir was adamant. "It was pointed out to me that mock-ups had been perfected to the point where it was impossible to tell them from the real thing," he wrote in his autobiography. "But I was unshakable in my belief in the influence of the setting on the actors, and fortunately I won the day. Gabin and Carette could never have played so realistically in front of an artificial background, if only because the noise forced them to communicate with hand signals."[28]

The crack German cinematographer Curt Courant and his assistant, Renoir's nephew Claude Renoir, installed cameras so audiences saw exactly what the engineer saw leaning from the cab: sinuous rails smoothly converging and dividing, stations passing in a blur, the train plunging into black tunnels, whistle shrieking. The movie's long opening sequence is the most spectacular view of a steam locomotive in action ever filmed. To get it, they bolted a camera to the left side of the cab. On the first try, they miscalculated the width of a tunnel. The camera was nearly knocked off and Claude Renoir came close to being decapitated when they entered it. The only time they resorted to a mock-up was for the scene where Gabin commits suicide by leaping from the train. "I could not ask Gabin to fling himself off a real tender," Renoir explained. "As he said when we were preparing the scene: 'Suppose the film fouls in the camera during the shooting. I should then have to do the scene again, so it's really better for me to stay alive'—a very sensible remark. So he jumped off a bogus tender on to a thick pile of mattresses."[29]

Renoir was delighted with the film and with Gabin's performance. "I regret only one thing," he said, "and it's that Zola didn't live to see Gabin play that character."[30] Gabin too was pleased with the result, calling *Bête* "one of my films that stood up best."[31] The public loved it, filling the Madeleine cinema in Paris for an exclusive run of 13 weeks after its premiere in December 1938. But again the politicized right-wing press, which detested Renoir for his communist leanings, panned it, while the panicked government censors at the General Commissariat for Information banned it by decree in August 1939, as "depressing, morbid, immoral, and a bad influence on young people."[32] As with *La Grande Illusion*, American reviewers were more objective. *Variety* called it "French production at its best.... Throughout, Gabin never misses."[33] At *The New York Times*, Frank S. Nugent found the story itself macabre and grim, but "we were conscious only of constant interest and absorption tinged with horror and an uncomfortable sense of dread. And deep down, of course, ungrudged admiration for Renoir's ability to seduce us into such a mood, for the performances which preserved it."[34] In his study of classic French films, Dudley Andrew called it "the apogee of poetic realism," with its "nearly ethnographic view of the conditions of the working man."[35]

Columbia Pictures liked the story enough to have Fritz Lang do an unsuccessful remake in 1955 entitled *Human Desire*, with an altered story line. Glenn Ford played a Korean War veteran returning to his job as a locomotive engineer and Gloria Grahame was a co-worker's femme fatale wife with whom he gets involved. The result failed to convince many critics. "[There] isn't a single character in it for whom it builds up the slightest sympathy," wrote *The Times*' Bosley Crowther. "And there isn't a great deal else in it for which you're likely to have the least regard."[36]

By 1939 Gabin was an undisputed *seigneur*, a grandee of French cinema. He could pick and choose among the many roles being proposed by producers salivating over the box office pull of his name on the marquee. He continued to prefer directors, screenwriters, and technical crews he was comfortable with. The rest of the cast, too, had to be what he considered the best that producers could find. A good cast, he always said, brought out the best in him, beautiful leading ladies made him look good. A poll done that year by the film magazine *La Cinématographie Française* had him number one in the esteem of French moviegoers, ahead of other first-magnitude stars like Fernandel, Louis Jouvet, and Raimu.[37] During this period, the magazine *Ciné Miroir* tried to analyze the Gabin myth, what it was about his persona that fascinated audiences. "Jean Gabin can be said to have created onscreen a character type that didn't exist before his arrival," it concluded, "the bad boy with a heart of gold, mocking, sardonic, sensitive, and generous, all of a piece, conscious of his strength but capable of putting it all on the line in the name of something higher."[38]

For *Le Jour se Lève/Daybreak* (1939, U.S. release 1940) Gabin again joined with the *Quai des Brumes* team made up of director Marcel Carné, screenwriter Jacques Prévert, and set designer Alexandre Trauner, with *Bête* cameraman Curt Courant, all working at their creative peak. The outstanding cast included the old pro Jules Berry, one of France's finest stage and screen actors of the 1920s and '30s who normally got top billing—and who very nearly upstaged Gabin; Jean admitted after the shoot that during certain scenes he stopped acting and just stood gaping in fascinated admiration at the older actor's *maestria*. It also included the caustic, street-smart star Arletty, and the luminous young Jacqueline Laurent, who had done several Hollywood films for MGM in the mid–1930s and was considered for the part of Nelly in *Le Quai des Brumes* before Michèle Morgan was chosen. With an original screenplay and dialogue by Prévert based on an idea of Jacques Viot, Gabin again played an innocent proletarian hoping to give meaning to his life with love, only to be flummoxed by a corrupt older man and the two women in both their lives.

With nothing but sheer timing, charisma, and Carné's demanding direction—he was punctilious and autocratic on the set, often re-shooting a scene time and again until he found it perfect and the actors and crew were exhausted—Gabin here goes further than ever before in creating a moving character of complex psychological and emotional depth. Compared by some to a tone poem or Symbolist drama, it climaxes the extraordinary series of his increasingly great films of the prewar period. It is also the last first-rate film he would do before the Second World War. After this summit it would be some 15 years before he made the comeback that enabled him to regain his status as France's most popular movie actor. Pauline Kael would rightly praise it as "perhaps the finest of the French poetic melodramas … a definitive example of sensuous, atmosphere movie-making—you feel that you're breathing the air that Gabin breathes."[39] We can only wonder how much finer, denser, subtler his acting could have become if the war had not abruptly interrupted his career and nearly ended it.

The film's storyline is simple, its whole interest is in the telling. As Carné himself

With Jacqueline Laurent in *Le Jour se Lève*, 1939. It was Gabin's last great film before a 15-year dry period caused by the war (Collection du Musée Jean Gabin).

said after Viot gave him the rough outline on three sheets of paper, "I had just had a *coup de foudre*. Not for the plot as such, which was nearly non-existent, or lacking totally in substance, but for the way it was structured. For the first time in the history of the cinema, it began at the end and developed through a series of flashbacks, the protagonist's visions of his past and the events that had made him a murderer."[40] Carné's instinct for drama was right—this would be considered the best film of his career—but his film history was wrong: the first movie to be told that way, *The Power and the Glory* with Spencer Tracey, was made nearly six years earlier, based on an original screenplay by Preston Sturges and produced by Fox. It's even possible that Viot, an adventurer, art collector of the Surrealist school, and general shady dealer, got the idea from that. (That great avatar of flashback narration, *Citizen Kane*, would come only two years later.) Hollywood did a remake in 1947 when RKO had Anatole Litvak do *The Long Night* with Henry Fonda in Gabin's role.

The film opens with a pistol shot, a door opening to show a man holding his abdomen and staggering toward a staircase, then falling down it. François (Gabin) has just killed Valentin (Jules Berry), a traveling vaudeville performer who does a trained animals act in provincial theaters. Police are called and he shoots at them through the door of his top-floor apartment. "What would they understand? Nothing," he mutters, much like Meursault after killing an Arab in Albert Camus' existentialist masterpiece *The Stranger*. "Suddenly you do it and it's done." They fire a fusillade through the door and window that he ducks. They settle in for a nightlong siege while he barricades himself in his small room and reflects on the recent past in a series of long flashbacks. They begin in a noisy foundry where François works as a common laborer—as the young Jean Moncorgé had in real life after leaving home—sandblasting parts while wearing a sort of hideous, dehumanizing hazmat suit. He looks up to see Françoise (Jacqueline Laurent), a beautiful, innocent-looking girl who is delivering flowers to the executive offices. Besides having their name in common, both are orphans. He falls in love with her but finds her strangely reticent. He understands why when he sees her leave the vaudeville show with Valentin.

He has a romantic interlude with the world-weary Clara (Arletty), Valentin's assistant, who has just left the show in disgust and tells François how sleazy and abusive her boss was. He confronts Valentin, who pretends to love Françoise because he is her father. François paces in his room, chain-smoking cigarette after cigarette, glimpsing himself in a wall mirror until he picks up a chair and symbolically smashes his own image. In another flashback Valentin visits him in his room and taunts him about being her lover. François seizes a pistol and shoots him. Coming back to the present, a crowd of rubberneckers and fellow workers gathers below. In one of his most famous angry outbursts, he goes to the window and harangues them furiously, hammering his chest with his fist while he screams: "Yes, I'm a murderer! But murderers are all over the place. Everybody kills, but they do it more slowly. Get out of here and leave me alone. You can read all about it in the newspaper. Newspapers are well informed, they know everything. What François? Don't know him. There's no more François. There's no more anything, so get out of here and leave me alone!" At dawn, the police stage their final assault, throwing tear gas canisters through the window. He presses the pistol to his chest and pulls the trigger as clouds of gas rise in the room. His bedside alarm clock goes off, with bitter irony, to signal the start of a new day.

Both Carné and Gabin went the extra mile to maximize the film's authenticity. The claustrophobic feel of Trauner's inventive set was increased by Carné's insistence that it be a real room with four walls, not the usual mock-up with a movable wall for camera access. Camera and sound crews had to enter and leave through the door, but this was blocked during the shoot when François braces it against the police with a massive armoire. That meant the crews could only access it through the window, which they reached via a ladder from the roof. Worse, from the crew's point of view, Carné had the besieging police fire real bullets; only a few sandbags protected them and Gabin crouched in the room as live fire blasted the lock off the door and pocked walls. One crewmember was slightly injured when a flying fragment hit him in the face.[41]

Jour showcases Gabin's prewar, poetic realist acting to perfection: the business of wearing black pants and shirt to increase the somber, tomblike atmosphere of the small room; contemplating himself reflectively in the mirror before angrily smashing it; crouching in a corner watchfully but calmly, seeming to accept that government, society, the world make men like him pay for a moment of uncontrollable rage when pushed to the breaking point. Defeated, alienated, having given up on love, he marks the night's passage of time by chain smoking, the burning down of each cigarette symbolizing the expiration of his last hours, reaching for the pistol when the pack is empty. Pacing back and forth, he hits his marks perfectly so shafts of light from below or above hit just his hands and brow. When he shoots Valentin, the camera does a tight close-up of his anguished eyes.

Of all Gabin's trademark angry outburst scenes over the years, his tirade from the upper floor window in *Jour* is the most famous and powerful. He prepared for it by staying on the set all day rather than taking a break, staying in character, stoking his mood with whiskey, reaching an explosive peak when Carné and the rest of the crew were ready.[42] By then he was almost in a trance, literally beside himself with choler. His emotional state at such moments was compared by André Bazin to that of the epic heroes of antiquity: "In the tragedies and epics of ancient times, anger was not just a psychological state amenable to treatment by a cold shower or a sedative; it was a special state, a divine possession, an opening for the gods into the world of humanity, through which destiny steals."[43] Getting into such a state always cost him, leaving him depleted and depressed afterwards.[44]

The film accurately reflected the anxious, despairing, *attentiste* mood of France in 1939. Many see it, like *La Belle Equipe*, as a metaphor for the death of the Popular Front and the end of the 1930s proletarian dreams of a better life.[45] The tear gas used in the last scene neatly symbolized the unprecedented use of it by Paris riot police against demonstrating workers in putting down a general strike in November 1938. As Edward Baron Turk writes in his fine study of Marcel Carné, "The film's subject, at least allegorically, is the downfall of the proletariat.... The actor who best embodied the vain struggle against dark forces was Jean Gabin. *Le Jour se Lève* provided Gabin with what is probably his greatest screen role. It also brought to formulation his persona as the common working man whose innate dignity is destroyed by social forces beyond his control."[46]

11

Storm Clouds of War

The panicky French government of Edouard Daladier predictably didn't like such decadent, subversive ideas. It banned *Le Jour se Lève* in December 1939, just barely beating the Germans at their own censorship/propaganda game; the Nazi occupiers would re-ban it a few months later just to make sure no Frenchman would inadvertently see it. French fascists later justified such action, declaring that "pimps, whores, and sordid love affairs were unfortunate subjects for French cinema."[1] The French public itself traditionally had nothing against the depiction of pimps and whores, *au contraire*. But in this case it was perplexed and disoriented by the film's unexpected use of flashbacks to narrate the action. "It was a big flop," Gabin said later. "The public didn't like the flashback technique. It began to be successful only after the war. I was 35 at the time, and as I recall, I was a fairly handsome guy. And Arletty, what a pretty girl! It's too bad they cut all the scenes where she was nude, like the one where she was in the shower and I was giving her her clothes. Today they would never have cut that. What a pity."[2] At a private screening before the Paris premiere in June, Gabin, always his most severe critic, was lukewarm. "It's not as good as *Quai*," he told Carné. "You're wrong," Carné replied. "It's better, and will age better too."[3] History shows that Carné won that debate.

André Bazin loved the film with a passion and saw it 30 times.[4] The fine postwar director Claude Sautet said he saw it 17 times in one month and four times in one day, "each time leaving the theater dazzled and engulfed by an inexplicable sense of pain and pleasure."[5] The Oscar-winning British actor Michael Caine said it was seeing Jean Gabin in *Le Jour se Lève* that convinced him to try a career in acting.[6] One reviewer who recognized its worth early on was the prominent, often acerbic British film critic Richard Winnington. Writing in the late 1940s, he said, "All the things that make *Jour se Lève* a bright confirmation of one's sorely tried faith in the cinema are not to be imitated, certainly not in Hollywood.... I have seen it four times and it still seems to have no flaw. It's absolutely national and absolutely universal. Hollywood must hate it a lot."[7]

Actually, Hollywood loved it and wanted it for its own. RKO bought the distribution rights to it in 1946 and, planning a remake, did their best to destroy all the prints of it.[8] Fortunately they failed, but it took a dozen years to find the original. They had Anatole Litvak make *The Long Night* in 1947 with Henry Fonda in Gabin's role. This being Hollywood, Fonda's character Joe isn't tragic, just a tiny bit alienated from society. Nothing to worry about: his friends support him, his girlfriend promises to wait for him if he goes to prison, and the audience leaves knowing he will be happy ever after.

Jour was especially important not only for its symbolism of France's political situation on the eve of the Second World War, but also because it marked the end of Gabin's first great period starting with *La Bandéra* and *La Belle Equipe*. This was when the Gabin myth of the proletarian character was developed and brought to its climax. His suicide amid the clouds of rising tear gas was the death both of François and of that archetypal character. After the war he would perforce be a deeply changed person and a different actor doing a different kind of films.

For the moment, though, he was enjoying life. That involved spending as much time at Saint Gemme as possible, hunting, fishing, and relaxing with Doriane and friends. On one trip back to Paris he was delighted to meet the American actor he admired most. Spencer Tracy was on a quick pleasure trip to Britain and France in May 1939, and while in Paris he looked up Gabin, whom he admired and whose career, particularly at the start, resembled his own in many ways. They went to a Montmartre nightclub one evening, where champagne lubricated Gabin's halting English but did little for Tracy's non-existent French. The next day they had lunch at Maxim's and Gabin, now well fueled with vintage reds, tipsily suggested Tracy stay in France and make a film. "We'll make one picture here," Gabin said, "and then we'll forget all about movies and go fishing. For a whole year." Tracy countered with the idea that Gabin come and make a movie in Hollywood. "I can hardly speak French," Gabin reacted. "How could I learn to speak English?"[9]

He would soon have no choice.

If Marcel Carné's masterpiece was indeed a flop at the box office, it wasn't solely because his innovative use of flashbacks surprised and confused audiences. With the storm clouds of war gathering all over Europe, Germany's brutal military support to Francisco Franco during Spain's ongoing civil war demonstrated what might be waiting for them. The French were in no mood for dark, pessimistic films and tortured souls. They wanted *entertainment*, but everywhere they looked were warning signs of catastrophe. Even when they held a world's fair in Paris in the summer of 1937, usually an occasion for amusement and relaxation, they came up against Picasso's shocking depiction of the horror on their southern border—*Guernica*, a mural-sized painting full of grotesquely stricken men, women, and animals shown at the Spanish pavilion, expressed the artist's revolt at the indiscriminate carnage wreaked by German and Italian warplanes on the Spanish Basque village of that name the preceding April. Nor were popular songs any relief. One called *Tout va très bien, Madame la Marquise* mocked France's head-in-the-sand posture with regard to the German menace: when Madame calls to see if all is well at the chateau, the servant answers that it has burned down and Monsieur has committed suicide, but not to worry, everything was fine.

They were encouraged by Premier Edouard Daladier's administration to believe everything would work out. Even if Hitler did something rash like seizing the Free City of Danzig, Poland's vital access to the Baltic, wrote one prominent columnist, accurately reflecting the attitude of his compatriots, "We will not die for Danzig."[10] Nor were they ready to die for Austria when he boldly annexed it in the Anschluss of March 1938. After appeasing Hitler with the infamous Munich Agreement in September of that year, allowing Germany to take the Sudetenland area of Czechoslovakia, Daladier admitted that he half-expected to be lynched on his return to Paris.[11] Instead, French pacifists hailed him for it. Public opinion was further tranquillized by the meaningless Franco-German non-aggression pledge the following December. As Jean-Paul Sartre, interviewed after the war, described French public opinion at the time, "In 1939, 1940, we were terrified of dying, suffering, for a cause that disgusted us. That is, for a disgusting France, corrupt, inefficient, racist, anti–Semitic, run by the rich for the rich—no one wanted to die for that until, well, until we understood that the Nazis were worse."[12]

More astute and clear-headed observers knew what was coming. One was William Bullitt, the U.S. ambassador to France who had been warning Washington of coming war in Europe for several years. He wrote a report to President Franklin D. Roosevelt in April 1939, saying, "It would be extremely unwise to eliminate from consideration the possibility that Germany, Italy and Japan may win a comparatively speedy victory over France and England."[13]

But anyone who paid attention could have noticed the signs that something was seriously amiss. For example, that suddenly the Louvre Museum was missing some of its prized possessions. Beginning in the autumn of 1938 the *Mona Lisa* and a number of other chefs-d'oeuvre had been quietly taken to the Chambord chateau in the Loire Valley. Within a year, nearly 4,000 of the museum's most valuable works would similarly be removed for safekeeping. Most went to various chateaux around the Loire, the Louvre borrowing trucks from the Comédie Française normally used for transporting stage sets, to haul them to the provinces. Thus when Hitler, Goebbels, and other top Nazis visited Paris in triumph, many of the museum's galleries were hung with empty frames, just as they were denied the pleasure of surveying all of conquered Paris from the top of the Eiffel Tower—its staff arranged for the elevators to malfunction that day, and the Fuhrer wasn't up to climbing the stairs. But such small victories were all France would have over the next four years.[14]

Jean Gabin and Michèle Morgan were to have their own personal *aperçu* of the reality of the menace. In October 1938 they began filming *Le Récif de Corail/Coral Reefs* (1939), a complicated, exotic Franco-German production with a mediocre screenplay about a manhunt and the attempt by a couple, played by Gabin and Morgan, to find a new life in Australia. Shot partially on location on the Cote d'Azur, it included an artificial islet in the Mediterranean that was supposed to look like a Pacific atoll—except when the set was damaged by waves, as it was repeatedly. As soon as the location shots were finished, they moved with relief to the more manageable UFA studios at Neubabelsberg in November for the interior sequences. It was their second movie together for Gabin and Morgan after *Quai*, and Micheline Bonnet, Gabin's faithful dresser, had tried to play matchmaker before filming began. Monsieur Gabin was very happy to have her again as his leading lady, she told Morgan, he had missed her.[15]

But they still did not get any closer than they had that memorable evening in Le Havre when they had celebrated her 18th birthday and Morgan had left him standing, bemused, at her hotel room door. "This time we never got beyond a curious sort of cama-raderie on the verge of flirting," she recalled of their time together on *Récif*.[16] One problem was Gabin's bad mood because he felt that contractual obligations with UFA had roped him into the project too soon after he had done *La Bête Humaine*; he didn't have enough time for his usual input regarding the screenplay. Nor could he make Charles Spaak's dialogue sound the way he wanted it. He therefore went along with it half-heartedly, and his performance showed it. That, plus the workmanlike but uninspired direction of Maurice Gleize, resulted in one of the least memorable of Gabin's films.

A more important obstacle to romantic involvement was the heinous, menacing atmosphere in the German capital. The cast had been put up in the sumptuous Pension Impériale on Berlin's chic main artery, the Kurfurstendamm. There they could hear the thump of boots on pavement as the *Sturmabteilung* and *Hitlerjugend* paramilitary organizations regularly paraded in their brown shirts. It put them in the middle of the events of the night of November 9, 1938, *Kristallnacht*, a term that lives in infamy because of its graphic reference to the glass shards that littered streets after synagogues, Jewish stores, and homes were smashed or burned by Nazi goons all over Germany. Hundreds were murdered, thousands rounded up and sent to concentration camps. Like Gabin, Morgan was horrified by what she was able to observe: "That night I was awakened by the sirens of fire engines and police cars. I opened my window and heard something like a storm, shouts, chanting, and shots, while in the sky shimmered the red gleams of fires. Did wars start like this? … In the morning I found a city disfigured by hatred; Jewish stores torn apart, burned and pillaged, with big white letters painted on them: 'Jude.' I felt overwhelmed by the savagery of that explosion of racism."[17] They had only one desire after that, to get out of Germany as fast as possible. Gabin vowed to himself not to set foot in the country again. When he did, six years later, it would be to visit a certain Eagle's Nest.

Michèle Morgan had a frenetic schedule in 1939. Hardly had she finished *Récif* when she began *Les Musiciens du Ciel/Musicians of the Sky* (1940), a tearjerker with her as a Salvation Army member who saves a petty thief from a life of crime before she dies on Christmas Eve. She would have liked to take a break, but she already had her next contract and the shoot was to begin in July. The movie was *Remorques/Stormy Waters* (1941), about an ocean-going tugboat crew based in Brest whose mission was to save ships in distress. Its captain was to be played by Jean Gabin, while Morgan would be a woman he rescues who becomes his mistress. So she wasn't too surprised when she received a phone call from Micheline Bonnet, who would be their dresser again. Whether Gabin had asked her to make the call or she just couldn't resist playing cupid, we can't tell. But she could hardly wait to give Morgan the news that Monsieur Gabin was going to divorce Doriane. He was free now. And he was delighted to be playing opposite Morgan again, talked about her all the time. In case Michèle didn't get the message, she suggested it would be a good idea for them to meet before the shoot began. Would it be all right if he called her?[18]

Five minutes after Micheline hung up, he did, and announced he would be by for her that evening. It was as if, tacitly, they had each already decided that this time would not end like that evening in Le Havre 18 months before. When Morgan returned home that evening after a day of filming, she found her apartment flooded with dozens of red roses, Gabin's signature wooing. He picked her up and they went out for dinner at a quiet little Paris restaurant with heavy white damask tablecloths and soft lighting. "We were very moved and impatient for each other," she remembered. "We flirted like lovers: our eyes never lost contact, our hands grazed without daring to really touch. Our laughter was forced and embarrassed, the silences dense. Every word was full of undertones." Dancing until dawn at a fashionable nightclub, Le Florence, followed, their movements so well matched that Gabin murmured, "You see, dancing is like making love, it's better the second time."[19]

After this first night together, Morgan admitted, "I was conquered, and couldn't wait to see him again. It was like being in a frenzy as we tried to catch up on all that time we had lost. We were going to have so little."[20] Gabin announced to Mique, his new pet name for her, that they were going to spend the weekend in Auron, a small ski resort in the southern Alps about 60 miles north of Nice, where they could be alone in the off-season.

It was a happy, intense couple of days, but already they were thinking of the future—and in different ways. She was mentally preparing for the day when it would be over. Whereas he loved her spontaneously, impulsively, without introspectively questioning how much he loved her and how long their relationship might last, she was already looking ahead to the day when their affair would cool, telling Gabin, "Jean, whatever happens to us, I would like to keep your friendship."[21]

Later, she realized that he took that to mean she was distancing herself, as indeed she was, perhaps unwittingly. He, on he other hand, wanted to live only for the moment, knowing that war was coming and he would be in it. "Don't forget that I'm a swabbie," he told her, "and if the navy calls me I'll have to go. Why not me? Because I'm in the movies? Actors have duties too. Do you see me asking for special privileges? That's not my style. The navy doesn't have too many chief petty officers, and I'm the right age."[22]

After one more lovers' escapade, this time to Deauville, they headed to Brest in July to begin the shoot with director Jean Grémillon. Ever turned toward the Atlantic, the great port now swarmed with French navy sailors in their white berets with red pompoms. With a certain pleasure of recognition from his days in the service, Gabin watched warships with martial names like *Invincible*, *Intrépide*, *Foch*, or *Surcouf* cruise in the harbor. While preparing to film the tugboat scenes on the *Cyclone*, he scampered up and down the boat's steep ladders and along narrow gangways with the ease of a veteran. As Captain André Laurent, he takes the *Cyclone* out one storm-tossed night to save a cargo in distress. During the operation he takes Catherine (Morgan) on board and she becomes his mistress. Just as he is tempted to leave his wife Yvonne (Madeleine Renaud), her chronic heart condition worsens and she dies in his arms. Catherine senses that his guilt feelings will always come between them and leaves.

Gabin and Morgan made no effort to hide their affair on the set and off—to hide it *any longer*, thought many working on the film, convinced wrongly that it had begun with *Quai*. She later described how it felt on the set that summer of 1939: "It was impossible not to think of war even if it wasn't a reality yet. It was crazy how carefree everybody seemed, how happy we appeared. I think we wanted to forget the threat, to have a little more fun, knowing that one morning we would wake up to face the terrible reality of war.... These were our last good days and I wanted to live them selfishly, fully, our free hours, our evenings, our rare days together were spent tête à tête walking through the streets of Brest, discovering little hotels or driving through the countryside and sometimes stopping in a discreet little inn, or lying on a beach, as if there were no film to be done, no rumors of war, only us, a couple like any other."[23]

The rumors ended on September 3. Preparing to film on the tug, the cast heard the wail of sirens in Brest and the answering thunder of ships' horns in the harbor signaling that France, like Britain, had declared war on Germany following its invasion of Poland. Technicians loaded up cameras and other material and everyone took the train back to Paris. In the station, posters were going up announcing general mobilization. The cast returned to the Paris studios for the rest of the shoot, including scenes of the *Cyclone* struggling against mountainous waves, which were shot in a basin 150 feet long and 12 feet deep.

On the first day Gabin had a scene in the studio, he didn't show up, puzzling Grémillon, who knew he was always punctual on the set. When he arrived late, the script supervisor quickly noticed that he was not in the right costume, a business suit. Instead, he had been called up as a chief petty officer and was in uniform. He had received his orders and come to say goodbye without further ado. "Cut the lights, that's all, everybody," ordered a resigned Grémillon, who understood that the days of making *Remorques* were over for some time to come; he himself would be drafted a few days later. Gabin and Morgan parted then and there on the set, in front of the crew. "It's better this way," Gabin murmured. "Give me a smile." He and Grémillon headed off to a café for a farewell drink, while Micheline tried to comfort Morgan: "You see, that's the way men are. When they go off to war they go have a drink, and we sit here like idiots."[24]

Gabin was sent to Cherbourg to serve as a gunner on a minesweeper. He was ready to interrupt his career to do his duty to his besieged country, but the reality was that there was very little to do in Cherbourg. Contrary to later accounts whipped up by Hollywood press agents of perilous action searching for mines in the English Channel, his ship spent most of its time tied up at the dock while its crew did make-work and he was bored to death. For them, the rest of the French military, and most citizens, this was not war, but the *drôle de guerre*, even if by October 1939 France had drafted some 2.6 million men and the country was mobilized to action. Schoolchildren were hastily evacuated from Paris, Metro stations turned into air-raid shelters, theaters and cinemas closed. But when no German attack materialized, the idea of a "phony war" took hold and France relaxed. Nightlife resumed, the children came back. All things English were suddenly popular. Everybody began singing a French version of Britain's cheeky "We'll Hang Out Our Washing on the Siegfried Line," dancing the Lambeth Walk, and wearing the newly fashionable color, RAF blue. Plucky little England was holding out, surely America, maybe even the Soviet Union, given the importance of the French Communist Party, would come to the rescue of France. But many began quietly renting or purchasing apartments or houses in the provinces. Michèle Morgan rented a small house in the Atlantic seaside resort of La Baule, just in case.[25]

The press discovered that Gabin was on the minesweeper in Cherbourg and did features on him with photos showing the movie star emptying buckets while on duty or hanging out his laundry. *France Magazine* put him on its October 24, 1939, cover with the teaser headline, "Who's this sailor?" It described him as a "real, fearless sailor, wearing his beret like a working man's cloth cap, with a cigarette dangling in the corner of his mouth." It claimed that he had been reproached by a strict constructionist gendarme for wearing his naval headgear like a cap on the back of his head instead of squared away.[26] He wrote regularly to Morgan, his envelopes marked by military censors "from somewhere in France." "It's not that I wanted so much to go to war," he recalled later, "but why declare war on the Teutons if it was just to sit there like fools. Sometimes I thought it was all a joke, but I never thought it would finish by a race—on foot, horseback, or car—to the South."[27]

Eight months later he was granted a two-week furlough and returned to Brest in the spring of 1940 for some final shots to wrap up *Remorques*. The last ones in the studio would not be finished until the summer of 1941, after the defeated French army had been demobilized and Grémillon could get back to work. By then both Gabin and Morgan had left France. He didn't see it until the war was over, and, hypercritical as usual about his movies, didn't much like it. But it made Gabin the first actor in either France or Europe to be paid a million francs, about $200,000, for a part. The film was also an important, if little noticed, step in his career. Since he began establishing the typical Gabin character in the early 1930s, it was the first in which he wasn't the proletarian plaything of implacable fate, but a solid pillar of society, a captain in the merchant marine giving orders with unquestioned authority to his crew. It was perhaps an unwitting change of direction; there's no sign that he deliberately planned it that way. But in retrospect it is clear that he was starting to transition toward a different persona.

French moviedom's "ideal couple" was back together briefly during his furlough. But Morgan, sometimes criticized by French reviewers as a walking icebox whose only facial expression was a dreamy look, never really committed to the relationship. Now she felt increasingly that it was already ending. Her analysis of it is worth quoting at some length, given her importance in Gabin's life at this critical time, and his bitter, if mostly silent, hurt at being dumped by her. "Imperceptibly, I was becoming certain that there was no future for us, that things would end the way they had begun, one evening," she wrote in her memoirs. "Our times together were always marked by long separations. How much had we really spent together? Four months total. And I sometimes think that if we had both been more open, we could have found the words that would have kept us together."[28] She further spelled out her tortuous rationalization of her behavior to Gabin's friend and best French biographer, André Brunelin:

> The dramatic events of those days certainly played a determining role in our separation. They made it especially brutal. But even without that, I always thought that what we were going through, Jean and I, had no future. The war and the debacle precipitated our breakup. Without that, and everything that followed, maybe we would have stayed together a while longer, but only for a time, no more than that. Of course, Jean had asked for a divorce, and I was free as he soon would be. But despite that, at no time did I imagine that what united us then would last, and still less that it could result in marriage. Was Jean thinking otherwise? Did he think of marriage? I don't know, but I don't believe so. We never talked about it.… What happened during those few days before shooting *Remorques* actually came too late, at least it did for me. I had wanted that moment in Le Havre when we were filming *Le Quai des Brumes*, despite having stupidly stopped him that evening.… But that summer of 1939 I was no longer as in love with Jean as I was a year or 18 months before. In truth, I think he was in love with me—I thought so at the time—but I didn't know how much until later, when I was in the United States, and even when I returned to France after the war, that he was more in love than I knew. Common friends have told me that Jean was upset for a long time after my departure for the U.S. I was barely 20 years old when all that happened, and I must have been a little egotistical.[29]

The war may have seemed phony to many, but thoughtful French writers were predicting disaster and blaming it on the French themselves. Drieu La Rochelle, who had been wounded in the First World War and thus was not called up now, wrote in December 1939, "The war has changed nothing, quite the contrary. The French are more divided than ever, behind the façade of general agreement resulting from their lethargy."[30] In May, André Gide wrote despairingly in his diary of his compatriots, "Oh incurably frivolous people of France! You are going to pay dearly for your lack of application, your heedlessness, your smug lolling among so many charming virtues."[31] Poet Paul Valéry confided to his notebook, "France expiates the crime of being what she is."[32]

What the nation had to make amends for was becoming a society that let itself slide into indifferent decadence as futile, self-seeking politicians squabbled over crumbs of power and place, fraud rotted its core, and Marxist labor unions and the Soviet-lining French Communist Party fanned discontent and unrest. While they danced on a volcano, as the French expression has it, they lost the spark of genius that had, from 1870 to 1910, made France a world leader in new industrial sectors such as aviation, civil engineering, automobiles, radio, and medical research. Now they would, as Gide warned, pay dearly for that.

12

Escape to America

With the German army now scything through French defenses, having simply gone around the Maginot Line's northern end, things happened rapidly. On June 10, the National Assembly voted to abolish itself and with it the Third Republic. President Albert Lebrun, Premier Paul Reynaud, president of the Senate Jules Jeanneney, and many members of the Chamber of Deputies slunk out of Paris after dark. Passers-by understood what was going on when they saw trucks being filled with filing cabinets and furniture pouring from government offices. In a broadcast on June 12, Reynaud told Parisians to flee any way they could; the next day Paris was declared an open city to save it from bombardment. After German troops entered it on June 14, non-coms could be seen strolling around snapping souvenir photographs of the Opera and the Eiffel Tower in what was virtually a ghost town.

On June 18 General Charles de Gaulle made his famous broadcast from London on the BBC calling on all Frenchmen to rally to him to keep "the flame of French resistance" alive. (He did not say, as has often been repeated, "France has lost a battle, but France has not lost the war." That was how an American wire service paraphrased his speech. He is said to have read it the next day and found it rather to his liking.) A week later, France accepted an armistice granting the German occupiers most of the north of the country, with Marshal Philippe Pétain head of a theoretically independent nation called the French State, its capital in the health spa Vichy. Antoine de Saint-Exupéry, the aviator-writer famous for works like *The Little Prince*, was flying reconnaissance missions as he saw his country collapse. "Everything was cracking up all around us," he wrote in *Flight to Arras*. "Everything was caving in. The collapse was so complete that death itself seemed to us absurd. Death, in such a tumult, had ceased to exist."[1]

Gabin left Cherbourg for Paris in mid–June, where he met briefly with Morgan, advising her to take her parents and head for that house in La Baule where they would all be safe. She agreed, saying she would set them up there and then come back. By her own account, she half-expected him to say he would go with her. Instead, his last words were "Au revoir, Mique. Be careful."[2] She wondered later whether he hadn't been waiting for her to ask him to come along. Both appeared incapable of expressing their real feelings at that moment. Possibly they remained inarticulate and oddly embarrassed because they didn't know themselves what each wanted of the other. In any case, this parting reinforced Morgan's sentiment that it was the end of their affair.

Amid the growing chaos of hundreds of thousands of Parisians packing up whatever belongings they could and leaving the city by any means possible, Gabin drove his Buick coupe to his apartment in rue Maspero, near the Bois de Boulogne. There he took some personal papers and his accordion. He also picked up a suitcase full of several pounds of gold bars that, like many French who always preferred tangible investments to paper money and government promises, he had begun buying a few years before as security. He took the bars to a business associate, a co-owner with him of a gas station and garage at the Porte d'Orleans, for safekeeping.

Then, threading his way through the thick snarl of departing traffic, he drove the 45 miles to Sainte Gemme Moronval to pick up Doriane, still his wife even though they were in divorce proceedings. He retrieved a few more gold ingots from a strongbox there, concealing them beneath the Buick's passenger seats. To his great regret, there was no way to fit his custom racing bike in the coupe. He threw Doriane's numerous suitcases—including, at her insistence, a splendid ermine coat she had vengefully bought two years before that just happened to be exactly the same model as one Gabin had given, secretly he thought, to one of his girlfriends—in the back of the coupe, and took highway RN 20 south. The tanks of an SS Panzer Division closing in on Paris were not far behind.

They were in the chaotic mass exodus of eight to ten million refugees fleeing south that month, not only from Paris, but also from northern France, Belgium, and Holland. With train service in the northern half of the country cut by the invasion, they travelled by everything from taxis and buses to cars and trucks, bicycles and horse-drawn carts. Many on foot pushed baby carriages loaded with their most precious possessions. The crowded roads made easy targets for the Stuka and Messerschmitt fighters that strafed them periodically, killing many and sending everyone else plunging into roadside ditches for cover. Gasoline was in short supply and was fought over in filling stations. When vehicles ran out they were abandoned where they were, further snarling traffic, which moved slowly at best when not immobilized beneath the summer sun.

Doriane began complaining and berating Gabin as soon as they left Sainte Gemme Moronval, blaming him for the situation they were in and for not having acted sooner. Finally he found the nagging unbearable. In the midst of still another sweltering traffic jam near the town of Montauban, 40 miles north of Toulouse, he blew up in one of those angry outbursts that were not always play-acting for the camera. This was the end, he told her, he never wanted to see or hear from her again. She could have it all. He left her the Buick, the gold, her suitcases and the ermine, and took off on foot with his accordion on his back.[3]

If he had stayed in Paris, Gabin could have enjoyed a semblance of normal life returning to the city. The Nazis were anything but dumb: they knew that they had everything to be gained by letting its theaters, movies, and cabarets reopen and operate more or less normally. By September, only three months after the fall of France, all the usual forms of Paris nightlife, from the opera to its numerous creative brothels, were doing a roaring trade with the thousands of German soldiers for whom the city was a paradise of pleasure that was nothing like home. Shows were often free for them, the menus of the best restaurants were printed in German, and feminine company easy to find with the many girls attracted by the uniform.

This form of bread and circuses diverted the French from more sinister ideas of resistance. It also flattered their preening pride by letting them pretend that, although they might have lost on the battlefield, their culture was still respected. Seeing swastikas flying everywhere on public buildings, or companies of Wehrmacht soldiers goose-stepping up the Champs Elysées to the Arc de Triomphe every day at 12:30 p.m., even complying with an annoying 11 p.m. curfew seemed to many an acceptable price to pay, especially if they could operate a good black market scam. As Hitler told his confidant Albert Speer, "Does the spiritual health of the French people matter to you? Let's let them degenerate. All the better for us."[4]

But Nazi tolerance extended only so far. As Alan Riding points out in his *And the Show Went On: Cultural Life in Nazi-Occupied Paris*, the victors' real objective, prompted no doubt in part by jealousy toward a culture that had long dominated Europe and tended to outshine Germany's, was to crush French cultural influence abroad. Joseph Goebbels, holder of a Ph.D. from Heidelberg and Hitler's Reichsminister for propaganda, made this clear when he gave his orders to the German embassy in Paris in November 1940. "The result of our victorious fight should be to break French domination of cultural propaganda, in Europe and the world," he said. "Having taken control of Paris, the center of French cultural propaganda, it should be possible to strike a decisive blow against this propaganda. Any resistance to or tolerance of this propaganda will be a crime against the nation."[5] Goebbels openly despised France, considering it "a macabre nation, bent upon pleasure, which has rightly suffered a catastrophe," its people being, he considered, "sick and worm-eaten."[6]

His tool for striking at French culture was his new Propaganda Abteilung, with some 50 offices throughout France and a staff of nearly 1,200, which also handled censorship of all French media and cultural institutions. Censorship was real but often unnecessary, because most of the press and many prominent publishers opted for self-censorship to avoid trouble. Major book publishers cooperated with the Propaganda Staffel, pledging they would not publish anything Germany or Vichy France had banned. That included "books which, through their lying and tendentious spirit, have systematically poisoned French public opinion; particularly targeted are publications by political refugees and Jewish writers."[7] As Jean-Paul Sartre said after the war, "During the occupation, we had two choices: collaborate or resist."[8]

Collaboration with the Nazis was a grey area, particularly for show business figures. When Maurice Chevalier sang on German-controlled Radio Paris, Edith Piaf and Mistinguett performed in cabarets or revues for audiences composed mainly of German soldiers, were they collaborating or simply trying to give Parisians a little much-needed entertainment? Some leading ladies, like Viviane Romance, along with many other actors and directors, made films in Berlin for the German-controlled French film production company, Continental Films. Jewish producers, directors, and actors were banned. Financed by Goebbels' propaganda organs, Continental made some 220 French films during the occupation, working with eminent directors like Robert Bresson, Jean Delannoy, Henri-Georges Clouzot and Claude Autant-Lara.[9] They had a captive audience—attendance at movies was 40 percent higher in 1943 than in 1938, as the French sought distraction from the daily misery of things like long lines for food and a bit of coal for heating. German authorities assured them that they would now have "wholesome films, which are worthy of the artistic heritage of the country and carry the stamp of the new order," as opposed to past productions made by Jewish producers who were no more than "vile speculators."[10]

A few performers chose active opposition to the occupiers. Josephine Baker smuggled intelligence about German troop movements to the Allies, Pierre Dac did Gaullist broadcasts from London, Jean-Pierre Aumont fought with the Resistance in Italy and the South of France. But most went along to get along and enjoyed a comfortable life. Some of Gabin's former leading ladies like Mareille Balin and Arletty took German officers as lovers, an activity known as *collaboration horizontale*. Arletty famously proclaimed, "In my bed there are no uniforms. My heart is French, but my ass is international."[11]

Many, like Danielle Darrieux, Micheline Presle, Louis Jourdan, Michel Auclair, and some producers found the good life on the French Riviera, particularly Cannes, home of the now cancelled film festival. They hung out at the sumptuous Grand Hotel, which some likened to an ocean liner immobilized by the war. As Darrieux remembered afterwards, "We were totally carefree. We'd have our feet done, we'd go to the beauty parlor all the time. We were very young, very pretty and fashionable stars, and we didn't give a damn about what was happening up north."[12] Micheline Presle concurred: "It was extraordinary. We'd meet the producers on the terraces, we'd go out on boats for picnics on the islands. We were far from the war."[13]

Michèle Morgan, having taken her parents to the rented house in La Baule, went on to join the merry band in Cannes. Earlier she had signed a contract with RKO, but had been putting off the decision to leave for the U.S. "It was like a vacation," she wrote later. "Swimming, tennis, cycling around town, and at the hotel in the evening we joked around like college students, laughing, shouting, dancing and improvising operas where we sang about episodes in our lives…. We needed to erase, to wash out the filth of the defeat, the world of our elders. The present helped us forget our fear of having no future."[14] After a few weeks of that, Morgan obtained a U.S. entry visa from the American consulate in Nice and an exit visa from Vichy on the strength of her RKO contract—during the occupation, French citizens could leave the country only for well-documented professional reasons or having persuaded the Vichy authorities of a plan to represent Marshal Pétain's France in a flattering light abroad—and prepared to leave via Spain and Lisbon. With no news from Gabin, she had written to Micheline Bonnet asking her to tell him *au revoir*.

She was packing her bags in October three days before departure, when Gabin called her at the Grand Hotel. After leaving Doriane with the Buick, he had managed to get to the seaside resort of Saint Jean Cap Ferrat, only a few miles from Cannes, where his friend Claude Menier, scion of France's biggest chocolate maker, had a villa. He had tried to reach her in La Baule and her parents told him her whereabouts. He took his time contacting her; he had arrived in Saint Jean Cap Ferrat in late June or early July, so that means he waited some three months before calling. Neither had he tried to join the refugee revelers in Cannes, though he must have heard of the little colony of movie people at the Grand.

As to Morgan, he felt their situation was ambiguous: they had said "au revoir" that day in Paris, but not "adieu" or the other things couples say when they put a definitive end to an affair. He decided to pick up the phone after Micheline, with whom he remained in frequent contact, tipped him that she was about to leave for the U.S. He was in Cannes the next day. They spent 48 hours together. It was either too short or too long, as the cool-headed Morgan described it, and more as friends than lovers, "a tender and sad epilogue." He told her she was right to go to "Olivode," as he derisively called Hollywood, joking that she'd be able to see The Greta (Garbo). More seriously, he said that if she stayed in France, the Krauts, as he always called them, would make her work for Continental.[15]

The Nazis had already tried to pressure Jean Renoir to work for the Vichyite French State, at which point he decided it was time to leave France. He and his future wife, the

Brazilian-born Dido Freire, managed to get to Hollywood via North Africa, Lisbon, and New York. René Clair, too, had fled with his wife and child via Lisbon to Hollywood, where he signed with Universal. Marcel Carné, on the other hand, decided not to leave, and went on to sign a contract with Continental, for which he was criticized after the war even though he made no movies for them, finding a way to make two with other producers in the unoccupied zone. As for Jean Gabin, Continental tried pressure, even blackmail, to convince him to work for them.

It had happened that summer. Shortly after the occupation began, Continental—eying a great propaganda coup for the Germans and Vichy if they had the most popular movie star of the day under contract—made Gabin an insistent offer. With typical Teutonic subtlety, they proposed to free his nephew, Guy Ferrier, who was then a prisoner in Germany, if he would do films for them. Though he was very fond of his nephew, he refused the deal. When that failed, they hinted that Berlin's patience was limited; refusal could mean his ending up in a concentration camp. They even threatened to requisition his handsome country estate in Sainte Gemme Moronval. In the face of all this, Gabin stubbornly repeated that he would not do pictures that could only serve Nazi propaganda, and left the ball in their court.[16] So, he told Morgan, he didn't know when they might come back at him again or with what new threats. He wasn't far from making the same decision she had, he said, providing he could obtain the all-important exit visa.

On the day of her departure from Cannes, Gabin drove her to Marseilles to begin the long train trip to Lisbon. At the city's cavernous Saint Charles train station they again felt the same self-conscious awkwardness they had in Paris three months before. As they had for the last 48 hours, each waited for the other to take the initiative, he hoping she would say, "Come with me," she wondering if he would say, "Wait, I'm coming along." When that didn't happen, he helped her find her compartment, hefted her bags into the overhead rack, and went to the newsstand to buy her papers and candy. Then he waited on the platform amid the crowd seeing off relatives and friends, many of whom were lucky enough to be escaping their war-torn, occupied country. Looking up at her as she stood at the open train window, he exchanged banalities. "It was like a scene in a movie," Morgan remembered, "but now the dialogue was by us and the words stuck in our throats. Nobody could tell that we had tears in our eyes. Jean on that platform was for a long time the last image I had of France, and of him. We would meet again, but it will never be the same. That was the day something ended. I never broke up with Jean, we simply parted."[17]

Gabin maintained his usual stoic reserve on the outside, but friends like Jacques Prévert confirmed that he was upset and depressed by the realization that this time he and Morgan were parted for good. Or not. She had booked passage the SS *Exochorda*, one of four American Export Lines sister ships known as the Four Aces that made the regular run from New York to Portugal, Spain, France and the Mediterranean. It was, at 9,400 tons, one of the smaller American transatlantic passenger ships, but offered a boutique service comparable to the more famous luxury liners. Shortly after seeing her off in Marseilles, Gabin had second thoughts back in Saint Jean Cap Ferrat. He hastily cabled Morgan at the ship, still docked in Lisbon, saying he would like to join her in Hollywood. He confirmed the cable with a letter in care of American Export Lines that was waiting for her on arrival in New York. But for her, it was over. She didn't want him to show up in Hollywood hoping to continue their affair. She replied by mail, diplomatically but firmly, that he could come if he wanted, but it should not be for her.[18]

But before he had her reply, he made the trip to Vichy that October to try to obtain an exit visa. He was received by Jean-Louis Tixier-Vignancourt, an extreme right-wing lawyer and politician who had promoted the establishment of the Vichy government and later unsuccessfully opposed de Gaulle in the presidential election of 1965. At Vichy he was in charge of the information department, which was Orwellian doublespeak for censorship. He informed Gabin that exit visas were the responsibility of Vichy's interior minister. He would attempt to obtain one for him, but it would take time. Gabin returned to Saint Jean Cap Ferrat empty-handed, only to find Morgan's disheartening letter waiting for him. Following his failure in Vichy to get the exit visa, Morgan's firm rejection was like a punch to the solar plexus.

He began wonder whether it was worthwhile after all to try to leave. He momentarily stopped taking any steps to get the visa or making plans for a departure, and concentrated on keeping in shape. He bought a new racing bike and pedaled for hours through the Provençal hills behind Saint Jean. He trained regularly with the professional soccer team of Nice and, now 36 years old, played benefit matches with a team of veterans. He did some water skiing off the beach at Saint Jean Cap Ferrat. Besides that, he did little but relax at Claude Menier's villa and try to improve his accordion technique. One thing did indicate that he seriously considered remaining in France during this period of doubt and hesitation: for his divorce proceedings with Doriane, he had the case transferred

Water skiing off Saint Jean Cap Ferrat while waiting for an exit visa from the Vichy authorities, 1940 (Collection du Musée Jean Gabin).

from Paris to the jurisdiction of Aix en Provence. If he stayed in the unoccupied zone, that would be closer. (The divorce would be granted by the court in Aix in January 1943, while he was in the U.S.)[19]

Then toward the end of the year, things suddenly began to fall into place. True to his word, Tixier-Vignancourt managed to obtain the exit visa for him from the Vichy interior ministry. He even hand-carried it to Gabin in Saint Jean in late December. It was good for eight months on condition that he do films favorable to the Vichy government; the profession stamped in his passport was "propagandist." That grated, and it would raise a few official eyebrows in the U.S., but Jean was in no mood to quibble. Past were the happy days when he would whimsically justify his longstanding refusal to work in Hollywood, pretexting that he was too French to adapt to American ways—one story said he had turned down an offer by Walter Wanger to remake *Pépé le Moko* at three times his usual fee because his favorite French wine didn't travel well.[20]

With that in hand, he cabled a friend named André Devan, formerly a prominent French producer who had been signed by Twentieth Century–Fox as a producer in Hollywood. Could Devan arrange the necessary entry visa to the U.S. and transportation to the West Coast? Devan cabled back that he could indeed make the arrangements. Moreover, Darryl Zanuck was eager to sign him to do five films for Fox.[21] The French press got wind of the deal and began overheated speculation. "Despite having the blues over leaving France, Jean Gabin is going to Hollywood," declared one. "What will Gabin do?" queried another. "Will he stay on the Côte d'Azur or will he pursue Michèle Morgan?" He gave an interview to the mass-circulation *Paris-Soir* that was published on February 10, 1941: "I'm leaving on February 12. Over there I'll hide out for five months with my valet and work on my English. I don't want to look like a nitwit. Once the film is done, I'll come back to France fast, because I can't live without it."

That contradicted the fact that his Fox contract called for five films, but he wanted to reassure Vichy that he would stay no longer than the prescribed eight months and not seek a long-term career in the U.S. Still smarting decades later from spiteful rumors that he skipped out to avoid the war and enjoy life in Hollywood, he gave an interview to French television in 1971 setting the record straight. "I refused to do films in France under the Occupation," he said. "I had a chance to get out and I took it. I didn't go to America for the fun of it. I made two films there because I needed the money to eat."[22] He could have taken this opportunity to remind that he had returned in time to see combat in the liberation of France, but, always modest about that, he didn't.

Gabin left Saint Jean in mid–February. He was accompanied by André, his valet who, in these times of duress, had become more of a friend than a servant, and Jose Samitier, a Spanish professional soccer player for Nice he had met during his friendly matches. Despite the fact that it would be a difficult, 1,200-mile train trip to Lisbon, he insisted on hauling along his accordion and his racing bike, fearing, in the case of the bike, that he wouldn't be able to find the equivalent in America. (The accordion was mainly a fetish, a symbolic link to the France of his working class origins to which he was emotionally attached, according to his daughter, Florence. There is no sign that he ever really learned it well; in any case, she told me, she never heard him play it.) Samitier's presence was especially useful in crossing Spain to Portugal, facilitating contacts with the local authorities.

They stopped off in Barcelona long enough for Gabin to obtain his American visa from the U.S. consulate. Though his films were relatively unknown to the American public, he was enough of an international celebrity for the press to cover him, and they caught up with him there. French papers published a photo of him reading about events in France in the Spanish newspaper *El Mundo*, while the United Press sent a dispatch published in *The New York Times* on February 17, 1941, datelined Barcelona: "Jean Gabin, the French film actor, arrived today on his way to Hollywood where he expects to resume acting. The collapse of the French film industry did what five years of Hollywood persuasion failed to do—convince Gabin that he should go to Hollywood. Many film concerns tried to get his signature on a contract."

When he got to Lisbon the scene was like something out of a movie thriller—or the Algiers of *Pépé le Moko*. There were spies from all over rubbing elbows with war profiteers looking to make a fast buck, beautiful women desperately selling what they could to get a passage out of Europe, emigrants and refugees offering everything from jewels and gold to valued artworks in exchange for berths on America-bound ships. Twentieth Century–Fox had booked Gabin on the SS *Exeter* of the American Export Lines, sister ship of the SS *Exochorda* that had taken Michèle Morgan to the U.S. four months before. (Only 18 months later, in November 1942, having become the troop ship USS *Edward Rutledge*, it was torpedoed and sunk off Casablanca.)

His arrival in New York was later described by *Photoplay* in the dramatic fashion of movie magazines:

> When the liner *Exeter* nosed up through New York harbor one blustery morning in March, a tall muscular man in a black turtle-necked sweater, a dark suit and an old fur coat, stood on deck eagerly watching the distant dock where he knew Devan awaited him. His once-blond wavy hair had turned grey. There was in his eyes the look of a man who has seen death and destruction and despair. But on his lips was the broad smile that has ingratiated him and his simple sincerity to so many French filmgoers in the years gone by. That smile was a smile of triumph. For the second time he had escaped seizure by the Germans![23]

Like most French of those days, Jean Gabin didn't do broad smiles; a shy, reserved grin was about as big an explosion of joy anyone ever saw him make. And he had never expressed publicly anything but aversion to foreign lands and foreign tongues in general, and America and English in particular. Now this rooted, consummate Frenchman was about to encounter New York in all its raucous, hustling intensity, followed by Tinseltown in all its gaudy, garish glory. As he stood at the railing of the *Exeter* watching the spires of Manhattan emerge, he was certainly far more melancholy and apprehensive than triumphant.

André Devan was indeed on the dock on March 4, 1941, to welcome Gabin to New York. He was accompanied by Sylvain Chabert, a wealthy French businessman and pillar of Paris nightlife before he left for the U.S. a few months before with his wife, the Franco-American chanteuse Irene Hilda, originally from Richmond, Virginia. He and Gabin had been friends since the 1920s, when they cycled together in the Bois de Boulogne, but he was still amused to see Gabin debark with his racing bike as if it were his most prized possession. While Devan set about making arrangements with Fox for Gabin's care and feeding in Los Angeles, Chabert took him under his wing. He showed him around Manhattan and served as interpreter for Gabin, whose English had yet to reach the level of pidgin. He introduced him to New York's growing French expatriate community, and, most important, where he could get a decent *bifteck-frites* and bottle of Beaujolais. In the evening they frequented nightspots with a large French clientele like the Maisonette, La Vie Parisienne, and the Glass Hat Club, where they sometimes caught performances by Irene Hilda or the torch singer Helen Stuart.

Also waiting for Gabin were the inevitable reporters. Despite his distaste for journalists, he gave several interviews through interpreters at the urging of Devan and Fox. *Photoplay*'s correspondent compared what he termed "the Spencer Tracy of France" to established French figures in Hollywood, finding him more vigorous than Charles Boyer, more vital than Maurice Chevalier, "with an earthy quality about him, a promise of tremendous power and drive not usually associated with a Parisian matinee idol." (That description shows how little Americans, even writers in the specialized press, understood who Gabin was and how much they underestimated his stature as a serious actor.) What, he predictably asked Gabin during a lunch at the fashionable Colony restaurant on Sixty-first Street, was his first impression of New York? "He thought a minute and then replied: 'The cars ... the endless stream of cars ... all moving about the city. It had been months since I had seen more than one automobile on the road at a time.'" Then the reporter paraphrased Gabin's impressions in his own prose more appropriate for fan magazine readers: "The chic, slim girls on Park Avenue ... the food at the smarter restaurants ... the luxury of hot water in his bath in his hotel suite ... these were the things that made his first few days in America seem like a lovely, restful dream after a disturbed nightmare."[24] *The New York Times*, also exercising a bit of poetic license, overlooked that Gabin had been on the Riviera for six months and seen virtually no action while stationed in Cherbourg. It described him colorfully as "a trim, blond-haired gent with a weather-beaten complexion which attested to the months spent aboard a French minesweeper in the early days of the war." Its reporter found that Gabin, though speaking through an interpreter, understood English "amazingly well for one who claims not to be able to speak the language." The story noted the striking coincidence that the American premiere of the five-year-old *Pépé le Moko* had just opened at the city's World Cinema. Whether that was a happy accident or due to astute timing by the theater owner, we can't tell, but *The Times* said Gabin "was quite pleased, to say the least."[25]

Besides Sylvain Chabert, Gabin dined frequently with the singer Jean Sablon, whom he had known since they had performed together in the 1923 operetta *La Dame en Décolleté* and later in his first film, *Chacun sa Chance*, in 1930. Sablon by now was an old New York hand, having first gone to the U.S. in 1937, where he sang on live CBS broadcasts, appeared on Broadway with songs by George Gershwin and Cole Porter, and made his first recordings in English. He returned to Paris for a while, but went back to America when the war started. He found Gabin feeling lost and homesick in New York, but not so depressed that he didn't ask whether Sablon knew Ginger Rogers, whose movies with Fred Astaire he admired. Sablon, having been acquainted with Rogers for some time, was aware that she had been intrigued by Gabin ever since seeing *Port of Shadows*, and also knew she happened to be in New York. It was obvious to him that his old friend Gabin wasn't asking to meet her just because he greatly admired her dancing. He invited them both to a dinner party at his Manhattan apartment. Gabin turned on the charm and his body language made up for his halting English. Rogers was visibly fascinated and they left together, but it seems they parted at her hotel room door.

13

Hollywood Alien

Gabin headed to Hollywood in mid–March to sign his contract with Darryl Zanuck making him, according to the entertainment press, the highest salaried star on the Twentieth Century–Fox lot. He eschewed flying, even though airlines were by then offering service from New York to Los Angeles, with several stops in between, in the new Douglas DC-3, some equipped with sleeping accommodations. He was following through on his vow never to take a plane again after nearly crashing into the Mediterranean in 1935. That meant boarding *The 20th Century Limited*, touted as "The Most Famous Train in the World," at Grand Central Terminal at 6 p.m., debarking at Chicago's LaSalle Street Station 16 hours later, then catching the *Chief*, Atchison, Topeka and Santa Fe's all-Pullman limited for another 63 hours to Los Angeles. Today, spending three days and four nights on the rails sounds like a grueling way to get across flyover country, but both trains were the ultimate in transcontinental travel luxury. *The 20th Century Limited* literally rolled out a red carpet at both departure and arrival, while the *Chief* was known as a rolling hotel for studio bigwigs and movie stars making round trips to New York.

Gabin loved it. In fact, it was one of the things he liked best about the U.S. He enjoyed the large, comfortable compartment where he could do his morning exercises, seldom leaving it except to stretch his legs. He took all his meals there, skipping the dining car to ensure privacy. Besides reading or taking a nap, he liked sipping a beer or whiskey as he watched America go by at a leisurely 60 miles per hour. During his time in America he made the trip often to New York, which he much preferred to the West Coast, to get away from what he considered the suffocating company town atmosphere and artificiality of Hollywood.[1]

He joined, but was never really part of, the wave of French directors, producers, screenwriters, production managers, and actors that began to flood into Los Angeles starting in 1939, when Jean Renoir arrived. Other directors like René Clair, Julien Duvivier, the Russian-born Léonide Moguy, and Henri Diamant-Berger followed, while Janine Crispin, Madeleine Lebeau, Victor Francen, Jean-Pierre Aumont, Micheline Cheirel, Marcel Dalio, Louis Jourdan, and, of course, Michèle Morgan were among the actors. Annabella, Gabin's partner in *Bandéra* who had a brief career with Fox in the 1930s and married Tyrone Power, recalled, "We lived as if in a dream. At one reception hosted by Warners, there were several gigantic dining rooms with walls covered in gardenias and carpets of the most immaculate whiteness sprinkled with brightly colored orchids."[2] The playwright and screenwriter S. N. Behrman, writing in *The New Yorker*, called the Hollywood of those days "a kind of Athens. It was as crowded with artists as

Renaissance Florence. It was a Golden Era. It has never happened before. It will never happen again."[3]

Charles Boyer had been enjoying a brilliant career there since the early 1930s, playing opposite stars such as Jean Harlow, Katherine Hepburn, and Greta Garbo. His impression of the West Coast after the depressing damp and discouragement of interwar Paris was of being in "a bath of light ... a marvelous country in which there was only youth, freshness and enthusiasm."[4] His positive reaction to America's youthful energy was just the opposite of Gabin's dismay at being separated from his roots. His ultra-Frenchness, his strong, innate patriotism, his open contempt for anything that smacked of nouveau-riche snobbery, worldly glitter, and pseudo-sophistication led him to snub, even scorn, much of Hollywood's movie community, including some of its French members.

He had little to do with Boyer. Good at holding grudges, often unfairly, Gabin disliked him due to a perceived professional rivalry back in Paris. He also disapproved of Boyer's taking American citizenship in the late 1930s, just when France was threatened with war. When it was pointed out to him that Boyer generously helped new French arrivals to Hollywood settle in and adapt, Gabin dismissed it as Boyer's trying to compensate for his guilt about abandoning France. Bad feelings had long run deep between the two and were exacerbated by the hothouse atmosphere in Hollywood. Gabin shunned Boyer's little group of French exiles who openly preached against the Vichy regime. Because of this and out of personal jealousy and spite, Boyer encouraged the rumor that Gabin was pro–Vichy. Gabin, accustomed as he was to taking direct action, convinced Boyer that he might be the object of a real-life enactment of one of his angry movie scenes if he didn't stop spreading the rumor.[5] But as always with slander, some of it stuck and many, both in the U.S. and France, continued to believe it.

Similarly, his friendship with Jean Renoir was marred for years by his reflexive rejection of French citizens who left their country in wartime and didn't return as soon as possible. Renoir, whose improvisational, unHollywood method of directing initially made him a hard sell at many studios, spontaneously sent Gabin a welcoming note saying he looked forward to seeing him in town. They did socialize for a while. But Jean turned against him when Renoir got his Hollywood groove and decided to stay on and take American nationality while France was suffering Nazi occupation.

The French community in Hollywood lived largely among themselves, as I have often seen when the French go abroad. They also tend to loosen up in ways they don't dare to at home. In America some even start to smile and call people by their first names. But usually they still prefer to socialize in their closed cliques, creating the *Clochemerle* atmosphere of a small French town with its jealousy, rivalries, and gossip, wherever they are. In 1930s Hollywood, the Franco-American director Robert Florey, who worked for Paramount and Warner Brothers, noted this. "They formed separate groups gathering together in the evenings for dinners or parties where no one spoke English and everyone complained about life in California," he observed. "While working at the studio—any studio—the French ladies would bring baskets of food and bottles of wine—hard to get during Prohibition—and organize picnic luncheons, drinking and laughing, speaking loudly in French at noontime to the amazement of the Americans not accustomed to this kind of behavior."[6]

Zanuck signed Gabin to do *Moontide*, a noirish film resembling the poetic realism of his recent films in France, with a somber screenplay by John O'Hara and Ida Lupino as female lead, to be directed by Fritz Lang. Shooting was to begin in about three months, during which Gabin was supposed to get his English up to speed. Gabin had enough star power and professional integrity to disagree with Fox right away, saying it would be at least six months before he would be ready to shoot. He had to be able not only to speak his lines correctly, he explained, but to feel them, the way he did in French, so they would come out of his eyes. And for that he had to *think* in English, which was going to require more time. Fox set him up in a bungalow at the Beverly Hills Hotel (with Marlene's help he would soon find a rental house that belonged to Greta Garbo perched in the hills). There were also a chauffeured Rolls Royce and a yacht at his disposal when he liked, but there is no indication that he used either. To handle his growing finances he engaged Bö Roos, one of Hollywood's leading business managers, whose clients included John Wayne, Fred MacMurray, Joan Crawford, Johnny Weissmuller and Marlene Dietrich.[7]

Marcel Dalio, the Jewish French actor born Israel Blauschild, whose parents died at Auschwitz and who escaped to the U.S. via South America, had known Gabin well since they had done *Pépé le Moko* and *La Grande Illusion* together. He had arrived in Hollywood a few months before Jean and called him to say hello. Gabin invited him over for the treat of a real French lunch—neither hamburgers nor Coca Cola, Dalio noted gratefully—prepared by his valet André. As they sat beside the swimming pool afterward, Dalio, who would later play the croupier at Rick's in *Casablanca*, nattered away about the local scene and mutual friends. "He listened to me in silence, taciturn, maybe indifferent, his mind certainly elsewhere," Dalio recalled, wondering what Gabin could have been ruminating. "After an hour or so he emerged from his silence with a sigh. 'You know,' he said thoughtfully, 'cattle really are a beautiful sight.' He was already in Normandy, counting his head of cattle."[8]

He told Dalio that if he wanted to see Greta Garbo, all he had to do was look down the alley where the trashcans were. She came every day at 4 p.m. "My heart was palpitating," Dalio recalled. "In a few moments I'm going to see 'The Divine.' I keep my eyes fixed on the little wall at the end of the alley, and soon I see a sort of Fantômas wearing a big hat, the face covered with a pair sunglasses, who stands on a trashcan to peek over the wall and watch us. Gabin says with a laugh, 'That's her.' It was really Greta Garbo. The house Marlene rented for Jean belonged to her, and from time to time she came to check on what was going on, to be sure those Frenchies were behaving themselves and not making love on the lawn or throwing empty camembert boxes in the pool."[9]

Gabin went to work on his English with a will. He dutifully worked several hours a day with a succession of three coaches over the succeeding months, paying special attention to the "th" sound and learning to aspirate the "h" at the beginning of a word that defeat most French. Fox force-fed him with private screenings of Clark Gable films, the idea being that Gable's English was the most typically American. He practiced it on everybody who would listen, from grocery clerks and studio technicians to his Filipino houseboy. An excellent mimic, he listened to radio commercials and could convincingly parrot the ubiquitous "No money down, easy convenient payments" and "Are you weak, rundown, sluggish?" as a party trick. The training cost Fox something like $85,000 before he could start *Moontide*.[10]

But, unlike Chevalier and Boyer, he was never really comfortable in the dreaded language of Shakespeare and tended to speak his lines mainly by rote—"I listen and when I've got it I give them an imitation," he confided to Michèle Morgan.[11] Whereas his superbly natural way of speaking his lines in French was one of the keys to his success as an actor, he always sounded stilted and felt uncomfortable in English; some compared him to a bad-tempered headwaiter in a French restaurant. Years later he refused to speak English unless absolutely necessary, and still seemed to smart over the experience. When he did films with American actors like George Raft and Robert Stack in the 1960s, he generally declined to speak it, feeling that since he had had to work so hard to learn English in Hollywood, they could try to learn some French.[12]

The contract inked, the Fox publicity department went into high gear. It gave him the full star treatment, billing him as "the Number One dramatic actor of the French screen." It worked hard to distinguish him from the French actors already familiar to the American public, presenting him as "All man ... a potent blend of working-class glamor and doomed romanticism." "He's the first rugged French star Hollywood has known," promotional material trumpeted. "The others—Maurice Chevalier, Charles Boyer—have all been the suave, sophisticated type.... He's a relief from the pretty boys," and sure to set feminine hearts palpitating.[13] *The New York Times* bought that line, dubbing Gabin "Charles Boyer from the other side of the railroad tracks."[14] The Los Angeles movie press treated him like the new king of Tinseltown. "Hollywood is a-dither," said *Photoplay* in a July feature. "For once it has been shattered out of its blasé indifference into teeming, fuming, fussing, feverish interest. Why? Jean Gabin is in town. Literally he is taking the place by storm. He is the man of the hour with every celebrity in town breaking his neck to get near him."[15]

Hollywood has never had anything against the gross, both as an adjective—philistine, coarse, tawdry, pick your synonym—and as a noun, as in the haul at the box office. The two dovetail neatly, the former underpinning the latter. As early as the 1920s the brilliant French inventor and creator of the world's first film studio, Léon Gaumont, went to the U.S. to demonstrate his new color film process to American producers. He came prepared to show them poetic footage of colorful flowers, delicate butterflies, lush landscapes. The Americans were unimpressed. "Where are the girls?" they asked impatiently. Gaumont cabled his office in Paris for cheesecake girlie shots and was better received.[16] The message was expressed more baldly in an ad for the U.S. release of a postwar Gabin film, *Voici le Temps des Assassins/Deadlier Than the Male* (1956): "Sex and murder mean money at the box office."[17]

As a litmus test of the different attitudes in America and Europe toward the nature of cinema, purely mass entertainment or what the French like to call the "seventh art" with some semblance of cultural potential—a dichotomy long recognized by the American practice of showing European films in "art" cinemas—Hollywood's handling and molding of French actors in the 1930s and '40s is revealing. This was the height of the studio system. Movie stars were produced by the dozen, with the image-makers changing everything from names to noses to give them what was considered maximum appeal to American audiences.

It didn't always work with European actors in general. It was a recipe for conflict with the recalcitrant, individualistic, idiosyncratic French in particular. For that matter, Hollywood's record of success with importing major foreign stars has been spotty at best over the years. The list of foreigners who failed to attain status equivalent to that they enjoyed at home includes the likes of Ivan Mosjoukine, Isa Miranda, Marcello Mastroianni, Hildegarde Knef, Alain Delon and Emmanuelle Béart, among many others.

Michèle Morgan, arriving in Hollywood before Gabin, got the treatment before he did. As thoroughly French body and soul as he, she explains in her memoirs, *Avec ces*

Yeux-là (*With Those Eyes*), that she never got over her shock at being viewed as a product instead of a person. To start with, the schlockmeisters at the RKO publicity office assured her all she had to do was look pretty, they would do the thinking for her. The first thing she had to learn was to say cheese whenever a photographer aimed a camera at her—an injunction that made her wonder what *fromage* had to do with it. With the cheese-smile firmly in place, she mainly had to field questions about her affair with Jean Gabin, the only aspect of her that really interested the American press. There was also the requirement, which she found humiliating, to hike her skirt to mid-thigh when she sat down during an interview.

In case it wasn't clear to her, an RKO publicity assistant explained who she was: "For the American public, you're 'the typical French girl,' sentimental but with a strong personality, shy but not naïve. You like perfume, intelligent men, Burgundy wine and cheese. You do like it, don't you? That's very French. Besides, it's in your file."[18] On the other hand, very French or not, her accent was a problem, particularly the French tonic accent stressing the last syllable of most nouns—"Say baNANas, not banaNAS," they explained. They assigned her a speech coach, expert at erasing foreign accents, who promised to having her speaking English "like an English woman living in America" in no time. He advised her that the fastest way to improve her English would be to find an American boyfriend. Lonely, she tried a few "dates," but found their conversation insipid—the impossibly handsome Robert Taylor talked only of his cattle ranch during a whole candlelight dinner, making it hard for her to suppress an inappropriate giggle. She balked at the requirement of an automatic goodnight kiss whether she felt like it or not, despite the best efforts of her RKO handler to explain the rules of the American dating game.

During her first months of this forced makeover, she couldn't help feeling "a sort of interior rage," as she put it. "I want to shout, 'I don't need to have my life exploited, or my personality shaped. I want to stay myself. You'll either take me as I am, or I'll leave.'"[19] She couldn't escape the feeling that Hollywood was crushing her personality, trying to make her look, and act, like every other young woman who had made the trip to the West Coast with stars in her eyes. Given RKO's determined attempt at remolding her, it's hard to imagine that this was an actress who, by being herself, would eventually play the female lead in nearly 70 films, be voted the most popular star in France ten times, and win the Career Golden Lion at the Venice Film Festival in 1996, not to mention a star on the Hollywood Walk of Fame. And she did it without playing the French sex kitten. ("My charm was not in my ass," was how she put it.)[20]

It was when she was cast, against her better judgment, opposite Frank Sinatra in his debut film, *Higher and Higher* (1943), that she realized how much the studio was trying to make her into something she was not. For one thing, it called for her to sing and dance with Sinatra, whereas she knew she had no real talent for either. For another, it involved a complete makeover by someone named Tommy, RKO's top makeup artist. When she saw the result in the mirror, she didn't recognize herself. The woman who looked back at her had redrawn eyebrows, remodeled lips, and a weird chignon on top of her head. "Something in me rebelled against it, a vague anxiety that I'd become a phony product. This beauty from a makeup box—but was it really beauty?—had turned me into an American girl like any other. I try to stifle that feeling. After all, weren't these the people who had created Marlene Dietrich, Joan Crawford, Ginger Rogers? And yet, all during the shoot I couldn't feel natural, I had the sensation of being separated from myself and the rest of the cast, as if someone else were playing the part. I felt I'd committed a monumental mistake."[21]

Thoroughly alienated from the studio system and from what she considered Hollywood's spurious lifestyle, she eventually came to agree with Julien Duvivier, who had arrived shortly before her. After the first few dazzling months of discovering the American Dream complete with outsized cars, big houses, and superb lawns under the California sun, he told her, Hollywood was like "living in a cemetery."[22] She later admitted that this was the most deeply unhappy period in her life.

Nothing could assuage it, not even the luxurious home in the style of a Norman French farmhouse she had built at 10050 Cielo Drive in Brentwood Canyon, north of Beverly Hills. (The house was later rented by Cary Grant, Henry Fonda, and Olivia Hussy. It became infamous in 1969 as the scene of the so-called Manson Family murders, in which the actress Sharon Tate, Roman Polanski's wife, was murdered.) Articulating the painful cultural isolation that she, Gabin, and many other French expatriates to Hollywood felt, she later explained, "Not to be able to speak my mother tongue with anyone meant being cut off from my roots. It's hard to imagine how much you can miss the shared complicity of simple things like fairy tales, children's songs and primary education. Having a history, a landscape, historic men, food and lifestyle in common is enormously important."[23] It was a typically French form of intense homesickness that immigrants from other countries, particularly northern Europe, don't seem to experience to the same extent. Nearly every French person I've known who lived in the U.S., and there have been many, had the same feeling of irremediable bereavement.

In Gabin's case, Hollywood's image-makers tried hard to twist him into a one-dimensional, American-style sex symbol. Every detail of his career was being managed by the studio, an entirely new and disconcerting experience for Gabin, who was used to much more freedom, independence, and respect. As the film historian Robert Sklar notes in *City Boys*, "No one could be guaranteed that the studio would manage careers wisely, or even attentively.... It was easier to pigeonhole or type-cast performers, to slot them into familiar genre categories, to use them as often as possible in repetitive roles."[24] Whereas in France he was taken seriously as an actor—André Bazin's tragic hero of contemporary cinema—in Hollywood he was merely a hunk to be sold to dreamy readers of lonely hearts columns.

Fox publicity pumped out titillating copy typecasting him with a vengeance, and the movie press faithfully echoed it. "Gals, we've seen him and can only say oooo la la, how you ladies will rave," went one column.[25] "Lusty and rugged, a real he-man, strictly a son of the soil," said another. "Despite his charming chivalry, you feel he could easily go primitive."[26] "Who is this Great Lover?" teased *Modern Screen* in July. The answer: "He's Jean Gabin, who has brought a new brand of oomph to Hollywood ... looks like an Apache, plays an accordion, and has made sizzling cinema love to Simone Simon, Annabella,

As seen by Hollywood, 1941. Studio publicity promoted him as a new sex symbol, the great French lover (Collection du Musée Jean Gabin).

Michèle Morgan."[27] The studio compared him, ludicrously, to Rudolph Valentino as a master of smoldering passion.[28]

Not only that, but, as swooning readers were informed, he wore turtleneck sweaters—considered exotic and erotic for some reason—and slept in the nude. For his publicity photos they tried to make him hot, a sort of French Ken doll, giving him an absurd, unflattering permanent, and tousling his hair in what was meant to be wildly romantic, seductive waves, which actually undermined his natural masculinity. They put an Apache-style red scarf around his neck and mascaraed his eyelashes, making his famous *regard* with his pale eyes appear almost feminine, which again was exactly the opposite of the macho theme of their promotions. He put up with this, painfully, despite his revulsion dating from his earliest days in show business, at the very notion of men putting on makeup. At one point they even considered changing his name to John, because in America Jean was a feminine name. Fox worried a lot about how to deal with his masculinity, seemingly unsure what to do with it. Probably that was because it was authentic, like the rest of Gabin's persona. What does a Hollywood studio, accustomed to creating artificial stars, do with an actor whose charisma, not to mention box office success, derives mainly from his authenticity? They never solved that dilemma to anyone's satisfaction. As the French film critic Georges Magnane wrote of Gabin's character in *Moontide*, "excellent at home playing men of the people, [he is] transformed here into a curious puppet, halfway between a gigolo and a sentimental bandit."[29]

Through interpreters, Gabin also lent himself to Fox-staged, fan-pleasing interviews, where the most urgent questions concerned what he liked about women, Americans in particular. He played along to the point of declaring, unconvincingly to anyone who knew him, that he found American women not only the most chic and beautiful in the world—"a new, better race of women"—but also the best dressed. They were, in fact, more attractive than French women, healthy, gracefully athletic, tanned, ready for good, clean, comradely fun. Clearly he had been well briefed by his Fox handlers.[30]

Presumably he was able to explain that satisfactorily to Michèle Morgan when he called her that summer. With both reluctantly being put through the Dream Machine processor, she would have understood why he had to make such totally out-of-character remarks. Gabin suffered just as much from alienation and solitude in "Olivode" as she did, but tended to internalize it more. They went to lunch at a faux bistro named Chez Oscar, complete with red-and-white checked tablecloths, for a life-sustaining pot-au-feu and a carafe of imported French red. She laughed more than she had in months, peppered him with questions about the common friends they had left behind, and teared up when he described life in occupied France. He explained the Nazi-imposed racial laws, the long lines for a baguette or a kilo of leeks, buying shoes on the black market with cigarettes, the humiliating daily Wehrmacht parade on the Champs Elysées—"that disfigured France he tells me about is my country, and I measure just how much I'm attached to it." He questioned her about her new life in America and quickly saw that she didn't have much of one, that, like him, she was just there to wait out the war. "I'll see how things turn out," he told her. "Who knows, maybe the day will come when I'll be able to help kick the Krauts out."[31]

Until then, Gabin could only try to keep up with the war in Europe in an era when news was slow to arrive. Even when it did, American media, like the American public, had only sporadic interest in the situation in France. The war as seen from Hollywood had something unreal about it; it took him an effort to realize that a whole continent was being subjugated while he basked in the California sun. An uncomfortable enough situation for a French patriot, especially when, like many of the French movie community, he felt an outsider. His friend and fellow actor Jean-Pierre Aumont had the same reaction to life there. "I missed Paris terribly," he said. "I couldn't walk around the way I like to so much. You know, especially in California, there are no pedestrians, they don't exist. And when I did walk, either the police stopped me to ask if I was in trouble, or very nice people—because they are very helpful—stopped, thinking I had had a flat tire: 'Where are you going, we'll give you a ride.' And if I replied, 'No thanks, I'm just out for a walk,' they looked at me like I was crazy."[32] It was the little everyday differences like that as well as the more important, that grated: Jean Renoir's sense of thrift was offended by the American habit of throwing out razor blades when they were still usable.

Gabin considered his time in Hollywood wasted and his two films there no more than a way to ply his acting craft to make a living while waiting to go back home. Like Michèle Morgan and several others, he was disastrously out of his element; even dressing up in a western shirt, with a silver-buckled belt, red bandana around his neck and big hat on his head didn't help. Of the French movie people there, only two, Boyer and Chevalier, were really successful. That was due to playing, in different registers, roles usually typecast to the point of caricature as the American idea of the typical Frenchman. Boyer the suave, worldly lover with the pencil-thin moustache was every midinette's dream, Chevalier was the whimsical, frivolous boulevardier always ready with a knowing wink and a sunny smile. Gabin was a more typical Frenchman than they, but his Frenchness was authentic, not studio-manufactured, and it was anchored in his working class origins. American movie audiences could not be expected to understand the mannerisms, slang, even the subtle ethical code that make up the identity of the French proletariat. He was deprived of that dimension in his Hollywood films, even if in 1943 Jack Warner thought him good enough to consider him seriously instead of Humphrey Bogart for the lead role of Matrac in *Passage to Marseille*.[33]

It was because of his very authenticity that he, even more than most other French actors trying to make it in the U.S., was handicapped by the cultural differences, even today deeper than most suspect, between the two countries. The result of being removed from his French context was a spurious hybrid light years from his persona in his previous movies. As he once explained his self-definition as a *national* actor, "I can't be international because I don't feel true, I don't feel sincere in another language. I'm a national actor because I need my everyday words to express myself and feel that I have my feet on the ground. I need the smells of my country, to feel that I'm at home, to have my own way of living, my way of eating. Otherwise, I know I'm no good."[34]

Gabin's largely subconscious rejection not only of America, but of everything non–French, manifested itself most clearly and involuntarily in his difficulty with the English language. Everyone who knew him in Hollywood agreed that he worked sincerely at learning it, if only because it was the key to earning a living in exile. But he simply couldn't feel it. In a crucial *Moontide* scene with Ida Lupino he even reverts to French at one point, spontaneously saying *je t'aime* instead of "I love you." It was the outward sign of his distressing alienation. "In English, I could hear myself speak and I felt that someone else was speaking in my place," he later explained. "It was like an echo and I felt completely out of sync. Nothing seemed to correspond to what I was saying, not my gestures, my body, or anything I felt physically, or thought. It was a very painful feeling.... I had the impression that I was no longer what I wanted to be, which was French."[35]

They were just good friends now. The affair of French moviedom's ideal couple had lasted only a few months, much less time than the public thought. So it didn't take long for Gabin to get to the point in that lunch reunion at Chez Oscar with Michèle Morgan. She had had time to get to know a lot of people in "Olivode" hadn't she? He just wondered if she happened to know someone he was interested in seeing, Ginger Rogers. As luck would have it, Rogers had been one of the few in the Hollywood set with whom she had friendly relations. She had even questioned Morgan about Gabin before meeting him in New York at Jean Sablon's apartment.

It happened at a big party at Rogers' lavish Beverly Hills home where RKO had arranged for Morgan's "coming out" shortly after her arrival. The *tout Hollywood* was there, from Olivia de Havilland, Orson Welles, and Mickey Rooney, to Ava Gardner, Humphrey Bogart and Clark Gable. Cary Grant had been assigned to introduce her around. ("Hello, my name is Cary Grant," he had said. "Does he think that in France we don't see movies?" she wondered.)[36] His duty done, he handed her off to Rogers, who paid her the compliment of showing her the famous basement soda fountain and making her a daunting chocolate-apricot milkshake. Then she had a few questions.

"How is Jean Gabin in real life?" she wanted to know.

"The thing about Jean is just that," Morgan replied, "he's always real, on screen and off."

"Is he as charming as he is in his films?"

"Oh much more charming than that."[37]

What Morgan didn't feel like telling Ginger, perhaps out of some residual jealousy, is the number of times in the past he had annoyed her with remarks like "Ah, Ginger Rogers! I like that girl. I'd like to get to know her."[38]

Morgan knew from personal experience that, despite his reputation as a ladies' man, his shyness meant he always liked to have some indication that he wouldn't be rejected; Micheline had often sounded her out in the past before Gabin made a move. So she was good enough sport to tell Jean not only that, yes, she knew Rogers, but that she seemed to like him. Seeing how much that obviously meant to him, she organized a small dinner party for them at her home. The two again found ways to communicate and, following their initial meeting in New York a few weeks before, Rogers was able to judge for herself how real and charming Gabin could be.

The Hollywood gossip mills began churning, but in fact there wasn't that much to report. Gabin sent her the usual flowers. They went cycling through Beverly Hills, they dined and danced in the fashionable spots where they were photographed, she smiling radiantly. But Rogers the All American Girl—or, as the fanmags put it, "simple and direct and of the people"—apparently didn't get far with Gabin. In her fluffy memoirs she minimizes the relationship, saying off-handedly, "I did have a few dates with the appealing French actor Jean Gabin" in May-June 1941, implying that things stayed purely platonic.[39] That wouldn't be surprising. She was up against the most formidable competition any woman could face.

The girl from Independence, Missouri's rival for Jean Gabin was the Berlin-born Lola-Lola of *The Blue Angel*. Depending on your point of view, Marlene Dietrich could be seen variously as the Blond Goddess of erotic fantasy, the Chaucerian Wife of Bath, or the Biblical Whore of Babylon, with whom the kings of the earth have committed fornication. The incomplete list of those Hollywood "kings" over the years included Brian Aherne, Jimmy Stewart, John Wayne, Gary Cooper, Michael Wilding, Kirk Douglas,

Harry Cohn, Sam Spiegel, John Gilbert, Douglas Fairbanks, Jr., Yul Brynner, and Frank Sinatra, not necessarily in that order. The majority of them were married.

In the real world beyond Hollywood there had been Maurice Chevalier and the German novelist Erich Maria Remarque. Later there would be Ernest Hemingway. There was also the besotted General James Gavin, the handsome young commander of the 82nd Airborne, who had a long relationship with Dietrich during the war. Adolf Hitler had sent his confidant Joachim von Ribbentrop to Paris in 1936 to ask her to return to Germany to make a picture and to be his mistress; she turned him down after considering the possibility of making a date with Der Fuhrer and then assassinating him. Add to that a number of American girlfriends who constituted her "Sewing Circle," plus Edith Piaf in Paris. All of this qualified as mere extracurriculars, because she had been married to Rudolf Sieber, an assistant film director and father of their daughter Maria, since the 1920s.

Jean Cocteau, who knew her in Paris and said, as only he would, that her name began with a caress and ended with the crack of a whip, called her "the most exciting and terrifying woman I have ever known."[40] For the Romanian-born actor Edward G. Robinson, a cultivated man with an excellent art collection who played opposite her in *Manpower* (1941), she was "the quintessential sex goddess."[41] John Wayne, in thrall to her for a lengthy affair beginning in 1939, recalled her as a torrid lover who was eager, responsive, voracious and willing to try anything. In a word, he said, "fantastic." George Raft said he would give a year's salary for one night with her, but probably didn't have to. What her feminine rivals called her is unprintable in a family publication, but James Gavin's wife Irma spoke for many of them when she finally admitted defeat and asked for a divorce: "I could compete with ordinary women, but when the competition is Marlene Dietrich, what's the use?"[42]

For this amoral woman, promiscuity—an old-fashioned word for an old-fashioned concept—was a way of life. She flitted from one lover to another with the animal-ease of a humming bird sucking the nectar from flowers. Besides, it had its utilitarian side, adding an extra dimension of ardor to her love scenes on the set with whomever happened to be her leading man. The extraordinary thing is that she unexpectedly, almost accidentally, seems to have genuinely fallen in love with Jean Gabin, insofar as she was capable of deep emotional involvement if not commitment.

They made an unlikely couple. She emanated cool, slinky allure if not actual depravity: a *Life* profile accurately called it "the heavy-lidded look of a seductive and world-weary hop-head."[43] Added to that was star glamor and intellectually sophisticated ironic self-derision, along with the kind of sulfurous experience associated with her famous line from *Shanghai Express* (1932), "It took more than one man to make me Shanghai Lily." Off screen she was often kind, solicitous, and extravagantly generous to everyone she knew, and some she hardly knew. She was cultivated, well-traveled, spoke three languages fluently, and preferred the company of brilliant men, from Erich Maria Remarque to Noël Coward, Hemingway, and Sir Alexander Fleming, the discoverer of penicillin. "I can pick 'em in a full room, just like that," she said. "I don't care what age they are."[44]

Conversely, despite his Montmartre street smarts, years immersed in the cosmopolitan French movie scene, and numerous love affairs, Jean Gabin was still basically shy, ingenuous, untutored, and uncomfortable around those with the kind of conversation and manners he associated with snobs and phonies. Although he routinely courted his leading ladies, he tended to invest heavily in his relationships. He was emotionally needy, insecure, and feared rejection. Ill at ease around people he didn't know well, he preferred socializing at home to attending fashionable social occasions. He knew contemporary theater and cinema from his own experience and, thanks to his friendship with Renoir, a bit about modern art. But high culture like opera left him cold—"It's ridiculous for a guy to sing while he's dying" was his peremptory judgment.

And yet the combination of wartime circumstances and psycho/sexual chemistry between these two antithetical beings produced what would be one of the most consuming, turbulent, and ultimately painful relationships either ever had. It's entirely possible, as the Dietrich biographer Charles Higham contends, that the men who most marked her were Gabin and Remarque, "the two men who, in one case physically and the other intellectually, penetrated her psyche most deeply."[45] Gabin, she recalled lyrically in her memoirs, was "*the* man, the superman, the 'man for life.' Nothing in him was false. Everything was clear and transparent.… He was gentle, tender, and had all the traits a woman looks for in a man. An ideal being, the kind that appears in our dreams.… I loved him very much."[46]

All autobiographies are self-serving, all arrange the truth, and Dietrich's *Marlene* is so flagrant in that respect that her best biographers discount much of it. But there is no objective reason to doubt that these words about Gabin, written 40 years after their last meeting in Paris and ten years after his death, reflect a deep-seated loss. Gabin, the opposite of a Don Juan, wasn't playing around, unlike most of her conquests. For him Dietrich didn't represent recreational sex or an introductory course for clean-cut American boys to Berlin-style European eroticism. Meeting her at a time of great dislocation and dismay in his life, he loved and needed her intensely.

Dietrich's daughter Maria was an interested and perceptive observer of her mother's tempestuous six-year relationship with Gabin, whom she considered the most sensitive and gentlemanly of Marlene's stable of lovers. "Dietrich's arms were waiting, ready to enfold him," she writes in her frank biography of her mother. "One of the great romances of the 1940s was born … and of course, Gabin suffered the most."[47]

14

Marlene

It happened gradually, for at first Jean Gabin was just another amorous target of opportunity. Dietrich had set her sights on him long before he got to Hollywood. They first met Paris in 1939 when there was some possibility that she would play opposite him in a French film noir called *Dédé d'Anvers*. They got together to discuss the script and struck up a casual friendship, but the producers backed out; the film would finally be done in 1948 with Simone Signoret in the title role. At the time, he found Dietrich's entourage, which included her usual lesbian friends and others he considered weird, repugnant. In any case, Gabin was preparing to do *Remorques* and had Morgan on his mind. But Marlene made a mental note to follow up when the opportunity presented itself.

It wouldn't be long coming. After her return to Hollywood, she got wind of Fox's interest in signing Gabin and urgently cabled her long-suffering complaisant husband, Rudi Sieber, in New York: "I HEAR GABIN MAY BE COMING HERE. FIND OUT. I SHOULD GET HIM FIRST."[1] After the news broke that he was indeed on the way, she said to her close friend and director, Josef von Sternberg, who had preceded her to Hollywood, "That unbelievable actor from that magnificent film, *Grand Illusion*—they are bringing him over to be in cheap American films? He probably can't even speak English. They will ruin him! He is perfect the way he is—and there will be no one to protect him. Can one still call France? Isn't Michèle Morgan in love with him? I could call her and find out where to reach him."[2]

She reached him first in New York in May 1941, during one of Jean's train trips back East to escape the idleness and alienation of Hollywood. He and Sylvain Chabert went to La Vie Parisienne for dinner. As soon as they entered, Marlene got up, ran over, and kissed him on the cheek, creating the sort of public spectacle she delighted in and he hated. She led him to her table and introduced him to Ernest Hemingway, whom she had known since 1934. He spent a boring evening while the two of them flattered each other and talked of old times in prewar Paris. But when they parted, Gabin and Dietrich agreed to meet again in Hollywood.

When they did, Dietrich had just finished doing *Manpower* (1941), inflaming her partners Edward G. Robinson and George Raft and generating rivalry between them, as their unscripted fistfight on the set suggests. With three top stars and an action screenplay about power line workers, the film was successful, helping her overcome her recent studio reputation as box office poison due to a string of mediocre efforts. Like Gabin's classic period of the 1930s, her series of seven exceptional movies with von Sternberg, from *The*

Blue Angel (1930) to *The Devil Is a Woman* (1935), was behind her. She was turning 40 and uncertain about her career, with a new crop of leading ladies like Ingrid Bergman, Lana Turner, and Rita Hayworth coming on strong, and Betty Grable challenging her legs. "Of course, I'm going to quit working," she told a reporter. "I want a chance really to see a bit of life before I die.... A film star's career ... can last only as long as one's youth lasts, and one's youth fades far quicker on screen than on the stage—I'm going to quit while I'm still at the top."[3]

She had managed to see a good bit of life, or at least of her leading men, in the previous two years. In 1939 she had done *Destry Rides Again*, an oater in which she played a dance hall queen named Frenchy opposite Jimmy Stewart as a deputy sheriff in the fictional western town of Bottleneck. The film was good enough to be included for preservation in the Library of Congress' National Film Registry as "culturally, historically, or aesthetically significant." For Dietrich the main interest, besides the much-needed fee, was Stewart. As the producer Joe Pasternak recalled, "She took one look at Jimmy Stewart and began to rub her hands. She wanted him at once."[4] She noticed that he read Flash Gordon comics on the set, so she wooed him with a life-size doll of the character. Hollywood rumor, confirmed by Maria Riva, had it that she became pregnant by Stewart and had an abortion, after which she dropped him as she had Gary Cooper (whom she dismissed as "neither intelligent nor cultivated, nothing but vanity"), her partner in *Morocco* (1930).[5] Next was John Wayne.

She met Wayne in the Universal commissary as they were preparing to film *Seven Sinners* (1940), where she is the naughty Bijou—Hollywood's view of French women was comically stereotyped—an itinerant barroom singer who sparks riots among aroused sailors stationed on small South Pacific islands. Particularly attracted is the handsome naval lieutenant Dan Brent, played by Wayne. As soon as she spotted him, she leaned over to director Tay Garnett and said in a hoarse stage whisper, "Daddy, buy me *that*."[6] Wayne was married to Josephine, the first of his three Mexican wives, but accepted Dietrich's invitation to her dressing room. "I wonder what time it is," she pretended, lifting her skirt to show a watch attached to a garter. "It's very early, darling," she assured him. "We have plenty of time."[7]

The time stretched out to several months or three years, depending on whom you believe. Wayne was enjoying what he called, according to biographer Marc Eliot in *American Titan: Searching for John Wayne*, "the best lay I've ever had," which ended his marriage with Josephine. When not instructing him in the finer points of carnal pleasure, Dietrich tried to improve his mind by introducing him to great literature. "Wayne was not a bright or exciting type, not exactly brilliant, but neither was he bad," she judged.[8] She persuaded him to switch from the Morrison agency, which had long represented him, to hers, Feldman and Blum. Morrison sued Dietrich for having "undue influence" over Wayne, proof of which was that their private detectives saw him leaving her bungalow at the Beverly Hills Hotel at 5 or 6 o'clock in the morning several times. In later life she discouraged the idea that she had had an affair with him, maybe to sustain her reputation for preferring intellectual men, maybe to assuage Jean Gabin's jealousy.

She was still seeing Wayne when she glommed on to Gabin in Hollywood in the summer of 1941. She got him out of the bungalow at the Beverly Hills Hotel and into the rental house in Brentwood belonging to Garbo, where he could hang his paintings by Vlaminck, Sisley and Renoir, and stow his accordion and bicycle. She helped him find French food supplies and records by Edith Piaf. Describing this beginning of their affair,

Dietrich recalled succinctly, "I got to know Jean Gabin when he came to Hollywood. He had fled from occupied France. As always in such cases, I was asked to help him get used to his new life. My task was to speak French, translate, and to hunt around for some French coffee and French bread. I had done all this for René Clair as well. But Gabin was supposed to perform in English. And he wanted to accept the challenge. So I taught him

Gabin and Marlene make their entrance at the fashionable Ciro's nightclub in West Hollywood, 1942. He made an impressive trophy that she liked to exhibit (Deutsche Kinemathek-Marlene Dietrich Collection Berlin).

English. He would hide in the underbrush of the garden that surrounded his home in Brentwood to escape his teacher—me."[9] Some of this is probably true, though it strains credulity to believe a man like Gabin would try to hide in the bushes at her arrival. Also, he had all the professional language coaching he could stand, and they spoke mainly French together, which was not much help with his English grammar and syntax.

In August she began filming *The Lady Is Willing* (1941), a screwball comedy in which she plays a single woman who wants to keep an abandoned baby and enlists the help of a divorced pediatrician (Fred MacMurray). Although she was already juggling Wayne and Gabin, there was always room for one more, and she was puzzled when MacMurray didn't become amorous. To keep her attention on the script, director Mitchell Leisen took her aside and gave her some Dutch-uncle advice: "Listen, Marlene, Fred's so much in love with his wife, Lilly, he couldn't care less about any other woman," he told her, "so you lay off. Just make the picture."[10] She swallowed her disappointment and got on with the job, only to trip over a toy fire engine on the set on August 25. Trying to protect the baby she was holding, she fell heavily and broke her ankle, which had to be put in a plaster cast. She finished the shoot filmed only from the waist up.

The incident might have cost her a government contract: the Office of Production Management had been discussing with her possibly using her famous legs in ads to promote alternatives to silk stockings, in short supply on the market due to the precautionary military buildup. Jean Renoir and his wife Dido were witnesses to how much she yearned for admiration of those legs. One night they went with her to a nightclub and Marlene kept asking Dido to accompany her to the ladies' room. She said it was to help protect her from all the women who accosted her there. But after several trips, they came to realize that what she really wanted was Dido to admire her legs in a sort of narcissistic ritual.

Dietrich could see that Gabin was lost in America and she claimed that aroused her maternal instincts. "I loved to mother him day and night," she remembered. "Helpless, Gabin clung to me like an orphan to his foster mother.... I was his mother, sister, friend— and more still.... The tough-guy façade and the macho stance were put-ons. He was the most sensitive man I knew, a little baby who liked best of all to curl up in his mother's lap and be loved and cradled, and pampered."[11] Again, allowing for Dietrichian hyperbole, it is certainly true that Gabin leaned on her for aid, comfort and support, as well as for a semblance of affection, which he always seemed to feel a lack of in his life.

But the sensitive soul wasn't the only thing Marlene admired in Gabin. She told friends he had "the most beautiful loins I've ever seen on a man," quite a compliment coming from a connoisseur like her.[12] She also appreciated, as with Wayne, the untutored, natural-man side of him, a refreshing change from her sophisticated European acquaintances. "Your head is empty, it sounds hollow there," she teased him in front of friends, tapping his forehead. "But don't change. You're fine just like that."[13]

Though Jean was basically a homebody, she dragged him out for dining and dancing at Hollywood's voguish spots, showing him off like a trophy. Sometimes a nightclub orchestra would spontaneously break into the *Marseillaise* when the conductor saw him enter. He detested that sort of special attention, but it pleased her enormously. She would stand at attention and sing the anthem—once friends heard him tell her, "I hate it when you do that French patriot act."[14] Other times she would take along a violin and play it at a restaurant table while flashbulbs popped and he looked embarrassed. In any case he disliked American nightclubs where, as he saw it, people came mainly to get drunk; he was disgusted by several brawls he saw in Hollywood gin mills. But he accepted going out with Marlene as part of their relationship. The part he liked best was when she turned *Hausfrau* back at home, cooking, scrubbing floors ("I do like a clean floor," she said), and turning the Brentwood house into a cocoon of French living as close as possible to life in provincial Angers or Dijon.[15] Their social life was almost exclusively with French actors and directors.

She consulted her library of French cookbooks to whip up dishes like stuffed cabbage and pot-au-feu, her specialty. "She was a star on screen and off, even when cooking stuffed cabbage for Gabin," recalled Marcel Dalio, who was part of their coterie, along with Jean Renoir, for whom Gabin's house was a virtual French canteen. "Of course, the gloves and apron she wore in the kitchen came from Hermès."[16] Annabella, with whom Gabin had made two pictures and who was then living in Hollywood with her husband Tyrone Power, went to dinner chez Gabin one evening. She later recounted to André Brunelin,

> Marlene kept going to the door, and opening it to see if he was coming, like the wife of a Breton sailor worried about her man being late. When Jean arrived, Marlene threw her arms around his neck as if she hadn't seen him for months, asking him how his day had been, if he wasn't too tired, and so on.

Marlene makes a spectacle of herself on an evening out, while Gabin puts up with it. He preferred her in her *Hausfrau* mode (Deutsche Kinemathek-Marlene Dietrich Collection Berlin).

He gave us an embarrassed smile, as if to say, "Sorry, but you see how much she loves me." I must say I was surprised to see Marlene run to get his slippers and kneel down to put them on his feet. After dinner she asked him to play the accordion and sing for us. She went and got it, put a rakish scarf around his neck and a cap on his head. He sang a few songs like *Viens Fifine*. It was charming and incongruous in that Hollywood villa with its pool and palm trees.[17]

The unintended consequence of Dietrich's well-meaning creation of a French nest for Gabin, her encouraging him to socialize almost exclusively with the French community and especially his faithful little clique of friends from Renoir to Dalio and Duvivier, was to isolate and alienate him even further from the country to which he had fled. Moreover, her open, expressed contempt for what she saw as the un–European vulgarity of American culture in general and Hollywood yahoos in particular inevitably colored his feel for the U.S and impeded his acclimation. Professionally, too, she was an obstacle to his relations with his American colleagues in the acting profession and the production crews whose support and understanding he required. Dietrich ultimately was part of the problem Jean Gabin had in adapting to America, not the solution.

She claims in her memoirs that she and Gabin never seriously quarreled, but that is patently untrue. With her affair with John Wayne continuing for several months after she joined Gabin and the flow of billets-doux from the likes of Remarque regularly arriving in the mailbox, Jean, always prone to possessiveness, had fits of jealousy in which he became violent and beat her. She took that as a sign he loved her. Her daughter Maria Riva said Marlene was glad he was, as she accused him of being "jealous beyond reason." That justified her calling him the worst thing in her lexicon, *bourgeois*. He called her "my Prussian," not always affectionately.

He worried not only about all her male bedroom alumni, but about her Sewing Circle lady friends as well. When she bought fancy lingerie, he wondered whether it was to please him or someone else. When she performed in Orson Welles' Wonder Show in Los Angeles, doing a mind-reading act in her "nude" gown for soldiers stationed there, Gabin insisted on working as a stagehand so he could keep an eye on her. In December 1941 she began shooting *The Spoilers*, once again playing opposite John Wayne. What might they be doing off the set, or even in her dressing room? And now that America was at war following Pearl Harbor, she was increasingly absent, claiming to be out promoting the sale of bonds as part of the Hollywood Victory Committee. Was that a cover for a new liaison?

Gabin left for a couple of weeks in February to do his first American film, *Moontide/Le Péniche de l'Amour* (1942, French release 1944), opposite the 23-year-old Ida Lupino. Dietrich, believing he was angry over her affair with Wayne, was afraid he would start something with Lupino. She began keeping a diary in which she noted her longing for him. It raises the question of who was suffering more, as well as the surprising possibility that Jean's earthy, elemental nature had, against all odds, awakened an authenticity of feeling she had not experienced before. The fact that she wrote it in French and left it where Gabin would find it when he returned looks like an effort at sentimental manipulation and helps explain the theatrical prose. But there must have been at least some real fire behind all that melodramatic smoke.

> February 15th. He has gone.
> February 16th. He is with me like a blazing fire. Jean, *je t'aime*. All I plan to give you is my love. If you don't want it my life is finished, forever. And I realize saying that does not prove anything—even saying "I will love you all my life long and afterwards too"—because even when I am dead, I will still

love you. I love you—it feels good saying it without you having to answer: "I don't believe you." However, if you were here I could kiss you and lay my head on your shoulder and believe that you love me. Because if you don't, all is finished for me—because if you don't want me anymore I intend to die.

I am in bed. My body is cold and I look at myself, don't find myself attractive, not attractive enough—I would like to be very beautiful for you. For you I would like to be the best woman in the world and I'm not. But I love you. You are all my heart, all my soul. I never knew what soul was. Now I do. Tomorrow I will sleep in your bed. It is going to hurt. But I will be nearer to you. I love you—I love you.

February 17th. I haven't slept. I took some pills at 3 a.m. but I was too cold to be able to sleep. I worked in the afternoon. I wait for you as though you were going to come back anytime from the studio. Please, my adored one, come back, please.

February 18th. I can't believe that only three days have passed since he went away. It seems an eternity to me, or a lost life. I am breathing, but that's all. I realize I am only thinking about myself. Maybe that is what one does when one really loves. I always thought that real love is not to think about oneself but that can't be true. I love him with every drop of my blood and I think only about one thing: being next to him—to listen to his voice—feel his lips—his arms around me—and I think that I want to give myself to him for life.[18]

A few days later she fell ill, with fever and tachycardia. She began to suspect that she was pregnant by Gabin—"but I can't have it if he is not free. And to have the child and say it is not from him, no, I don't want to think about that." She decided to go to La Quinta, a desert spa two hours' drive southeast of Los Angeles with luxurious bungalows that was popular with the Hollywood crowd for vacations or assignations. Her feelings about the possible pregnancy were thoroughly conflicted. "If I have his child," she confided to her diary on February 28, "I am going to ask him to decide what we are going to do. I don't want to hide myself the last five months. If he wants, I'll have the child as though we were married. I don't give a damn what people think. I wouldn't be able to kill that child. But if he wants to, I'll do it.… I hope that this time I am not pregnant because I am afraid he would stay with me for that reason and not because he loves me."[19]

On March 6 Gabin joined her at La Quinta and they made up. *The New York Times* caught up with her on March 9 and headlined "Marlene Dietrich Ill." The story had her "convalescing from an illness at the La Quinta Hotel," where she was expected to remain two more weeks.[20] Rumors flew that she had had an abortion. But a phone call she made to her faithful confidant Rudi Sieber appears to contradict that: "After all the joy, Jean really loving me, something terrible has happened. I'm not carrying his child after all. How is that? I didn't douche on purpose. Funny, no?"[21] Maybe that was the truth. But given her talent for fabulation, it's also perfectly possible that she and Gabin decided on an abortion, maybe because his divorce from Doriane had not been pronounced and he wasn't free any more than she was due to her marriage to Rudi.

Gabin's first American film had so many problems to start with, it's a wonder *Moontide* turned out as well as it did. Darryl Zanuck had expected him to start filming three months after his arrival in Hollywood. Gabin's English needed twice that much time to become barely acceptable. Then he didn't like the script as written by John O'Hara based on a novel by Willard Robertson. It was too wordy and stilted for his acting style. Mark Hellinger, the producer, asked screenwriter Nunnally Johnson to rework it, streamlining the dialogue and attempting to square the circle by keeping the dark, sinister tone while still giving it a happy ending.

In its final version Bobo (Gabin) is an itinerant longshoreman on the California coast who saves Anna (Lupino, who shared top billing with Gabin) from drowning herself in the

In Western mode with Dietrich at La Quinta, circa 1943. She might have been convalescing from an abortion (Deutsche Kinemathek-Marlene Dietrich Collection Berlin).

Pacific. He takes her back to the bait shack where he is temporarily living and they fall in love. His parasitical sidekick, Tiny (Thomas Mitchell), is afraid of losing his friendship, and the money Bobo gives him, to Anna. He tries to convince him they should get out of town because, he claims falsely, Bobo murdered a man during a drunken brawl before passing out and forgetting it. Bobo confronts Tiny on a seawall and the two fight, with Tiny falling to his death in the sea. Bobo and Anna have their wedding at the bait shack.

The shoot didn't begin until November 27. At Marlene's urging, Gabin had insisted that Fritz Lang, the Austrian-German who had done the Expressionist films *Metropolis* (1927) and *M* (1931), be the director, not knowing that he was one of Dietrich's old lovers. Lang didn't like the script, detested Zanuck, and found it constricting to do most of the shoot in the studio. Searching for a way to get out of doing the film, Lang took Gabin aside and provocatively told him he and Marlene had had an affair. Gabin blew up and made a scene with Dietrich, who feigned innocence: "With that ugly Jew? You must be joking, *mon amour.*"[22] Gabin's reaction, as Lang hoped, was strong enough for Zanuck to release Lang from his contract on December 12 to keep his French star happy. He turned the film over to Archie Mayo, who had recently directed *The Petrified Forest* (1936) with Bette Davis and Humphrey Bogart. Marlene cattily denigrated the film, later saying, "He was shooting an idiotic film, the title of which I've forgotten, but he spoke correct English—I personally saw to that!"[23]

She spent the first four days of the shoot on the set, less concerned with Gabin's English than with evaluating to what extent the female cast members might eventually

With Ida Lupino in *Moontide*, his first Hollywood film, 1942. Fox tried hard to Americanize Gabin, but he wasn't comfortable in English and he overacted to compensate (Collection du Musée Jean Gabin).

be rivals. She needn't have worried about the attractive young British star Lupino, who, although she got along well with Gabin, was recently happily married to the actor Louis Hayward. He even refused to kiss Lupino's hand during one scene, saying, "There'll be no hand kissing in my pictures. The Hollywood idea of a Frenchman making love exists only in Hollywood. The French detest the gigolo type of Romeo as much as do the Americans."[24] The movie was chaste even by the standards of the day, with only a few clinches, and Gabin's Bobo insisting heavily several times on no hanky-panky before they were duly married, to the visible disappointment of Anna.

But that didn't deter Fox from playing up their screen romance to the max. The publicity department had already tried to position him as "the greatest romantic star of Europe, who became world famous through his love scenes." Now it ballyhooed that they had added $100,000 to the movie's budget for 15 extra shooting days of additional romantic shots.[25] It targeted the female audience exclusively. "Different!" screamed one ad. "Jean Gabin is not only an altogether new type, girls! He's got a different technique of lovemaking. Don't ask! See it … in *Moontide*, his first American picture!" Another showed three girls with a reference book trying to learn how to say his name. Was it Gabbien? Gabbuni, Gabbean? "No wonder girls want to get that name right (pronounced Gab-BAN, now say it again), he's a man who'll thrill you!"

Moontide opened at New York's grand Rivoli theater on Broadway on April 29, 1942, to mixed reviews. *Photoplay*, with its tendency to shill for the studios, lauded it lavishly. "We think this is the equal of, if not better than, Monsieur Gabin's French pictures.... Gabin gives an unforgettable performance ... so good Charles Boyer's toupee is turning grey with envy.... The sensation of the month." It confidently predicted an Oscar for "the touselheaded Frenchman."[26] But if *The New York Herald Tribune* called it "[Gabin's] triumphant initiation into Hollywood film-making,"[27] others were less kind. *Variety* found Archi Mayo's direction sluggish and failing to generate suspense, while Gabin didn't convey enough warmth and personal feeling. Bosley Crowther of *The New York Times* liked what he called Gabin's "strapping masculine charm," but felt that this had been exploited by Fox to sell a mediocre film that didn't show him at his best. "Mr. Gabin is an old favorite of this department for his memorable French films," he wrote. "He is much better than *Moontide* and that still isn't giving him his due." But here he was being wholesaled to American audiences, for "seldom has an actor's frank allure been quite as deliberately and as obviously dished up in amplitude as is Mr. Gabin's strange enchantment in this ponderously moody film."[28] The way the lights and camera caressed his face, eyes, and thatch of hair—almost as if he were a glamorous female star—showed him off to cover up a poor screenplay, he concluded.

Even that was too generous to this aborted attempt to Americanize Jean Gabin. He had done his homework, helping revise the script, working on his English, even going slumming around the docks in San Diego to get a feel for the people and place. But for anyone who knew and loved his great films of the previous five years, it was an embarrassment. Fox tried to use his poetic realist films, particularly *Le Quai des Brumes*, as a template, complete with waterfront setting and swirling fog. It also had similar oddball characters like the homespun philosopher Nutsy (Claude Raines), Ida Lupino playing a waif much like Michèle Morgan's, and a seaside shack as refuge. But it didn't come off as anything but an obvious counterfeit. The story required a tragic ending, but Hollywood demanded a happy one. That was obviously impossible if they were to attain the integrity that Gabin's films typically possessed. They even domesticated Gabin's character, strangely dressed in a western-style shirt with a neck bandana, having him help Anna pick out material for curtains and pillowcases, and prettying up the shack where they live.

Obviously ill at ease in English—some of his lines are barely intelligible, despite a manful effort to pronounce words like "threshold" that do not come trippingly off the French tongue—he tried to compensate by doing the one thing he never did in a previous film: he overacted. Instead of the understated, natural acting synonymous with the Gabin style, he made whimsical faces, curiously thrusting out his lower lip to try to look fanciful while spouting words of wisdom on what Hollywood considered that clichéd French specialty, love. The grotesque result is Gabin doing an American imitation of Gabin. Later he preferred to forget the film, explaining that honoring his contract with Fox was the price he paid to get out of occupied France, and he needed the money to eat while in exile.

Gabin went to New York for the premiere. Also in the audience at the Rivoli, at his side, in fact, was Ginger Rogers. They went out together several nights, and Gabin seemed to want to make sure they were seen and reported on. As Rogers put it in her memoirs, "His longtime girlfriend, Marlene Dietrich, was hot with fury when she found out."[29] That is precisely what he wanted. He had been jealous of Marlene and her legion of lovers long enough, now it was his turn. Hollywood fanmags were glad to help promote the idea that he was hesitating between the two of them. In "The Love Dilemma of Jean Gabin," *Photoplay* explained that "he had to choose between Marlene Dietrich and Ginger Rogers. That wasn't so easy, even for a man like Jean Gabin, [with] more sex appeal than any other male in the profession. He fairly vibrated with sheer animal magnetism."[30]

This little episode was brief, just enough to get the message across to Dietrich that two could play that game. (Rogers seemed to like French men but never understood them. She later married Jacques Bergerac, a French actor who soon tired of her approach to healthy living, which besides ice cream sodas required spending nights on the terrace in sleeping bags; they divorced after three years.)

When Gabin got back to Hollywood, he and Dietrich had another scene-cum-reconciliation. Shortly thereafter, he gave an interview to a movie magazine describing his favorite feminine type: intelligent, worldly, with the mind of a man and the heart and body of a woman.[31] Only one woman in Hollywood fit that description. Marlene had won again.

15

Free French

She might have won the competition for his affections, but Marlene couldn't make Jean Gabin happy in Hollywood. That summer a Los Angeles reporter noticed his melancholy. "When you talk with him you can't fail to notice the emotional tension—the dilemma—he is in," he wrote. "He isn't really gay about his romance with Marlene—he wasn't gay during his brief romance with Ginger…. Gabin is like a man who doesn't know which way to turn; there is the pain of perplexity in his eyes. He sings, whistles, yells lustily, but somehow there's always a note of pain in his voice."[1]

How could Hollywood, for all its sun, palm trees, flashy cars and private pools, not be a painful existence for Jean Gabin? He who dreamed of a farm in Normandy, who had never liked or understood anything that was not French, was cut off from his beloved country, now conquered and occupied. He had lost contact with most of his friends and family. He worried that some might have been killed or sent to concentration camps. He felt guilty about living comfortably in California while they were suffering. On top of that, he was caught in a double bind, harassed on one side for not supporting the Vichy regime, accused on the other of being a pro–Vichy collaborationist. His situation was untenable. Two events brought that home to him.

The Vichy government was on his case. It had granted him a visa to leave the country on the condition that he serve as a useful propagandist in America. Since his departure it had seen no films starring Jean Gabin that glorified Marshall Pétain's collaboration with the Nazis. Moreover, the visa's eight-month validity was now past deadline. Pétain wanted France's favorite movie star back as a token validation of his regime's legitimacy. The French consul in Los Angeles, Georges Achard, wrote him on December 27, 1941, to say he should return to France as soon as possible. If he didn't, he implied, Gabin would be considered a defector. "As you know," he wrote, "our country needs to unite its material and spiritual forces to overcome the misfortune that has befallen it. The authorities, the people themselves, believe that you hold an important place in this rallying of national unity, and your prolonged absence would be seen as a defection in these painful hours."[2] The tone was cordial, but the threat of being considered a defector, not to say a traitor, was there.

It was no coincidence that the consul wrote less than three weeks after the Japanese attack on Pearl Harbor. Now that the U.S. had entered the war, Vichy feared that well-known French actors who had fled to Hollywood might side openly with the Allies against it. Achard had also notified Michèle Morgan, René Clair, Julien Duvivier, and Jean Renoir that it was their duty to return to the motherland. Vichy insisted that Gabin and his exiled cohorts come back and make censor-approved pictures for the German-controlled Continental Films.

Jean Renoir was the only one in the group who replied in writing, and that was a sly dig at the lack of freedom for moviemakers under the Nazis. "For personal reasons I would be very happy to make a film in France," he said. "I am ready to look at any proposal made by a truly French production company."[3] He knew, of course, that this was an impossible condition to satisfy in occupied France. In the absence of a reply from Jean, the consul wrote again on January 5, 1942. This time the tone was curt, reminding him in no uncertain terms that the French embassy in Washington demanded an answer urgently. Gabin, eschewing a written reply, phoned him to say simply that he preferred to remain in the U.S.[4]

Left diplomatically unstated was Gabin's determination that when he did return, it would be as a member of the Free French Forces to rid France of its occupiers and those who had collaborated and made deals with them—including Achard himself. That, however, was not obvious to those who had intercepted Achard's letters. Thanks to his entanglement with Marlene, the Federal Bureau of Investigation had him under surveillance, suspecting him of being not only pro–Vichy, but possibly a conduit for collaboration with the enemy. Why, the Bureau wondered, were French authorities recalling him after only a few months in the U.S.? Was it time for him to deliver information he had been able to glean as a spy? Thus began the second event that convinced Jean Gabin he had no future in America.

The curious case of the FBI's investigation of Marlene Dietrich and Jean Gabin began in earnest with a call to the Bureau's Washington headquarters in May 1942. The middle-aged lady caller said she had information indicating that Marlene Dietrich was involved in a "collaboration movement in the United States and France." It was suspicious, the lady said, that she was German, married to a German, and with certain activities in France. She was probably an active agent in the U.S. working for the Vichy government. She was sure that Dietrich's goal was to get French stars like Jean Gabin to return to France and make films for Continental as a way of promoting Franco-German relations. Miss Dietrich, she said, had even gone so far as to invite State Department officials to tea in Washington to further her aims. "She had absolutely no business delving into this," she said indignantly. "It shows how Miss Dietrich's personality influences well-intentioned men." As for Gabin, she believed he was no more than an easily manipulated puppet in Marlene's hands.[5]

The woman who concocted this tissue of errors, half-truths, and falsehoods—Dietrich had been an American citizen since 1939, had refused to work in Nazi Germany, her films were banned there, she publicly called Hitler an idiot, and Germany had branded her a traitor—was Mrs. Mabel Walker Willebrandt, a 53-year-old former assistant attorney general during the Harding and Coolidge administrations of the 1920s. Originally from western Kansas, Mrs. Firebrand, as she was dubbed by the press, had been in charge of some of the Justice Department's biggest prosecutions during Prohibition, taking on tough bootlegging rings and arguing more than 40 cases before the Supreme Court. Now she had her own law firm with offices in Los Angeles and Washington, D.C. She often did work for MGM and the Screen Directors Guild.[6]

Darryl Zanuck had hired her to see what she could do to expedite Jean Gabin's request for an extension of his American visa, then bureaucratically bogged down in the

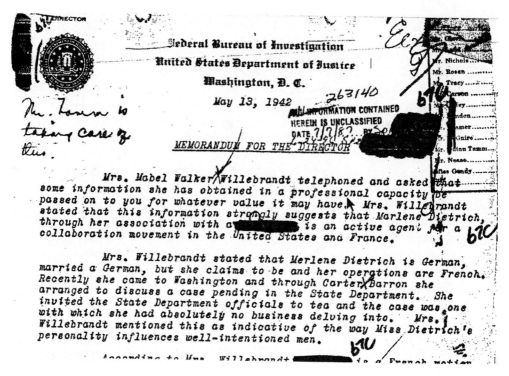

First paragraphs of the FBI memo for the director of May 13, 1942, relating Mabel Willebrandt's declarations that sparked the Bureau's surveillance of Gabin and Dietrich (FBI document, vault. fbi.gov).

Immigration Service. To her considerable displeasure, she found that Dietrich was trying to pull strings in Washington to help Gabin obtain the extension. Marlene was treading on her turf. Worse, Dietrich was upstaging her with impressionable officials at State by, of all things, inviting them to tea and, who knows, giving them a glance at the famous legs. Mabel wasn't one to be trifled with. Thus the barrage of innuendo she unleashed to the personal attention of FBI director John Edgar Hoover. The irony was that Willebrandt was supposedly acting on behalf of Gabin. He had no idea that, out of sheer pique, she was sending information to the FBI sowing suspicion of Dietrich and him.

It had been many years since she had been the Justice Department's scourge of scofflaws, but she still had clout in D.C. Hoover jumped to it. The Dietrich file, available online at the Bureau's website in its Freedom of Information/Privacy Acts Section (The Vault), shows that three days after receiving Willebrandt's allegations, he sent a two-page letter to the FBI's Los Angeles and Washington field offices outlining them and demanding swift action. Hoover wrote,

> It was the opinion of Mrs. Willebrandt that Miss Dietrich is directly connected with these collaborationists, that she is an active agent and that there is some means of direct communication between them. She mentioned that film people are either so uneducated or so vain that they are easy prey to such designs. It is desired that an immediate discreet investigation be undertaken by your office concerning Miss Dietrich in order to ascertain whether she may be engaged in activities inimical to the national defense of the United States. The Bureau should be kept promptly advised of all developments in this connection. It is desired that the Washington field office make arrangements to interview Mrs. Willebrandt further for any additional information she may have concerning this matter.[7]

When the Los Angeles Special Agent in Charge, R.B. Hood, didn't react fast enough, Washington sent a follow-up rocket saying the director wanted this handled "most expeditiously," with daily teletype reports on the progress of the investigation.

Hood and his agents got going with active surveillance of Marie Magdalene von Losch, as Dietrich's file was officially labeled, based on her original name. They intercepted her mail and cable traffic and listened to her phone calls from May 28 to June 13 at her home address of 828 Birchwood Drive in Beverly Hills. (The office continued doggedly to report on her activities to Washington for months after that, even as the Treasury Department was awarding her a special citation for her patriotic bond selling tours across America.) They interviewed Willebrandt, persons she suggested, and virtually everyone who had an opinion of Marlene—many of whom were glad of the chance to spread a little venomous slander. Mabel started bobbing and weaving with her allegations, sometimes suggesting that because of what she termed Dietrich's "terrific love affair with Gabin" she could be a conduit for collaboration. Gabin was living with her, and she was convinced that Dietrich controlled all of his activities and opinions. Because of her, she said, he had broken with former friends who had tried to steer him away from her. On the other hand, she fudged her accusations by saying that she had "absolutely no information as a basis for any possible espionage activities on the part of Miss Dietrich."

They talked with the jealous Erich Maria Remarque, who took the opportunity to pretend he simply couldn't understand why she would want to have an affair with Gabin, casting suspicion on their motives. They shuffled through the anonymous letters that came in. One informant said he personally had heard Dietrich sing the Nazi Horst Wessel Song at a dinner party, another claimed he knew for a fact that she had "toasted with champagne the bombing of England." One from Chicago had noticed her swing through the Middle West promoting war bonds and visiting military installations, where she learned about the latest Army equipment; might she not be a new Mata Hari under the guise of selling bonds? Another source described as a radio and movie actor called agents to say Dietrich was so pro–German she wouldn't even let her daughter ride horseback on an English saddle. Mark Hellinger, her producer for *Manpower* and Gabin's for *Moontide*, was no great friend of theirs when talking to the Feds. He told agents that deep down she was still pro–German, but not really subversive, "too stupid to be a spy." He intimated that while Gabin was seeing Ginger Rogers, Dietrich was plotting various unspecified actions against Rogers, which showed that she was, as he put it quaintly, "effeminately cruel."[8]

The FBI wheels ground exceeding fine. They knew she drove a 1940 Buick coupe convertible registered in name of R. Sieber; that she had a safe deposit box at Central Hanover Safe Deposit Co. number A104 (annual rent $14.40); that she bought flowers at Holchester's, 6327 Yucca St., and sent flowers twice to Sieber and once to von Sternberg; that she owed accountants Schwartz and Froehlich in New York $250; that she was being dunned by the IRS for back taxes; that her maid from Germany had been with her 16 years; that her husband Sieber lived in a New York hotel with a Russian woman who had previously lived in Moscow, Berlin, Constantinople, and Paris, and he had done so for the last ten years. When she took the train to go back East, they knew what compartment in what car she was in on the *Chief*. They monitored her sex life, reporting overlapping affairs with Gabin, Remarque, and Wayne. A memo to Washington in July quoted an informant who stated that everybody around Hollywood knew "Dietrich has never been able to 'hold a man.' She gets them and loses them, 'affairs' ranging from one day to approximately six months." According to this informant, she also reportedly "had veered from the norm and had had affairs with well-known women in Hollywood, one of these being [the actress] Kay Francis. Another was [name redacted]'s wife to whom Dietrich reportedly gave a large sapphire ring."

Gabin himself was the subject of a separate, less intensive FBI investigation of whether he was pro–Vichy. One sign of this, they thought, might be that he refused to join other French members of the Hollywood community in a group organized by Charles Boyer, the so-called French War Relief Committee, to demonstrate ostentatious public support for de Gaulle's Free France. In fact, he had shunned them because he didn't like Boyer and, anyway, ostentation was contrary to his nature. As the investigation went on, Gabin came to realize that one source of slanderous rumors was none other than Boyer, who had long been envious of his greater screen success. According to FBI documents, Gabin resolved to put a stop to that in his usual way: one day he went to Boyer's home, grabbed him by the throat, and threatened to strangle him if he didn't stop.

The rumors dried up, but Gabin's relation with Dietrich was itself a reason for suspicion by the agents, possibly making him guilty by association. And the unfortunate fact that his exit visa was approved by the Vichy authorities and the profession mentioned in his passport was "propagandist" took some explaining. (The Hollywood slurs based on such details were often enough to smear him in New York. Louis Sobol, the longtime Broadway columnist for Hearst newspapers, said *Moontide* was good, but he refused to review it because the word around town was that Gabin was a collaborator.)[9] However, even Mabel Willebrandt proved to be indulgent, if disparaging, toward the man who had fallen for Marlene's wiles. He was, she said in her final analysis, "the simple, ordinary, peasant-type of Frenchman who not only does not know enough to be engaged in any subversive activities, but would not do so." Her target wasn't Gabin, after all, but Dietrich, whom she considered a threat to her business with Zanuck.

The FBI wasn't taken in by her allegations for long. Still, the Los Angeles office had to humor Hoover with dutiful daily progress reports at a time when anti-subversive hysteria was sweeping the country—the forced evacuation from their homes of more than 100,000 Japanese-Americans, and their internment in detention centers, had just been ordered by President Roosevelt. In a case synopsis dated July 13, 1942, an agent at headquarters noted Willebrandt was simply unhappy because Dietrich was also in Washington working to straighten out Gabin's visa status. "These developments, it is apparent, incensed Mrs. Willebrandt and it is suggested that she made this complaint concerning Dietrich through spite." It concluded that nothing in the investigation indicated Dietrich was engaged in espionage. As for Gabin, the Bureau decided that there was no reason to believe he was guilty of any un–American activities or aiding Vichy.

The last bit of information the Feds received on Gabin came from Marlene herself on June 25, 1943. After interviewing her, Special Agent in Charge Hood reported to Washington that "Gabin, with whom she was closely associated for some time, and who you will recall was the subject of an investigation of some length by the Los Angeles office, is leaving on Monday, June 28, for New York City, where he will board a transport for England. There he will become associated with the Free French, and he expects soon to see action on the front.... Dietrich expressed pleasure at this turn of affairs, whereby Gabin would now be able to definitely show the people in Hollywood that he is not pro–Vichy."

Gabin later explained why he finally decided in mid–1943 that he had to return to France and join the battle for its liberation:

If I ever doubted in 1940 and 1941 that France would be liberated some day, after the Americans got into the war there was no longer any doubt. I was convinced that the Allies would win the war and Europe and France would be free. At least that was my hope, for all sorts of reasons, but mainly because of my desire to return to France. I was sick at the idea of what would become of me if the Germans won and I had to end my days in the United States. So it was clear that I couldn't just stay there and be well paid to make faces in front of a camera, while others were dying so I could go back home one day. I imagined that some of my friends in France must be fighting—I learned later that there weren't that many—and getting themselves killed, executed, or deported. I couldn't see myself returning without having done anything to help, just going back and saying, "Hi, pals, how are you doing?" I wouldn't have dared look them in the eye or shake their hand, and I wanted to be able to without being ashamed. It's for all those reasons that I left to fight in that bitch of a war, even if I was scared to death.[10]

As mentioned by Dietrich to the FBI, Gabin did indeed take the *Chief* back to New York in June 1943. But it would take much longer than she indicated for him to enlist, receive an assignment, and do all the necessary paperwork to satisfy the U.S. and French authorities. De Gaulle's *Forces Françaises Libres* had a recruitment and public relations office in Manhattan known officially as the *Mission Militaire Française aux Etats-Unis*. On this trip he saw its head, Captain Sacha de Manziarly, who welcomed Gabin's offer to volunteer. But his initial reaction was that he would be more useful if he would do a film promoting the Free French in the U.S. (Jean-Pierre Aumont, the only other prominent French film actor in Hollywood to fight with the Free French, had a similar experience; they enlisted him only after he did the propaganda film *The Cross of Lorraine* [1943] with Gene Kelly for MGM.)

As Jean's experience with the FBI showed, the American public suspected the French generally of collaboration with the enemy, and had only a vague idea of the fledgling Resistance movement. Hollywood had set out to capitalize on that. Resistance films became a profitable subgenre, with titles like *Paris Calling* (1941), *The Cross of Lorraine* (1943), *Passage to Marseille* (1944), and the most famous, *Casablanca* (1942). Universal had its own cycle of war films. It announced plans in June 1943 for one called *Passport to Dakar*, with a $1 million budget, Julien Duvivier as producer and director, and starring Gabin. That morphed into Gabin's second and last Hollywood effort, *The Impostor/L'Imposteur* (1944, French release 1946).

Shot from August to November, *Impostor* has a simplistic, by-the-numbers screenplay that only a propagandist could love. Gabin, the only actual French actor in it, plays Clément, who is in prison for killing a policeman. On the eve of his scheduled execution, the prison is bombed by the Luftwaffe and he escapes in the chaos. He joins a truck of soldiers heading south, which is also hit by German planes. Clément, the only survivor, takes the uniform and ID papers off a dead sergeant named Lafarge and boards a ship carrying a unit of Free French soldiers. They debark in West Africa, and Clément/Lafarge is decorated for bravery and promoted to lieutenant after a battle in Chad. An old friend of Lafarge shows up and reveals that Clément is impersonating him. Court-martialled and demoted, he is sent to the front line, where he dies a heroic death and is buried in an unmarked grave.

There seems to have been many a wink and a nudge between Duvivier and Gabin in the script. In many ways it resembles their earlier film together, *La Bandéra*. In both movies he plays a murderer on the run who becomes a soldier and finds redemption fighting and dying in Africa. Some of the screenplay's details are insider jokes for anyone who knew Gabin well: his best friend in *Impostor* is named Monge, echoing Gabin's real name, Moncorgé; in civilian life he owned a farm in Normandy; the ID papers he steals,

Gabin (left) checking the script with the American actor Allyn Joslyn on the set of *The Impostor*, 1944. A propaganda film promoting the Free French, it was the second and last picture Gabin did in America (Collection du Musée Jean Gabin).

glimpsed during the film, say he was married in a town called Mériel. Gabin got top billing, with his name in giant characters even before the title rolls. But he again had trouble with the English dialogue, often speaking nearly unintelligible lines through clenched teeth. Ads for the film screamed that in this one Gabin was "Killer! Lover! Liar! Man!"

By the time it opened in Washington, D.C., on January 27, 1944, Gabin had left to join the Free French. That added an extra punch to studio ads, which could call him a soldier on and off the screen, whose whereabouts now were a military secret. But most critics found the screenplay slow and verbose, with Gabin's talent largely wasted. As Bosley Crowther put it, "That moody French actor, Jean Gabin, in his second American-made film, is still waiting sadly for a picture to compare with some of those he formerly made in France. Even with Julien Duvivier, a fellow Frenchman, directing him, he is giving the piteous appearance of a man drifting vaguely out to sea."[11] The showbiz press was more indulgent. *Variety* thought it gave Gabin "a forceful opportunity for a top characterization,"[12] while *Hollywood Reporter* found it was "a stirring war melodrama so ideally suited to the rugged characterizations associated with Jean Gabin that it is impossible to imagine any other star in the title role."[13] Trade magazines brightly advised theater owners to boost attendance with captured German equipment in the lobby. Gabin knew its weak points; he refused to do the dubbing into French for fear of disappointing his fans at home.

Gabin spent much of the second half of 1943 trying to enlist with the Free French Forces. His first hurdle was to negotiate his contract with Darryl Zanuck, who legally could require him to do three more films for Fox. Seeing that his ballyhooed French star's box office appeal wasn't as great as he had hoped, suspecting that his Hollywood career was going nowhere for any number of reasons technical and personal, and sympathizing with his desire to liberate France, Zanuck let it be known that he wouldn't object to canceling the contract. The simple fact is that, from a purely commercial point of view, he had miscalculated Gabin's star potential for Fox. Hollywood typecast most foreign actors as aristocrats or peasants, gay blades (Chevalier) or Continental lovers (Boyer), and his strong screen persona, established in a peculiarly French context, was none of the above. As David O. Selznick said, "There are very few great movies, and therefore very few great parts. And even fewer great parts with an accent."[14]

Freed from his contractual obligations, Jean went back to New York in July. This time, knowing that Captain Manziarly was again going to ask him to do public relations in the U.S. for the Free French, making the rounds of fashionable parties wearing a handsome uniform bearing the Gaullist Cross of Lorraine, he did an end run on him. Instead, he went to see the New York office of the Free French Naval Services, the navy having been his original service branch when he was called up in 1924 and again in 1939. Not only were they glad to enlist him for the duration of the war with serial number 22550FNFL43.[15] They promoted him to the rank of Fusilier *second-maître*, roughly equivalent to a Marine buck sergeant. The promotion to noncom from his previous rank of private was attributable more to his prematurely gray hair and growing paunch than to any new leadership qualities developed in Hollywood. "Besides," he remarked tongue in cheek, "I looked better in a noncom's cap than in an enlisted man's French navy beret with a red pompom."[16]

Next he had to convince de Gaulle's representatives that, movie star or not, he really did want combat. By November, he could argue that, with *The Imposter*, he had now done the propaganda film they wanted. But the French Naval Mission office in Washington, which had responsibility for his file, was skeptical that the 39-year-old actor recruited in New York could handle combat. It contacted him on November 26 with three options, two of which were wacky by any standard. He could, they suggested, enter France as a war correspondent covering the Resistance, but since their quota for French journalists was full, he would have to go as a newsman for a foreign publication. It took a fine French military mind to propose that to Gabin, with his low opinion of the press, and anyway he was supposedly already enlisted as a navy Fusilier. Or maybe he could find a civilian job with the cinema section of the Free French Information Services. Again, he had to make clear that he wasn't looking for a civilian position. Finally, they conceded, if he really wanted to see action, he could serve with a unit in North Africa.[17] It's to Gabin's considerable credit that, repeatedly offered options that would let him pretend he had done something for the war effort while saving his skin in a cushy civilian job, he stubbornly insisted on a combat role.

He finally got it. He was assigned to command an anti-aircraft unit on the Free French Naval Forces ship *Elorn*, an Algiers-based, lightly-armed replenishment oiler whose mission was refueling ships on the high seas. Named for a river in Brittany, the 11,000-ton ship could carry 8,600 tons of fuel oil and was scheduled to sail back to Algiers from Norfolk, Virginia, in January. Refueling ships wasn't his idea of combat, but he accepted it.

Until then, Gabin had to kill time in New York. He filled some of his leisure hours writing a stream of love letters to Dietrich back in Hollywood. The yearning ache he felt is palpable. "*Ma grande*, my love, my life!" went one. "You're here before me, I look at you.... I'm alone, like a kid lost in the crowd. Is it possible to love this much? Do you think that one day we will be together again and will live together, the two of us, only the two of us? Would you wait for me.... Will God want me to find you again, you, the greatest of all?... You are in my veins, and my blood, I hear you inside of me.... For the first time, I tell you: I need you for all my life or I'm lost."[18]

It didn't take many of these to convince Marlene to join him in Manhattan at the Hotel Pierre, where they usually stayed on their past trips. They made the rounds of their habitual watering holes, from La Vie Parisienne to El Morocco, where they were seen dining and dancing, she in a clinging black dress and feathery hat, he in his naval non-com's uniform. In more serious moments he told her he was giving her some of the things he had brought with him from France, including the accordion and racing bike, as well as the Sisley, Vlaminck and Renoir paintings. "I didn't want to keep anything," he recalled after the war. "I left with the feeling that I was going to die in that war, but I had to do it to be reconciled with myself. I was scared to death of it, and they say that in battle it's the ones who are afraid who die first. I was no hero, but I felt that if I had had to stay in America for the rest of my life, I would have died of boredom anyway."[19]

16

Oldest Tank Commander

Dietrich accompanied him to Norfolk, obviously relishing the drama of her role as the woman seeing her man off to war. The evening before he sailed, they had dinner in a restaurant in nearby Hampton. Afterwards they took in a particularly appropriate war movie, *Action in the North Atlantic*, with Humphrey Bogart as a stoic, unflappable merchant marine officer on a tanker in a convoy dodging German submarines. On January 14, 1944, their car pulled up to the dock just before the 2 a.m. deadline for crew to be aboard the *Elorn*. Other crew members watched, goggle-eyed, as the two movie stars said goodbye. "We swore an eternal friendship to each other like little children, and I remained alone on the wharf, a poor, forsaken little girl," was how Marlene described the leave-taking in her inimitable, self-dramatizing prose.[1] The ship sailed at 10 a.m. the next morning. Jean Gabin would never again set foot in America.

All during his period of active duty, Gabin insisted that he was only Jean Moncorgé, just another naval person. It was hard to escape the aura of celebrity, but at least his captain agreed on his identity. One day while he was on watch as an anti-aircraft gunner, the captain came up to him.

"It seems that you're a movie actor in civilian life?"

"Yes sir," replied Gabin.

"I never go to the movies, I don't like them at all," the captain continued. "My sister, who's very pious, thinks movies are unhealthy, not at all moral. People always kissing each other on the mouth—it's disgusting."

"I guess it's a question of personal taste, sir."

Later on during the nearly three-week voyage, another officer came up to the captain and asked if it was really Jean Gabin who was on board. The captain said he didn't know anybody by that name.

"The actor!"

"Oh, Moncorgé. I don't know how he is as an actor, but as a seaman he's damned good."[2]

Gabin had his first taste of war two weeks after leaving Norfolk. On January 28, German subs began harassing the convoy south of the Azores. Although the *Elorn* was an oiler, it was equipped with enough armament to serve also as an escort for Liberty ships carrying American materiel to Allied units in Europe and North Africa. Coordinating with other escorts, it dropped depth charges to keep the subs at bay.

Then, after passing through the Straits of Gibraltar, Gabin had the chance to prove his mettle as a gunner. Stuka dive bombers, their eerie sirens wailing, attacked the convoy near the Algerian port of Cherchell. As he directed his anti-aircraft crew to fire at the strafing planes, he remembered the Humphrey Bogart film he had seen with Dietrich. "I kept thinking how calm he was in that movie, and here I was shaking so hard with fear that my helmet nearly fell off my head," he recalled. "I tried hard to hide my fear from my men. What a jerk that Bogart was. I'd like him to be here right now in my spot and see how calm he would be under real fire. I often wondered whether it wasn't thinking so hard about Bogart that saved me from cracking. I should have sent him a thank-you note."[3]

The *Elorn* docked in Algiers on February 2. Gabin debarked into a city much changed since the days of *Pépé le Moko*. Now it was teeming with Free French officials planning the liberation of France, and American military preparing the Allied offensive in Sicily and mainland Italy scheduled for that summer. He was supposed to return to Norfolk with the ship six days later, but was determined to find a way to fight in France. One day he accidentally ran into a lieutenant commander with the American navy named John Lodge. Gabin knew him slightly from Hollywood. Lodge had been an actor there before the war, notably playing the male lead opposite Marlene Dietrich in *The Scarlet Empress* (1934), as well as acting in several major British and French films. Fluent in French, the younger brother of Senator Henry Cabot Lodge, Jr., was now serving as liaison in Algiers between the American and French fleets.

He invited Jean to join him at a dinner for senior Allied military and Free French officials. Among them was Louis Jacquinot, a prominent prewar French politician who was now a member of de Gaulle's National Liberation Committee based in Algiers. As luck would have it, he was also head of Free French naval affairs, thus Gabin's civilian chief. During their conversation, Jacquinot proposed that, instead of volunteering for combat at his age, he make films with the new Free French propaganda unit being created in Algiers. Once again, Jean had to repeat that his aim was to fight; if he had wanted to continue acting, he would have stayed in Hollywood. Jacquinot was disappointed, but he was willing to get Gabin off the *Elorn*. A few days later he was assigned to be a drill sergeant at the Fusiliers' boot camp, called Sirocco, a few miles around the Bay of Algiers.

It had been three months since Dietrich had said goodbye to Jean in Norfolk, and she was pining. "My lonely 'child' lost all contact with me," she wrote in her memoirs. "I was terribly worried. Where was he? I knew he needed me, and I could sense this longing from the other side of the ocean."[4] Again she was writing for maximum dramatic effect. She knew where he was, and given the impassioned tone of his letters, there was no need to "sense" his longing. She was going to find a way to see him, if only briefly. She had been doing USO shows for troops as part of the Hollywood Canteen. With her Washington contacts, it was a simple matter to get a foreign assignment.

On April 4 she took off from LaGuardia Airport in an Army Air Forces C-54 with a USO troupe in her tailor-made uniform from Saks Fifth Avenue. By April 11 she was in Algiers and ready to do her first show with the comic Danny Thomas—and with Jean Gabin in the audience. She sang her trademark *See What the Boys in the Back Room Will Have*, hiked up what she called her nude dress to play the musical saw between The Legs, and looked, as Thomas recalled, like "every woman in the world they were hungry for rolled into one."[5]

But during this episode only Gabin would have her. For the next several weeks he would leave Camp Sirocco in the evening in his dress uniform for their rendezvous after the USO show. Often they would dine with generals and admirals, which made Sergeant Gabin, with his scrupulous respect for military hierarchy, ill at ease. One night the British

The navy Fusiliers drill sergeant in Algiers, 1944. Gabin had to pull strings to avoid making propaganda films and remain in a combat unit (Collection du Musée Jean Gabin).

press magnate Lord Beaverbrook was in Algiers on business and invited Dietrich and Gabin after the show to his suite at the grand Aletti Hotel on the port. As they stood on the balcony they could see flashes of tracer fire over the Mediterranean as RAF Coastal Air Force Beaufighters downed 3 Luftwaffe Junkers 88s and a Dornier 217.[6] The couple made no attempt to keep their liaison quiet; many in Algiers, including Gabin's recruits at Camp Sirocco, thought she was his wife. Their wartime idyll came to an end in May, when Marlene left for Naples with her USO troupe to entertain Allied soldiers in the Italian campaign.

But she had had ample time in Algiers to advise Jean on his financial affairs, to her own considerable benefit. After her departure, he sent letters to the Bignou Gallery in the Rolls Royce Building on East 57th Street in New York, and his Los Angeles business manager Bö Roos. He informed the former that he had made presents to Madame Marlene Dietrich of four of his paintings being held at the gallery: *La Femme au Chien* by Renoir, *Les Saules* by Corot, *Les Plaideurs* by Daumier, and *La Cathédrale de Saint Denis* by Utrillo. All, of course, were extremely valuable. In his letter to Roos he confirmed that he had made that request, specifying that he was acting on her advice. He further requested that Roos cancel an IOU signed by Dietrich in the amount of $10,000, and that he make available to her all funds then in his account with the Beverly Hills branch of Bank of America.[7]

Developments like that raise the question of to what extent Marlene manipulated Gabin. The two were opposites in ways that made him uniquely vulnerable to her. He was sincere and guileless, she cunning and unsentimental, instinctively doing whatever necessary to survive, if possible to dominate. Although she had moments of spontaneous generosity, her daughter Maria Riva accused her of habitually using those around her, from her husband Rudolf Sieber to innumerable lovers and casual members of both sexes in her endlessly evolving entourage. She exploited them all for her emotional and financial needs. She may have been as attached to Gabin as it was possible for her, but he was also an impressive, reassuring testimony to her continuing appeal and erotic power. If he agreed with her advice to give her money and valuable presents, who was she to refuse? As she once wrote to Maria after still another gift from Gabin, "at first I did not want to accept them and then I sometimes think that I am very stupid always feeling like that. Jean has so much property [in France]—is really a rich man."[8]

That April, Gabin's military career took another turn. Preparing Free French Forces for the Allied invasion of France, Charles de Gaulle decided to create a navy Fusilier tank regiment and attach it to General Philippe Leclerc's 2nd Armored Division. The new unit, dubbed the *Régiment Blindé de Fusiliers Marins* (RBFM), or Navy Fusiliers Armored Regiment, was an afterthought hastily put together with some 5,000 troops. It was equipped with American M-10 tank destroyers (TD) with three-inch direct-fire guns designed to engage massed German Panzer main battle tanks in firefights.

As soon as he heard of the new combat unit, which was in training in Morocco, Jean volunteered for it. When his request through channels to staff headquarters got bogged down, he made an urgent demand directly to naval affairs minister Louis Jacquinot. While Jacquinot was dragging his feet about authorizing Gabin's new assignment—maybe still hoping he would have second thoughts and join the propaganda unit—the RBFM was heading to the Algerian port of Mers-el-Kébir to board a transport for England, where they were scheduled to hook up with the Allies. They sailed on April 29, just as Jacquinot's message assigning Gabin to the unit finally reached its commander, too late for Jean to join it. RBFM tank crews would be without him when they hit the Norman beaches at Sainte-Mère-Église on August 3, 1944.

Jean was frustrated and disappointed that bureaucratic snafus kept him from making the departure for the Allied march through Normandy. But even if he wasn't yet returning to France in person, the possibility of the French public seeing their favorite star at this critical time upset the Vichy authorities. Taking no chances that his image on the screen could cause an unwelcome rise in patriotic morale, they suddenly prohibited his films. *The New York Times* headlined on May 8: "Jean Gabin's Films Barred in France." As the story reported, "Vichy France has placed a ban on all films featuring Jean Gabin, French cinema star who went to the United States in 1941. No reason was given, but presumably M. Gabin is considered an expatriate de Gaullist [sic]."[9]

It would be October before Jean set foot on French soil and joined the fight, fully 18 months after he had first enlisted with the Free French services in New York. Through no fault of his own, he therefore missed the Battle of Paris that he had had been longing for the last five years. As a gesture to de Gaulle, American forces delayed their entry into the city so Leclerc's 2nd Armored Division could liberate it from August 19 to 24. The battle climaxed with the surrender in Paris at his Hotel Meurice headquarters by General Dietrich von Choltitz, the commander of occupied Paris who had refused Hitler's order to destroy the city.

Then there was the victory parade down the Champs Elysées, and the ringing speech by de Gaulle in which he conveniently forgot to mention any part played by the Allies in the liberation. To this day, most Frenchmen born and bred can still recite this part by heart: "Paris outraged! Paris broken! Paris martyred! But Paris liberated! Liberated by itself, liberated by its people with the help of the French armies, with the support and the help of all France, of the France that fights, of the only France, of the real France, of the eternal France!"[10]

But if Paris and most of France were liberated, the war wasn't over. Much remained to be done to defeat the German army throughout Europe. Jean swallowed his disappointment and got on with soldiering. He trained with tank destroyers and qualified as crew chief, making him the oldest tank commander in the French army. He did this despite suffering from claustrophobia and a debilitating, obsessional fear of fire. Friends and family had always noticed how he nervously ground out cigarette butts repeatedly, avoided anything to do with electrical wiring, was wary of burning candles or fireplaces, and always double-and triple- checked heating and cooking appliances at home before going to bed.[11] He knew full well that, of all the branches of the army, the tank corps was the one where he had the highest risk of being roasted alive in a steel box.

Gabin finally sailed for France with the rest of his unit in October on the French cruiser *La Gloire*, which had to thread its way through mines to reach the port of Brest. From there he went to Maisons-Lafitte, near Paris, to join the 2nd Armored Division as a tank instructor while waiting for it to move out toward the Rhine for mopping-up operations. In November he wrote a letter to Marlene from an undisclosed location:

> My adored love, my life,
>   Not a second passes that I don't think of you, and I live in the hope of soon being near you. I too, my love, am tired, so tired, and my morale is so bad. I'm tired of being alone without you. Months, years pass and we're losing the best part of our lives. I don't mean to complain, my love, because there are those worse off than I, but you see, at my age the years pass swiftly. And that makes thirty years that we've lived in a state of war. How you must be cold, my life, because if I judge by the freezing climate here where we are, it's a terrible cold that penetrates to the bone. So I imagine that where you are it must be worse. Be careful, my angel, I love you more than ever. I miss you awfully.[12]

Shortly thereafter, he joined the 2nd Platoon, 2nd Tank Squadron of Leclerc's rapidly advancing division at Phalsbourg, in the Moselle region 25 miles northwest of Strasbourg.

They moved on to Hottviller, closer to the German border, to support American troops against the German counter-offensive in the Sarre Valley and northern Vosges mountains. He took command of a tank named *Souffleur II*. The first *Souffleur* (*Blaster*) had taken direct hits by two rounds from a Jagdpanzer tank destroyer and caught fire. Two of its crew, trapped in the turret, had burned to death. Gabin was aware of this, but instead of taking it as a bad omen—like many actors, he was superstitious—he chose to believe that the same fate couldn't happen to another tank with the same name.

His own name, he insisted all during his time in uniform, was not Gabin, but Moncorgé. As one of his crew members, Roger-Charles Legendre, recalled in a documentary, "My platoon leader told me, 'Your new tank commander is somebody you know, Moncorgé.

"I said, 'I don't know any Moncorgé.'

"'You'll recognize him,' he replied, 'it's Jean Gabin.'"[13]

As a commander, he was appreciated more for his simplicity and devotion to duty than for his movie star status. "We all knew Jean Gabin from *Pépé le Moko*, *Gueule d'Amour*, and *Le Quai des Brumes*," Raymond Thiébault, the driver on *Souffleur II*, told a television documentary. "But the man with us was Jean Moncorgé, a comrade, and we

The oldest tank commander, Sergeant Moncorgé (center), in the field with his crew (unidentified) in 1945 (Collection du Musée Jean Gabin).

Working on the *Souffleur II* during a maintenance stop. Gabin, who had an obsessive fear of fire, knew that crew members of the original *Souffleur* had burned to death when it was destroyed in a firefight with German tanks (Collection du Musée Jean Gabin).

were impressed by the fact that, being a property owner and having a certain status, as they say, he chose to be with us like that and take such risks. At 40, he risked it all, whereas it would have been easy for him to avoid the war. I doubt many men would have voluntarily sacrificed their whole career to go into combat."[14]

Besides the obvious danger and hardship of soldiering, Gabin endured the specific conditions of tank warfare, particularly days of standing exposed in the tank turret. Although he wore the standard safety goggles, his eyes were filled with the dust and diesel fumes from the vehicles ahead. For the rest of his life, he suffered from chronic conjunctivitis and avoided strong light, including paparazzi flashbulbs.

On March 9, 1945, he was given a few days' furlough and went to Paris, where he presented an evening of friendly boxing matches at the Velodrome d'Hiver for the benefit of the navy's charitable works. His first time back to the city in five years was a shock. There were shortages of everything from food and heating to clothing, gasoline, and taxis. He got a glimpse of how ugly vengeance and settling of scores among the civilian population were going to be during and after the Liberation. Spiteful *comités d'épuration* were set up to blame, accuse, and punish members of every professional sector, including the arts and cinema, against whom a case of collaboration with the German occupiers could be made.

Marcel Carné and Henri-Georges Clouzot were officially admonished for signing contracts with Continental—though Carné never actually made the movie—with Clouzot banned from filmmaking for two years. Another director, Jean Mamy, was executed for making what was alleged to be a propaganda film. Arletty was put on trial for taking a Luftwaffe officer as a lover and sentenced to two years' house arrest. Maurice Chevalier was jailed for collaboration and released only on condition that he perform at Communist Party fund-raisers. Danielle Darrieux, Viviane Romance, Edith Piaf and many others of the showbiz community were arrested, questioned, and finally released after public humiliation. They were the lucky ones. Many women throughout France who were accused, often falsely, of sleeping with German soldiers, were molested and paraded through the streets before having their heads shaved in the public square. Mireille Balin, Gabin's glamorous partner in *Pépé le Moko* and *Gueule d'Amour*, was caught with her lover, a young Wehrmacht officer, trying to escape to Italy. He was killed, she was beaten and raped by Resistance members before being imprisoned for several months and later dying in poverty.[15]

Disgusted by the venomous post–Liberation atmosphere that was developing in France, Gabin was actually glad to rejoin the war-tested camaraderie of his unit near Bourges, in central France, where it was awaiting orders for its next mission. They weren't long in coming.

With the Battle of the Bulge largely over, the Allies decided to attack the Atlantic Wall, the immense German system of coastal defense fortifications running thousands of miles along the coast of Europe from Scandinavia to the Franco-Spanish border. In France alone, nearly a million men had been conscripted to build it with reinforced concrete casemates housing artillery and anti-aircraft batteries; many of the nearly indestructible things are still in place on French beaches.

The French army was assigned to help take the Royan Pocket, a German enclave in and around the city of that name, and one of the German army's last strongholds in post–D–Day France. Hitler, wanting to deny use of its port to the Allies for resupply following the Normandy invasion, ordered it held to the last man. It was defended by 8,000 troops in 218 casemates and other concrete works, 180,000 anti-personnel and 35,000 anti-tank mines. The attack began January 5, 1945, with tons of incendiary and anti-personnel bombs being dropped by the RAF and the Army Air Forces to soften up defenses. With Royan 85 percent destroyed and nearly one-quarter of its civilian population killed, the main assault started April 14 involving some 30,000 Allied and French infantry, 1,200

8th Air Force bombers, and 25 ships of the French Naval Task Force bombarding the city from offshore. In one of the biggest battles of the Free French Forces, Gabin's tank regiment opened the way for the infantry attack with direct fire at casemates and blockhouses for two days and nights, while also fighting off prowling Panzers. The German garrison surrendered on April 18. Two days later, Adolf Hitler committed suicide in his bunker in Berlin.[16]

The end was nearing fast, but the Allies feared the Nazis would create a National Redoubt along the lines drawn up by Heinrich Himmler in case of defeat. The logical place was the Berghof, Hitler's vacation residence known as the Eagle's Nest in the Obersalzberg area of the Bavarian Alps near Berchtesgaden. Jean's unit was ordered to participate in mopping up operations in the area.

On the way, they stopped in Landsberg-am-Lech, west of Munich, where de Gaulle was inspecting the 2nd Armored Division. While Gabin was standing in the turret of the *Souffleur II*, he heard a familiar voice calling his name. Marlene had been entertaining troops in the area and, as she described it:

> I asked an officer to get me a Jeep, and I set out to search for Gabin. Finally I found his division. Evening descended on a great number of tanks standing in a field. I began to walk and look for gray hair under the caps of the "Fusiliers Marins." Suddenly I saw him from the rear. I called out his name; he turned around and said "*Merde!*" That was all. He jumped out of his tank and locked me in his arms. I had hardly regained my breath when a signal sounded for the tanks to line up in formation. He climbed into his vehicle again, and soon all you could see was a cloud of dust and all you could hear was the growling of motors.[17]

The Eagle's Nest was an anticlimax. With all German resistance having been cleared out, Jean parked his tank at the bottom of the mountain—it was too wide and heavy for the road up—and took a Jeep to the Fuhrer's former residence. He came back with kegs of Hitler's white wine that he shared with the crew. Three days later the war ended with Germany's unconditional surrender signed at Rheims.[18] Counting his two previous call-ups, Jean Gabin had served a total of 3 years, ten months, and 20 days of active duty with the French navy. He was awarded the *Médaille Militaire* and the *Croix de Guerre*, and officially cited for showing "the highest qualities of determination, courage, and military valor."[19]

When René Clément directed *Is Paris Burning* (1966) about the liberation of Paris, with an all-star cast from Jean-Paul Belmondo to Anthony Perkins and Orson Welles, he asked Gabin to take a part. He refused, saying he'd fought in a real war and had no intention of playing the soldier for the camera.[20] In a later television documentary on Gabin, his son Mathias remembered, "Papa spoke very little about the war. When he did, he would say, 'I was just Moncorgé. Gabin didn't exist any more.' His wartime service was sacred to him. That's why he never wanted to play military roles in movies after that."[21] For the rest of his life, he never missed a bibulous reunion with his tank crew. Their bonded, undemanding comradeship, the experiences they had been through together, were more important to him than any show business or motion picture people he worked with. He often said in later life that they were the only real friends he had ever known. His last wish, faithfully respected by his family, was to be symbolically joined with them.

17

Gray Years

July 14, 1945, marked the first time in six years that France could celebrate the fall of the Bastille. Towns and villages were again festooned with fluttering tricolors, band and accordion music filled public squares, there were fireworks and dancing till dawn from Paris to Perpignan. Charles de Gaulle, head of the Provisional Government of the French Republic—he would resign six months later in disgust over futile political squabbling—reviewed Free French and Allied troops at Paris' Place de la Bastille, where its 150-foot column was swathed in flags, the huge cobblestoned square decorated with an enormous V for victory and de Gaulle's Cross of Lorraine. From there, the parade of troops and motorized vehicles proceeded on to the Champs Elysées and up to the Arc de Triomphe.

Jean Gabin, demobilized a few days earlier, had left his Fusiliers unit and returned to Paris, where he took a room at the Hotel Claridge. Located halfway up the avenue, it was an old prewar haunt of his when he wanted a change from apartment living or had a new lady friend. Today he would not participate in the parade. He had signed up for the duration of the war, he explained when rejecting his commander's informal request that he remain on active duty long enough to command the *Souffleur II* one last time. He wanted out as soon as his papers came through. After 27 months fighting with the Free French Forces, he felt he had done his duty, his conscience was clear. But he stood at the window and watched the parade that morning with mixed feelings as the *Souffleur II* clattered into view. "From my room I had a front-row balcony seat for the parade," he recalled. "Standing in the turret was my second-in-command, Le Gonidec, or Gogo as I always called him. He looked happy to be there. It was ridiculous, but I couldn't help blubbering like a baby."[1]

War and exile were over for Gabin. He was back home in the beloved France that he had longed for from Hollywood and helped to liberate in combat. But re-entry would be harder than he imagined. He was beginning the greatest period of debilitating doubt, emotional instability, and professional frustration of his life. It was all the more painful for being in his own country among his own compatriots. It was what he came to think of as the entr'acte in his life and career. He called it his gray period.

His first taste of what postwar life would be like came with the reaction of Parisians to his appearance. Walking in the street or taking the Metro—taxis were still rare—he couldn't help overhearing the remarks of passers-by who noticed his gray hair and lined face. That hurt. Then, when he drove to Sainte Gemme Moronval to check out his house, he found a ruin. Since it was the finest property in the region, German troops had set up a campaign headquarters in it. When the war turned against them with the Normandy landings, they determined to take revenge on the French star who had refused to come back from America and make films for Continental. First they took all the photos of Gabin they could find in the house, nailed them to tree trunks, and used them for target practice. Then they ransacked the interior, destroyed all the furnishings, and vandalized the whole place before leaving.[2]

He could, and would, have a new house built there. But what hurt even more was that many of his fellow Frenchmen either deliberately ignored or were unaware of his Free French service. Admittedly his actions the last five years made him an easy target. For the envious, the vindictive, it didn't take much to create the impression was that he had abandoned his country after the invasion and spent the war years comfortably in American exile, while they suffered under the Nazi jackboot. And it didn't help that, as everyone knew, he had taken a German woman as his mistress. Many, like Jeanne Witta, who had done continuity on the set of *Le Jour se Lève*, said he was "just back from America" in 1945, choosing to overlook that his route back took him through Stuka attacks, months of instructing recruits in an Algiers boot camp, and piloting a tank destroyer against German Panzers. "Like so many others, Gabin took off for the U.S.A. when the Second World War started," she wrote venomously in her memoirs, "and then he came back with Marlene Dietrich."[3]

He was branded by those who wished to slander him as "one of those actors 'made in U.S.A.'" who were returning home now that it was safe. Even his old friend Arletty, so thoroughly compromised herself, lumped him together with those who had shirked their duty. "They were all part of the big farce," she sneered. "I saw them during the debacle of 1940. They were worried about only one thing, missing the last plane to New York. They didn't give a damn about France … spending four years in the Hollywood paradise." And she added a bitter afterthought, referring to how she was treated at the Liberation for sleeping with German officers: "Ah, Gabin, good old Gabinos. He was with Marlene Dietrich. We had the same kind of whores: he his Prussian woman, I my Prussian man."[4]

Professionally too, the road back was going to be strewn with obstacles. Inevitably, the war had changed Gabin, as it had affected James Cagney, Jimmy Stewart, and many other actors whose careers were disrupted by forced absence from the movie set. When he left France in 1941 at the age of 37, he was the undisputed number one star, far more popular even than top box office draws like Fernandel and Louis Jouvet. Now the public, critics, movie directors and he himself wondered whether he could make a comeback. "Gabin has returned from America transformed," went one fan magazine article, "with his hair prematurely grey, his face saddened and defeated like someone who is lost.... Will he be able to resume his life as an actor, find a role equal to his stature as a classical hero of antiquity lost in the quotidian tragedy of our time?"[5]

Articles like that showed that both reviewers and the public expected to see him on the screen again as he had been during his great period of the 1930s. It was an impossible, unrealistic expectation, if only because of his new appearance. "I couldn't play the same parts I did before the war, and that made me awkward," he explained to a television interviewer later. "I had to feel my way. The public was very demanding. They wanted to see me the way I was before, but I was older and you could see that in my face."[6]

Gabin was not alone in Paris. Marlene Dietrich had been there since June with her USO troupe and joined him at the Claridge when he arrived. But on July 13 she and the troupe were shipped back to the U.S. Jean asked her to take care of shipping his things from Hollywood to Paris, which she did, putting Rudi in charge of the details. But as her stay in the U.S. lengthened, he suspected that she was seeing some of her many male admirers, and said so in the stream of letters he wrote her. He urged her to come back to Paris and make a film with him that he was planning. Maybe they could get married. She replied she was ready to do both. But of course it was mere Dietrich-speak that she didn't expect him to take at face value. In his need, he did.

The uniformed Gabin and Dietrich in Paris, July 1945. She was still touring with the USO, his civilian clothes were in Hollywood (Deutsche Kinemathek-Marlene Dietrich Collection Berlin).

She tried to allay his jealousy with a letter in August, saying, "Angel, you are completely crazy, and you drive me insane with your doubts." She claimed that Rudi was ready to give her a divorce and she would come and live with him at the Claridge, but first she had to go to Berlin to see her mother: "I hope you understand this—after that, I am all yours. If you are sweet to me, I will stay with you for the rest of my life—married or not married however you want it. But, if you want a child, then it is better if we marry."[7] What she didn't say was that it wasn't only her mother she wanted to see in Berlin. Also waiting for her there was the dashing 38-year-old supreme commander of Berlin's American Zone, General James Gavin.

He had sent her a coy cable saying, "The 82nd [Airborne Division] is looking forward to seeing you soon."[8] Their affair went on through the autumn, he signing his letters "Your Jimmie." For a while, everyone seemed to know about it except Gabin. "He wants to marry me," she told Mitchell Leisen, who had directed her in *The Lady Is Willing*, "but I can't be an army wife. What would I say to the other army wives?"[9] She also told him she had moved in with Gavin for two weeks. Jean began to see the light, but only through a glass darkly. For the moment he was in denial, seeming not to know quite what to make of it, only that it hurt. "I know that you are in love," he wrote to her, "What you don't know is how much I suffer."[10]

Marlene was back in Paris by September, but the course of her true love with Jean was far from running smooth. They found an apartment on the elegant Avenue Bugeaud near Porte Dauphine that had belonged to Josephine Baker before the war. (Baker was horrified when she learned of it: "When I think that German cow is sleeping in my blue satin sheets," she bristled.)[11] Gabin's depressed state worsened, his anxiety over how he would make a comeback made him bad tempered, even violent, when they fought over trivia. In a letter to Rudi, Dietrich complained, "Takes me so long to get used to the ways of Jean. Why his nerves are in such a state I can't explain…. He came out of the war all in one piece and is not happy about anything…. I cannot pull him out of his depth…. We have had a fight every night."[12] Many mornings she had to use makeup to cover the bruises.

Still, he needed to do a film, and he wanted to do it with Dietrich. That gave rise to a fiasco that, among other collateral damage, led to a falling out with two cinema professionals he most liked and respected, Marcel Carné and Jacques Prévert.

Recalling the success of their two great classics of the 1930s, *Le Quai des Brumes* and *Le Jour se Lève*, the two of them very much wanted to do another picture with Gabin. In the spring of 1945 they saw a ballet by the modern choreographer Roland Petit called *Le Rendez-vous*, with haunting music by the Hungarian-born composer Joseph Kosma. With a story line about wartime racketeering, collaboration, betrayal, and a tragic love affair, they thought that as a movie it would be the perfect vehicle for Gabin. He agreed, as long as they had a role in it for Marlene. He and she signed contracts with Pathé and co-producer RKO in late June. The screenplay didn't exist yet, but Gabin was confident Carné and Prévert would produce a good one. He was right on that score, but he reckoned without the capriciousness of Dietrich, whose contract gave her script approval.

Prévert got to work on the screenplay of *Les Portes de la Nuit/Gates of the Night* (1946), the talented Alexandre Trauner did the sets, and Kosma wrote the music for a song expressly for Dietrich with lyrics by Prévert that would become a worldwide favorite called *Autumn Leaves*. But the project soon ran up against objections by the two stars, especially Dietrich, who carped about everything. She didn't like what she saw of the developing screenplay. It cast her as an unglamorous housewife married to a black market racketeer, while her father had been a collaborator during the war. She feared that her German accent wouldn't go over well with the postwar French. She needed more glamor. She wanted nothing to do with anything touching on sensitive wartime subjects like the black market and collaboration. She made dozens of suggestions for changes. One was sexing up her part by having her character pay a taxi driver after pulling up her dress to show The Legs and taking franc notes from the top of her stocking. She didn't even want to sing *Autumn Leaves*; she called it *merde*.

For his part, Gabin was uneasy about playing a former Resistance fighter after all the flack he had taken for his years in Hollywood. Deeply in thrall to Marlene, he drove Prévert crazy by looking over his shoulder as he wrote, constantly asking, "What will La Grande say?" "What will La Grande think?" Concerned about all the pre-production bickering, and worried that the screenplay's extramarital affair might offend American audiences, RKO withdrew its support. Things came to an unpleasant head in January, when Dietrich, exercising her right to script approval, withdrew. The role wasn't right for the new style she wanted to create for herself, she claimed. She also criticized the screenplay for giving a bad impression of France under the occupation—quite a reach coming from a German, even a Francophile German. Gabin yielded to her judgment, refused to do the film without her, and failed to show up on the first day of the shoot. Though he pretexted a scheduling conflict with another film he was planning, he had been paid in advance and was sued for breach of contract.

Carné, left holding the bag but relieved to have the querulous couple off his back, took Edith Piaf's advice and cast her protégé, a newcomer named Yves Montand, in Gabin's role; the relatively unknown Nathalie Nattier got Marlene's. They couldn't come close to the star power of Gabin and Dietrich. Despite Prévert's proficient screenplay, Trauner's excellent noir sets evoking a shabby postwar Paris, and a song like *Autumn Leaves* that everyone loved, the film flopped. Carné later regretted his choice of Montand, then a lightweight just beginning in motion pictures, compared with Gabin. Montand himself declared the error cost him 20 years of his career.[13]

It was a regrettable episode all around that left everyone—except the heedless Dietrich—unhappy, and that dug Gabin deeper into his slough of despond. Due to his emotional obsession with Dietrich and her pernicious influence on him, Gabin missed out working with two of his favorite moviemakers. Worse, he was prevented from doing what, with his presence, could have been a better picture and his successful re-entry into French films. "That was a big mistake," he said later. "I should have done that film, and Marlene too."[14]

In 1937 a novel called *Martin Roumagnac* by the French writer Pierre-René Wolf caught Gabin's eye, or probably Doriane's, and he bought the film rights to it. He had been trying to sell it to producers and directors ever since, but they rejected it as a banality about a small-town *crime passionnel*. He finally found a producer on the strength of his name and signed a contract for it in mid–1945, with the shoot to begin the following spring. He saw to it that Marlene would have a part.

But the wild oscillations of their relationship continued, with Gabin more and more unhappy about her increasingly obvious affair with "Abelard," as she code-named James Gavin in a romantic reference to the unhappy medieval love affair of Héloïse and the French theologian Abélard. In November he sent her a farewell note which might have been intended to make her choose between them. In any case, it showed how distraught he was. "Ma Grande, I have just left you,' it said. "I realize I have lost you forever.... I know that this letter is stupid and ridiculous in such a moment when you have such deep grief [Dietrich's mother had just died in Berlin]. Please forgive me. I am deeply sad too. I don't know what to do next. I hurt, I hurt so much. I feel alone. I don't know what's going to happen. Doesn't matter! Adieu. I will never come back."[15]

He did, of course, though Dietrich moved out of the Claridge and into a room at the Elysee Park Hotel a short walk away. They went ahead and started the film. In *Martin Roumagnac/The Room Upstairs* (1946) he played a graying, middle-aged building contractor in Clairval, a fictional small town in the French provinces. He meets Blanche Ferrand (Dietrich), a beautiful, widowed adventuress with tarty, frilly dresses and a past to match. The script has her from Australia—an unconvincing attempt to explain her German accent—who, just as improbably, runs a bird shop with her uncle. She has her eye on a rich local notable and hopes to get him when his sick wife dies. Meanwhile, she entertains the deputy mayor in a room above the shop. She becomes Roumagnac's mistress as a mere dalliance; he's only a small-town hick who doesn't even know how to dance or which fork to use in a fancy nightclub when they go to Paris for a weekend. Naively head-over-heels, he builds her a handsome villa, goes into debt for her, neglects his business. After a friend convinces him she's been playing him for a fool, he goes to the villa, strangles her in a Gabinesque fit of rage, and sets fire to the house. Arrested and accused of

With Dietrich in the nightclub scene, *Martin Roumagnac,* **1946. It was their only film together and one of his worst (Collection du Musée Jean Gabin).**

murder, he's acquitted by a sympathetic local jury, only to be shot dead by a young admirer who loved Blanche from afar.

The film attempted to continue the Gabin myth of the 1930s: he was again a naïve, untutored sort more sinned against than sinning, who kills his treacherous paramour in a fit of rage and is himself killed at the end. It was how producers, directors, and the public still wanted to see him, but at 42 years old he was too mature to be convincing as an innocent fatally entangled in the wiles of a woman and the ways of the world. Admittedly a potboiler, the film got a mixed reaction from reviewers. Most of them found Dietrich ludicrously miscast as a provincial strumpet with an extravagant wardrobe. She had spent weeks before the shoot shopping in Paris for dresses and hats to wear in the film, making her, as one critic mocked, "the envy of every lady bird-seller in France." Gabin coached her on how to speak like a provincial shopkeeper, slurring her words instead of speaking academic French. But Marlene's heart wasn't in it from the start, and afterward she called it "a disaster … maybe three people saw it and all hated it."[16] Gabin himself was rumored to have tried to get all copies of it destroyed years later, but that might have been to get rid of as many traces as possible of his affair with Dietrich.

Their tension off the set was visible in the heat with which they played their fight scenes. When they argued, it was with an extra dose of ferocity, and when he strangled her, he did so with such angry force that she was unconscious for several seconds. He was seething with hurt and jealousy that spring. Noël Coward said they argued all during a dinner he had with them in Paris, she insisting she had to have her independence like all great actresses, citing Sarah Bernhardt as an example. He retaliated, saying he was going to start an affair with an actress he'd recently met named Maria Mauban.

It didn't help matters that Walter Winchell reported in his column that Dietrich and "a very young general" would soon marry.[17] In May, she asked Jean what he wanted for his 42nd birthday, and he said he'd like to see the Sisley, Vlaminck and Renoir paintings he had left her. They were hers, of course, but he would be happy if he could see them on the walls of his room at the Claridge for a while. She cabled the U.S. and the paintings duly arrived and were hung to his satisfaction.

But days after his birthday their relation took a new downturn when she announced she had accepted an offer from Paramount to play a gypsy in *The Golden Earrings* for $100,000. "I need money," she told Gabin, "American money, real money!"[18] He countered with a final ultimatum: he asked her to stay, marry him and have his child, otherwise it was over between them. It's hard to believe he didn't realize that she would not, *could not* accept marriage with him. He may not have known that she was actually three years older than he and physically unlikely to have another child. But he could have observed, as many did, that she had never divorced Rudi because their façade of marriage protected her from proposals like his. (At a dinner party in 1963 she told Robert Kennedy, "I hate marriage. It's an immoral institution.")[19] She left for Hollywood in July, as soon as the last scenes of *Roumagnac* were shot, taking the three paintings back with her. Jean took her to Orly airport and carried her bags to the plane on the tarmac. She was jaunty in an elegant suit, flouncy hat, and two-tone summer heels, he trudging dejectedly beside her in a work shirt and jeans.

They continued to exchange letters for a while. In August, still aching, he wrote a loving farewell note, saying "You have been, you are, and will remain my one and only true love.… I just remain with an immense sorrow, a deep pain within me and infinite grief."[20] At summer's end she gave an interview to the French movie magazine *Cinévie* that was dismissive of him and whatever they had had together: "I don't know what the future holds, and I don't want to. To each his own life. Jean's destiny is France, mine is Hollywood. There are turning points in every road. I've always conceived my life primarily from a professional angle. And I must say that my profession has been more important geographically than emotionally."[21]

It amounted to a cold public goodbye from a woman who had given every sign of loving him for five years, and who only a few months earlier had professed herself willing to live with him any way he wanted. By November Gabin's attitude toward her had changed radically. He sent her a cauterizing note full of bitterness.

> So that was your Great Love. I have been a fool for years, Marlene, but no longer. You like your independence, you like to have sex when you want, and it's your right. I don't ever want to see you or meet you again. I don't even want to see you in the film we've done together and that marks the end of our story, and it's been quite a story. Whatever you might think, I have been absolutely straight with you, and until now, as I promised in one of my letters, I have not seen any other woman. You will understand that that stupidity on my part has lasted long enough, and now it's my turn. I'm not limiting myself any more, I'm going to *baiser* a beauty.[22]

They both attended the *Roumagnac* premier, she with Rudi as chaperone, and he ignored her.

The beauty was named Maria Mauban, a 22-year-old French starlet Gabin had met in a Paris nightclub while Dietrich was on one of her trips to the U.S. He saw her from time to time, and in July 1946 a mass-circulation Paris scandal sheet headlined that they were going to be married.[23] Later that year, he called Dietrich at the Paramount studio where she was making *Golden Earrings* and told her he was indeed going to wed Mauban. Of course nothing came of it. The young starlet was then making her first film and needed a bit of publicity, while Gabin was brandishing the Mauban threat the way he had Ginger Rogers back in Hollywood, to provoke Marlene.

But in his present distressed mood he needed, as he always had, a woman in his life. In that too he was the archetypal Frenchman. As amorous knights they had swooned before ladies of the medieval court, as kings they had appointed official mistresses, as presidents they often have been known as much for their midnight escapades as for their politics. Still today, French men yield more sway to women than any other males in the Western World. *Liberté, égalité, fraternité* might be the country's official motto, but the unofficial one is *cherchez la femme*.

Following Maria Mauban, the woman Gabin found at this chaotic time in his life was a 31-year-old singer and nightclub owner named Colette Mars. He was starting his next film, *Miroir* (1947), a mediocre gangster movie—"I prefer to forget that one," he said later—in which he played the owner of a shady gambling club who is killed in a final gangland shoot-out. During an evening's conversation with her at Mars' club, Gabin suggested she try acting. She agreed, and he helped her learn the trade on the set of *Miroir*, where she played, most appropriately, his mistress.

He wooed her with the usual armfuls of flowers and dancing the *java* in Montmartre hot spots, but she initially resisted, with some difficulty. "I was surprised to see that a man could still court a woman in 1947 the way Jean did," she remembered. "It was sweet, tender, full of delicacy and charm. How could I not have been seduced?"[24] How, indeed, and after she was, Gabin quickly got serious and proposed marriage. Again, he had picked the wrong woman to start a family with. Like Marlene, Mars wanted to keep her independence and her career, and wasn't interested in having children. She knew his possessive, jealous nature would have meant the end of that. After Michèle Morgan and Dietrich, Colette Mars was the third woman who rejected his proposal of marriage. He would have to *chercher* elsewhere.

The one thing he was sure of now was that it would not be Dietrich. After leaving Paris to do *Golden Earrings*, she had kept up a steady drumbeat of torrid letters and cables, trying to reel him back in. Most went unopened. When he bought an apartment in rue François Premier, near the Christian Dior flagship shop, she bought one nearby on Avenue Montaigne that she kept for the rest of her life. Charles Higham recounts in his biography of her that she often asked him to accompany her to a sidewalk café across from Gabin's building; there they would sit for hours, she hoping to get a glimpse of him coming or going.[25] One evening in 1949, she stalked him to a restaurant and got a table near his. He refused to look at her. When she got up after the meal and pushed past him, deliberately grazing the back of his chair, he cut her dead.

He bought a gravesite in Normandy, she took one next to it. When a reporter asked Gabin whether he was going to do another film with her after *Roumagnac*, he replied coldly, "The old woman is too unstable."[26] Marlene made at least one more attempt at a rapprochement with Jean. While she was doing a show at Paris' Olympia theater in April 1959, she wrote him a three-page letter in which she recalled their years together and asked him to come see her show for old times' sake. She gave it to Jean-Jacques Debout, a popular singer appearing in her show, who managed to get it to him during a lunch with mutual friends. As soon as he saw the familiar handwriting, Gabin balled up the three pages without reading them, threw them in an ashtray, and set fire to them.[27]

Did she really love him as much as she pretended? Or was he simply the one who got away? The war made many people do things they wouldn't have done if their lives hadn't been turned upside down, if it hadn't seemed there might really not be a tomorrow. Jean clutched at Marlene because, despite being German, she created a little corner of France in Hollywood. In normal circumstances, I doubt that Jean, the earthy man of the people, would have given the flighty, cosmopolitan Dietrich the time of day. She wasn't his kind of woman at all. Proof of that was that when they met in Paris in 1939 to discuss the script of *Dédée d'Anvers*, he paid no attention to her. The war brought them together. Their relationship couldn't stand the strains of peace.

Gabin, no longer the matinee idol, could feel his career slipping away. "Gabin is dead," declared one critic. In the absence of the political romanticism and dashed utopianism of the 1930s, he could no longer personify the doomed proletarian rebel. Due to that, as well as to his prolonged absence from the French screen, he had lost the status that allowed him to pick and choose among the best directors and screenwriters. Nor could he dictate terms to producers, who didn't know what to do with him. They now considered him a good but ordinary actor whose glorious past that was more of a burdensome handicap than an advantage. When Michèle Morgan tried to intervene on his behalf with a producer, saying nothing fundamental about Gabin had changed, the producer's reply was telling: "Yes it has. He's not as marketable as before."[28]

Not only he had changed. Postwar French society was fast evolving in ways that obliterated many things Jean Gabin had represented in earlier films. Slowly at first, then with dizzying acceleration over the next 30 years, the France that Gabin—basically a man of the 19th century—had known and loved began disappearing before his eyes. It was the start of the *Trente Glorieuses*, the three decades from 1950 to 1980 that saw France change faster and more profoundly than even the protean United States. It was not changing in ways that suited Jean Gabin.

The Catholic religion that constituted the wellspring of French culture during millennia, making France known as the eldest daughter of the Church, was losing its hold on the faithful. They opted with alacrity for the pleasures of consumerism, leaving the great cathedrals echoing to the steps of foreign tourists. The village café, the center of social life where workingmen often spent some 25 percent of their pay, began to disappear, and with it a vibrant form of social interaction. Local shops, from the butcher, baker, and cheese maker to cobblers and tobacconists, closed as huge regional hypermarkets with 40 or more checkout lanes drained their customers. Due to sudden industrialization, farming began its decline from some 30 percent of the population to around 5 percent, radically altering demographics, the economy, and politics.

The provinces started losing whole segments of their citizens as they flocked to the cities, where they were housed in the ugly, impersonal, often crime-infested warrens that sprang up around urban areas. The famously tight-knit, multigenerational French family slowly unraveled as women found life in an office more fun than founding and caring for a family. With that, the traditional home cooking, *la cuisine bonne femme*, that was the basis of France's justly famous food, was consigned to cookbooks that gathered dust on kitchen shelves. Pizza parlors and Chinese takeout joints soon outnumbered bistros; France, to the delight of many and dismay of some, would become McDonald's second-biggest market in the world.

On the horizon was the chaotic, uncontrolled immigration from former colonies that diluted the country's identity and created national self-doubt about what it meant to be French. Above all, in the 1950s was created the European Common Market, later European Union, bringing with it forced-march standardization and homogenization that would gradually erase national idiosyncrasies. The inevitable result was that Gabin's homeland, always so proudly different, was becoming like everywhere else, losing the specific, pungent personality he had rendered so well on the screen.

But one first-rate French director was still willing to give Gabin a shot at a poetic realist film. René Clément, who was just beginning a brilliant career in feature films and who had a hit with his first, *La Bataille du Rail/The Battle of the Rails* (1946), about French railway workers sabotaging German troop trains, signed him for a Franco-Italian production. *Au-delà des Grilles/The Walls of Malapaga* (1948) was shot on location in Genoa with a screenplay by Cesare Zavattini, a leader of Italian neorealism. It contains many of the noir elements of *La Bandéra, Pépé le Moko,* and *Gueule d'Amour*: a runaway who has killed his unfaithful mistress, has his pocket picked, falls on hard times, briefly finds love, and is ensnared in a police trap.

Pitching up in Genoa after stowing away on a tramp steamer, Pierre (Gabin) meets a kindly waitress named Marta (Isa Miranda) who is separated from her abusive husband. She shelters him and they have a brief idyll amid the shadowy back streets of a Genoa seemingly plunged into perpetual night. Eventually he is denounced to the police and arrested. The film, technically deft and with moments of fine acting, was good enough to win an Oscar for Best Foreign Language Picture. (Ironically, it was Marlene Dietrich who presented the Oscar.) At Cannes, Clément also got best director prize. Gabin, unshaven and unkempt for the part, here looks truly haggard, gaunt, tired, and middle-aged beyond what the role calls for. He has lost all youthful appeal, but is not yet patriarchal. Still, he turns in a convincing performance stamped with his natural gravitas. As a creditable transition film, it was a necessary step toward developing a new screen persona.

He would make ten more films before finding that filmic identity. Many were flops at the box office as he and directors struggled to define his place in French cinema, and the public adjusted to a different Gabin. Several of these won awards. But he couldn't help feeling out of place. The influential critics at *Cahiers du Cinéma* snubbed him as old hat, and new stars like Gérard Philipe, Jean Marais, Daniel Gélin, and many others were coming on strong. Audiences, too, wanted a new style of movie. The old pro could be forgiven for a certain bitterness at the new turn his profession had taken. "Motion pictures are ugly right now," he told a magazine. "There are too many beginners. Too many young people who do one film and think that's all it takes. The press is responsible for that. As soon as a director or an actor does a film you say they're terrific. So naturally it goes to their head."[29]

But some of the new stars knew they had much to learn from him. "I went to see Gabin's films over and over," said Daniel Gélin. "It was to see one expression from him, one look in his eyes. Jean was my real mentor. He explained to me that it was all in the eyes. I hung around the sets where he was acting to observe his scenes. He was a master of technique. He knew the characteristics of every camera lens being used, and noticed if the lighting wasn't quite right. When he played a scene, he knew exactly how it would look on the screen."

His technique was still as solid as ever. It would take time, work, and a new personal equilibrium rooted in a settled family life to make it fit the new age of motion pictures.

18

Dream Realized

Jean Gabin's gray period in his career wasn't over, but his life was about to get considerably brighter on the personal level. In late January 1949, dining with friends at the Colony Club near the Etoile, later to become the three-star restaurant Taillevent, he zeroed in on a tall, blue-eyed blonde on the arm of a prominent businessman he happened to know named Fred Sanet. The next day he called Sanet and said that if it wouldn't be treading on his romantic turf, he would like to meet the lady he had escorted that evening. Sanet replied they were just friends and he would be glad to give Gabin her phone number. Shy as always when approaching women, Jean asked his friend to set up a date with her for him at the Colony Club.

Thus he got to know Christiane Fournier, known professionally as Dominique, a 30-year-old mannequin. Originally from Vichy, she had had a son named Jacky from a brief liaison when she was 22. Going to Paris, she was working as a hairdresser in an upscale beauty parlor when the fashion designer Nina Ricci, a regular client, noticed her willowy elegance and got her a modeling job at Hermès in rue du Faubourg Saint Honoré. From there she moved to the exalted Lanvin high fashion house a few steps away. Due to her remarkable resemblance to Dietrich, she was assigned to model a dress called *Marlene*.

Read into it what you will, but Jean was unaware of that detail at the time. All he knew was that she had a style he liked. For starters, she physically resembled several of the significant ladies of his past, from Brigitte Helm to Michèle Morgan, and of course Dietrich. More important, he also liked what he saw of her character that evening over drinks. She was simple and unaffected despite being one of Lanvin's star models. Neither was she particularly impressed by being with a movie actor named Jean Gabin, since at the time he was not one of her big-screen favorites. They were immediately at ease with each other as they talked about their jobs and plans for the future. She was excited about an upcoming trip to Spain and Morocco to present Lanvin's latest haute couture collection.

He told her about a play he was rehearsing called *La Soif* (*Thirst*). He invited her to the dress rehearsal at the Théâtre des Ambassadeurs, across the street from the American embassy on Place de la Concorde. "Jean was very handsome," she remembered. "More handsome than in the films some years before that had made him famous. Now he was more mature, more virile, his traits hardened and marked by life, the war, and the fear he had known in combat. But the hardness was softened by a generous smile and eyes that had a joyful, almost childlike twinkle when he was happy. It was impossible for a woman who had the luck to meet him not to fall in love with him."[1] Their 14 years' difference in age didn't bother her, she liked older men.

Gabin courted Dominique with his usual old school courtesy. He refused to rush things, adding chivalrous touches that, as Colette Mars had noted, were rare in those days. At 44, with a becoming thatch of gray hair and an actor's presence, he bore little resemblance to the proletarian toughs she had seen him play on the screen. He made a point of always being impeccably turned out in bespoke suits and shirts from Sulka and Opelka, two of the best men's tailors in Paris. He not only sent her flowers, but had them sent to her every working day at Lanvin at precisely 5 p.m., the hour of their first meeting at the Colony Club. After the play had opened, he would go by Lanvin to pick her up well before curtain time. Punctual to a fault, he would arrive too early and stand on the corner, trying to look inconspicuous in dark glasses and turned-up collar, prompting her colleagues to call out teasingly, "Dominique, your guy is here!" They usually went out for a light collation of caviar, smoked salmon and vodka, then headed to the theater, with supper after the show. They talked of everything but Marlene Dietrich; he was pleased to see that Dominique was the first woman he had known since the war who had not raised the subject. After two weeks of that, they went back together to his room at the Hotel Baltimore on Avenue Kléber where he was living. It was February 19, Saint Gabin's day.

He told her he wanted to have a child with her and she agreed. It was the first time in his life, through two marriages and at least half-a-dozen serious relationships, that a woman actually expressed willingness to have his child, Dietrich's unconvincing professions notwithstanding. But Dominique was still uncertain whether he was serious. She found out in early March, when she was due to make her trip to Spain and Morocco for Lanvin. He told her flatly she wasn't leaving. She was, he said, instead going to quit Lanvin and marry him. She did both. The wedding was on March 28, two months to the day after their first meeting. The wedding was at the palatial *mairie* of the 16th arrondissement, followed by dinner at Maxim's with a few friends like Marcel Carné and Henry Bernstein, author of *Le Messager*, the film version of which Gabin had done in 1937, and of the play he was then acting in. It wasn't long before Dominique announced the news he had been hoping for. She was pregnant.

Henry Bernstein—the English spelling of his first name was due to his American mother—had been one of France's most popular playwrights and theatrical producers before the First World War, with dozens of hits. Thin

Jean and Dominique in 1949 shortly after their marriage in Paris. She left her position as a star mannequin at Lanvin for him (Collection du Musée Jean Gabin).

skinned, he had fought a number of sham duels on the field of honor with critics and other authors, nobody of course being harmed. He and Gabin had crossed paths in America during the war, which he spent in New York living well at the Waldorf Astoria. On returning to Paris he resumed direction of the Ambassadeurs theater. He often liked to write for a specific actor whose style he admired. In 1948, while Gabin was doing *Malapaga* in Genoa, Bernstein decided he would be his next star. The result was *La Soif*, a play in which three thoughtful characters reflect on love, friendship, jealousy, and desire.

It was a radical departure for Gabin in two respects, showing his willingness and determination to try something new as he struggled to find his place in postwar show business. First, accepting a role not only as an artist, but one engaged in conversations among Parisian sophisticates about age-old conundrums of the human condition couldn't have been further from the action characters of his past. Second, Jean hadn't been on the boards in nearly 20 years, and then it was to do revues and operettas. He had never done legitimate theater involving a lengthy text. For a movie actor who deliberately avoided studying his lines until shortly before going on the set, the better to achieve a more spontaneous effect, this was a major technical challenge.

His agent, André Bernheim, argued that the role Bernstein had created for him was the way to restart his career. Gabin hesitated, feeling certain that taking the stage was, as he put it, like entering the lion's den, with the critics just waiting for him to make a mistake.[2] Besides, he was convinced that his success in films was due mainly to his photogenic face and the intimate way he spoke his lines. Neither was much help in a theater, where most of the audience couldn't see the expressive look in his eyes or nuances of facial expression, and his voice had to be distinctly audible in the back row. But on the chance that the play could represent a much-needed breakthrough, he agreed to play Jean Galone, a middle-aged painter in quest of inspiration who is involved in a triangular love affair. His partners were two old pros of the stage, Madeleine Robinson as his vacillating mistress, and Claude Dauphin as his childhood friend who tries to steal her from him.

Gabin always suffered from stage fright, but the evening of the play's Paris premiere in February 1949 was worse than anything he had experienced on a movie set. This was a gut-wrenching panic attack that, in its intensity, he compared to that day of combat on the *Elorn* under fire from strafing, dive-bombing Stukas. Sneaking a peek through the curtain at the audience as it settled in—a mistake that did nothing to help settle his nerves—he saw that the *tout Paris* was there, including some of the most prominent figures in show business and all the critics from the major newspapers. "I thought to myself, 'Old boy, this time you've made the biggest mistake of your life,'" he recalled later. "The only way you can get out of it is to fake a sudden illness. Get sick right now and let them cart you off to the hospital. Or just walk out the door. But don't get on that stage, they'll cut you to pieces."[3]

Just then, a stagehand knocked on his dressing room door and said, "Five minutes, Monsieur Gabin." If anything, the warning should have worsened his panic. It had the opposite effect. He was suddenly struck by the idea that it was with this stage name that his father would have been called in his dressing room. He thought how much Ferdinand, who longed to do serious theater, would have liked to be in his place right now, acting with top billing in a piece by the famous Bernstein at one of the most prestigious theaters in Paris. He resolved to do this one for him, a sort of posthumous gift from his good-for-nothing son. It was a simple psychological trick, but it steadied him and got him through the evening. He did the whole play in a sort of trance, ignoring the audience and acting as if Ferdinand were the only spectator.

The critics praised Bernstein's play, his first in nine years, for its deft dramatic construction and for his willingness to take on the big themes of love, loyalty, and hunger for life even as the end draws near. As for Gabin, they acclaimed him as they hadn't since the 1930s. "*La Soif* brings us a revelation: Monsieur Jean Gabin, positively admirable in the role of Jean Galone," wrote the prominent novelist Francis Ambière in the magazine *Opéra*. "Here making his stage debut, he hasn't moved me so much since *La Grande Illusion*. A few bad films had lowered him in my esteem. What a comeback, and what a discovery! Sobriety, intensity, truth—Monsieur Gabin has it all."[4] Lucien Guitry, writing in *Vogue*, called Gabin "that rare phenomenon in the history of show business, a screen personality we have admired for twenty years who reveals in *La Soif* that he is also a first-rate stage actor."[5]

Gabin deployed his habitual thoroughgoing professionalism in *La Soif*. He never missed a performance, even though the play ran successfully for a year and Claude Dauphin opted out after six months. He maintained the same exhausting peak of emotional intensity night after night, whether the audience was good or sat on its hands. And when the script called for him to collapse from a stroke in the second act, he fell heavily to the floor, invariably bruising himself despite the advice of his partners to take an easier fall.

However, when the run ended, he refused to do the usual tour of the provinces with the play. He had proved to the critics and to himself that he could do theater and do it well, that he still deserved to be one of France's favorite actors. But compared with the greater flexibility of acting in motion pictures, he found the inevitable, well-known constraints of theater—having to perform every evening without fail, feeling up to it or not—seemed like a form of slavery. He also found other details of theater life galling, such as not having dinner until after the show, often followed by insomnia from the tension of acting. He preferred to stick with films as long as he could. As it turned out, he could for another 26 years and 59 films. He would not do theater again.

In fact, he was already busy doing a new picture with Marcel Carné. Gabin had bought the film rights to the novel *La Marie du Port* by the prolific Belgian writer Georges Simenon, who produced some 500 novels during his lifetime. He convinced the producer Sacha Gordine to back it, and wanted Marcel Carné as director. Carné, still smarting over the way Gabin and Dietrich left him in the lurch with *Les Portes de la Nuit* in 1946, took some convincing. That fiasco had hurt Carné's reputation, with producers avoiding him the last three years. Gabin finally got him to come around and renew their friendship, pointing out that he too had taken a hit: Pathé had sued him for breach of contract, costing him $60,000.

They began filming on location in Cherbourg in mid–1949, when Gabin was able to get away from performing in *Soif* during its month-long summer break. Things got more complicated when the play resumed. He had to be on the movie set in the Paris suburbs at 11 a.m. to do the interior scenes, then dash to the theater by 8 p.m. for the play. That kind of stress might help explain why Gabin looks drained of vitality and older than his 45 years in the film, with bags under his eyes, his hair looking thinner and grayer.

In *La Marie du Port*/*Marie of the Port* (1950, U.S. release 1951) he plays Henri Chatelard, a middle-aged bachelor who owns a restaurant and movie theater in Cherbourg. He's bored with that, and he's bored with his mistress, Odile (Blanchette Brunoy), for whom the feeling is mutual. Odile's attractive, manipulative, 18-year-old sister Marie (Nicole Courcel) catches his wandering eye in nearby Port-en-Bessin, where she is working as a waitress. She teases and toys with him, alternately advancing and retreating. Meanwhile, Odile seduces Marie's titular boyfriend in a room above the restaurant, where Henri discovers them. Eventually he capitulates to the tough-minded Marie who, without sleeping with him, gets what she wants: a bourgeois marriage with a man of comfortable means, letting her escape from life as a waitress.

Like *Martin Roumagnac*, this was a transition film for Gabin, who was getting further and further away from his tough, romantic outsider persona. Instead of a leather jacket he wears well-cut double-breasted suits, rather than slapping his women around he accepts that because of his age he is at a disadvantage vying with younger men for their favors—he just laughs it off when he discovers his mistress in bed with one. Likely benefiting from the synergy generated by his success in *Soif*, Gabin was liked well enough by the public to make the film a hit at the box office. As Pauline Kael later put it in her *New Yorker* review, "Here he is seen weathered and aged; the passions of his early roles have given way to worldly-wise skepticism." All in all, she found it "a highly civilized film, simple in theme yet meant to be subtle in the great French tradition."[6] From Gabin's perspective, the film had another, more long-term advantage: he discovered that Simenon's writing style and themes fit him well in screenplay form. Over the years, he would do many more pictures based on his novels, including the famous *Inspector Maigret* series.

With his new marriage, a baby on the way, a successful play and, almost simultaneously, a creditable movie under his belt, things were looking better for Gabin. That had not gone unnoticed by Doriane. Their divorce had been pronounced in January 1943, but she felt she had not received a fair settlement. A vindictive Jeanne Mauchain now resurfaced and began a series of acrimonious legal proceedings to try to obtain a better deal, which to her meant half of his total wealth. She had always been a smart negotiator, as she showed when she served as Jean's agent. Now she coordinated her legal case with a barrage of interviews designed to give judges and public alike the impression that she was wronged by an ungrateful man, a poor, abandoned woman reduced to living on a pension of a few hundred dollars a month.

"I was four years older than Gabin when we met," she declared to a mass-circulation newspaper. "At that time he was lazy, with no ambition or education. He was just an insignificant actor without much talent playing second-rate roles. Fortunately I had some money, and was able to help him despite his bad character. It took me years to teach him how to knot a tie, to walk correctly, and to behave properly in polite company. If he was able to become a great actor, it was entirely due to me; without me, my connections, and my money, Gabin wouldn't have existed." According to her, all his great films of the 1930s, from *La Bandéra* to *Les Bas Fonds* and *Pépé le Moko* were her doing, including the iconic scarf he wore in the Casbah.[7]

Jean wanted above all to avoid anything that could endanger the happiness he had just begun to experience with his marriage and coming fatherhood. He also wanted to shield Dominique from the petty squabbles and slanderous rumors he knew Doriane was capable of generating indefinitely. He decided to put an end to her campaign himself, without waiting for an appeal court's decision. Most of his wealth was in valuable real estate that he had bought before the war: land on a residential street in the upscale Paris suburb of Neuilly, an apartment building on rue Maspero in the best part of the fashionable 16th arrondissement, his handsome rebuilt property in Sainte Gemme Moronval. He sold it all and gave her half of the proceeds which, although the sum was never made known, must have meant upwards of a million dollars for her at the time. Exit Doriane.

Enter Florence Moncorgé-Gabin, born on November 28, 1949, in the Paris suburb of Boulogne Billancourt, where one of the best maternity clinics in the Paris region was located. Gabin, delighted when Dominique became pregnant—though he was so anxious about her condition that he insisted she enter the clinic a week before the contractions began—was ecstatic when Florence arrived, even if she was a surprise. The state of pediatrics didn't permit accurate forecasting of a child's gender, but for some reason the couple had been firmly expecting a boy; all of Florence's baby clothes had been embroidered with the initials J-M, for Jean-Marie. No matter, Jean's dream of starting a family was being realized. Two more children, a boy they named Mathias and another girl, Valérie, arrived in short order.

Jean had lived a good part of his life in hotels and liked it. After marriage, he had trouble settling down to a permanent address. The Gabins lived in Versailles when Florence was born, but Jean soon bought a house in the best part of Neuilly and began renovating it. The work was barely finished when he spotted a handsome villa back in Versailles, sold the house in Neuilly, and had the villa redone top to bottom. But before moving in, he discovered that the boy who had occupied the room destined for Mathias had died of cyanosis. Superstitious as always, he immediately resold the villa and moved the family to a house he bought in Deauville, where they stayed several years. As Dominique recalled, "We moved over 20 times. Six months after each time we set up housekeeping, he would say, 'I think we made a mistake.' And off we would go to start over again." She once showed him an advertising leaflet for a mobile home and jokingly suggested they buy it; since they moved all the time, she said, they might as well have a house on wheels. He was not amused.[8]

Dominique, whom Jean began calling Maman, was herself not especially amused by the way he changed with marriage and paternity. He had impressed her with his trim physique and sartorial elegance while he was courting. But, no longer feeling the need to look good, he soon put the beautiful suits away, along with the socks that matched his ties, in favor of his habitual turtleneck sweaters and cloth caps. He seemed to take on a little more weight with each child. She had married a man known as a great seducer of beautiful women and a pillar of Paris nightlife, and quickly became the wife of a homebody who avoided even going to the movies or the theater because he disliked being recognized in public. (The only way new actors came to his attention was watching their old films on late-night television. Florence remembers that he "discovered" Paul Newman only after seeing *The Sting* long after it was released.)[9]

"Mother wasn't too pleased with the way Papa changed after their marriage," Florence told me during an interview at her home near Deauville. "When they met he was slim and elegant, but later he actually seemed to want to age prematurely. He let himself go, developed a paunch, and didn't bother with dressing well. One evening he even took her to a restaurant in Paris wearing his bedroom slippers."[10] Sentimental, he shied away from public demonstrations of affection, covering his feelings by acting gruff. Dominique once said she couldn't remember his ever holding her hand in public.[11]

She soon learned that Jean Gabin's idea of a good time was to come home, put on his slippers, have a scotch or white wine, and watch TV while having dinner. "You can't imagine," he said, "what a pleasure it is for me to watch other actors work while I'm having dinner."[12] During a shoot he would call her every afternoon to know what would be on the table when he got back, preferably heavy traditional dishes like cassoulet, petit salé, boeuf gros sel, and andouillette grillée, usually accompanied by a light Beaujolais or a white Alsace like Sylvaner.

Conversation centered on sports like soccer and cycling, plus endless disquisitions on the good and bad points of his favorite racehorses. At one point, Dominique suggested in jest that maybe the Gabin family should learn to neigh, the better to discuss his favorites at the Longchamp, Auteuil, and Vincennes tracks.[13] What he never talked about at home was his films. "I knew of course that Papa was an actor," Mathias remembered, "but it was only after his death that I realized how important he had been, and even longer after that that I discovered what he represented for France."[14]

He paid little attention to the children's grades in school, considering their health the most important thing. Although an atheist, he sent Florence and Valérie to a Catholic school in Paris run by the American Marymount sisters to introduce them to English and the right manners, not to mention Coca Cola and cornflakes. As a result of his indifference toward their studies and the disruption of frequent household moves, none of the three obtained the French secondary school diploma, the *baccalauréat*. He reasoned, to the dismay of Dominique, that he had gotten along well enough in life without one. But he was uncompromising on the values he tried to inculcate. "His principles were closer to those of a man of the people than of the middle or upper classes," Florence said. "They were based on rectitude, loyalty and honesty. He would tell us, 'In life you have to hold your head up high, and for that you have to walk straight. You can have failings, but you have to be decent.' For him there were the 'good guys' and the others were 'shit-eaters.' He never gave us any pocket money. His position was that money had to be earned."[15]

Gabin worked hard at being a model French *père de famille*, despite being in a profession requiring frequent absences—and providing frequent temptations—in which it wasn't always easy. In fact, he worked too hard at fathering in some respects. His gnawing anxiety and uncompromising character made life difficult for the family, especially for the children growing up in the 1950s and '60s, an era so radically different from that of his own childhood and adolescence. As Florence remembers, "My father very much wanted to have children, but deep down he wasn't ready for the responsibility they represented. For him, kids were like toys that he didn't know how to make work. Mother was ready to have more, but he said stop."[16] He worried constantly that they would get sick or have an accident. If they caught a cold or ran a slight fever, they had to stay in bed and he checked on them almost hourly. For fear of a fall or a fire, their bedrooms were never higher than the second floor and he installed bars on their windows; they were forbidden to take an elevator, there might be a mechanical failure.

Jean's strict views on life and old-fashioned tastes led inevitably to conflict with the children. He hated rock music, considering virtually any popular singers after Maurice Chevalier and Tino Rossi worthless. Electric guitars were incomprehensible. Florence, a headstrong, romantic adolescent, was the first to rebel. "When we listened to rock music, he would say, 'We've gone completely decadent,'" she told me. "'Either those guys scream while they wiggle their hips, or they don't have any voice.' We had arguments all the time. He believed I was living in an unreal world and it drove him crazy. He would hold his head in his hands and say, 'My poor girl, you're living in a fantasy world, you'll never get anywhere in life. What are you talking about? Come back down to earth.'"[17]

At 17, she fell into a serious depression that took several months to cure. As an adult she worked in films, including doing continuity on Gabin's last one, *L'Année Sainte/Holy Year* (1976). They had serious arguments over her boyfriends, whom he considered worthless playboys. Her younger sister Valérie, too, felt uncomfortable with his overly-protective rules and restrictions. After his death she had a falling out with the family, went to the U.S., and worked for a while as taxi driver in Miami. Back in France, she worked on the crew of a couple of films and produced some short subjects. His son Mathias, on the other hand, followed closely in his father's footsteps, doing his military service in the navy and then running a stud farm in Normandy. He shunned show business, but his son Alexis Moncorgé became an award-winning stage actor; the French press loves to underline that he is the grandson of Jean Gabin.

Directors and producers had stopped calling. Gabin decided the time had come to diversify his activities. If nothing else, maybe he could even realize another of his childhood dreams, that of owning a farm and cattle. "Papa always said acting wasn't a real profession," Florence explained. "It was only a temporary job. What he wanted was something solid he could count on, and that was land and cattle. He could always make a living with that, and the children would be sure of having something to eat."[18]

Seriously considering becoming a full-time farmer, in July 1952 he bought a Norman property called La Pichonnière near the village of Bonnefoi, 90 miles west of Paris. The place was dilapidated, with chickens roosting in the living room and the bathtub full of seed, but it came with 104 acres of pasture. He had it rebuilt from the ground up—workers found gold pieces in the old farmhouse that were struck with the likeness of Louis XVI; Gabin conscientiously turned them over to the local tax office.

He paid special attention to the stables. Remembering what he had learned in Mériel at Auguste Haring's farm, he made sure each stall measured exactly 54 square feet and was absolutely flat, because cows gave less milk when they felt crowded or off-balance. He kept on buying parcels of land until he had 370 acres, when the average French farm at the time was a few dozen acres. It didn't take long for the locals to start raising their prices and selling out to the movie star from Paris who paid cash. Higher land prices would eventually create resentment against him because they made it hard for other farmers in the area to extend their own holdings, or for youngsters starting out to gain a foothold.

He also began purchasing black-and-white Norman cows and a few bulls. In an era when most French farmers still milked their cows by hand, he installed electric milking machines. Instead of having the arable fields plowed using the customary hefty Percheron draft horses, he bought the area's first Massey Ferguson tractor and enjoyed driving it himself. At this time, too, he began breeding racehorses, particularly trotters; his jockeys wore his racing colors, violet cap and yellow jersey.

They were his passion, or as the French say, his *danseuse*, an increasingly expensive one, as time went on. Now able to indulge the taste for horseracing developed when his father took him to the races—"If you ever get rich, buy racehorses," Ferdinand had advised him—he became a fixture at the tracks in Paris and Deauville. Better, he built his own track with small stands near La Pichonnière, the Hippodrome Jean Gabin, where the Jean and Dominique Gabin Prize is still run every July. "Someday I hope to have a champion that I can take to the Roosevelt Raceway in New York," he told *The New York Times* in 1964. "But of course that's not up to me, it's up to the horse."[19]

The gentleman farmer at La Pichonnière, where Gabin built his own racetrack. The farm was the realization of a childhood dream, the horses became an expensive passion (Collection du Musée Jean Gabin).

Meanwhile, Jean decided the farmhouse wasn't comfortable enough for him and the family. He built a three-story manor on a nearby rise that he called La Moncorgerie, playing on his real name. On each chimney he proudly placed a large monogram "M." It became the family's vacation and weekend retreat. When doing a film, he made known to his directors that shooting had to be over each week by noon Saturday so he could start the two-hour drive to Bonnefoi. The imposing house and farm became tourist attractions, with some uninvited strangers venturing as far as the front door for a glimpse of him, much to his vocal displeasure.

He took this new role as seriously as any he acted before the camera. It wasn't Marie Antoinette playing shepherdess at Versailles, but a real,

At the races in Deauville in the 1970s. The daily tip sheet was his favorite reading material (Collection du Musée Jean Gabin).

producing farm. "Being a farmer is much more serious than being a movie actor," he said. "I do movies to make money, money that I count not in francs but in heads of cattle." Eventually, he had an operation with up to some 400 head and 70 racehorses.[20]

But Gabin's happiness due to his marriage, paternity, and new farm wasn't enough. He was still suffering through the worst patch of his film career. In the early 1950s that made him anxious, even anguished. He doubted seriously that he would be able to support his growing family over the long term. Dominique remembered that these were the years when he would ask her in late-night desperation, "What can I do? All I know how to do is to be an actor." He lost confidence in his talent and began to doubt that he could regain his popularity with the public and critics. Partly by doing mostly second-rate Italian or Franco-Italian pictures, he managed to keep relatively busy. But what she remembered about these years was that when he was congratulated on a decent one, he would say, "Yes, that one was okay, but what about the next one?"[21]

One of the good ones was *La Nuit est Mon Royaume/The Night Is My Kingdom* (1951, U.S. release 1953). Gabin plays Raymond Pinsard, a locomotive engineer—again—who loses his sight when a boiler explodes. The predictable screenplay takes him through the stages of denial, despair, attempted suicide, and eventual acceptance when he begins a relationship with a woman blind from birth who teaches Braille. Gabin turns in a tour de force in a role where he, whose strong point is his expressive eyes, plays mostly in dark glasses and has to express emotion only through his voice, facial expressions, and mannerisms. It won him the Volpi Cup for Best Actor at the 1951 Venice Film Festival.

Still, he was most often cast as merely another befuddled bourgeois male, the pathetic plaything of domineering wives, scheming, unfaithful girlfriends, and disloyal acquaintances. Neither public nor critics were buying the new, vulnerable Gabin. As one unforgiving reviewer wrote, "A passive Gabin isn't the Gabin we know. However great an actor he is, this part isn't right for him. There are certain rules of drama that you can't violate with impunity. You can't make a cuckold, even a happy one, out of the actor who's been the army deserter in *Le Quai des Brumes*, the officer in *La Grande Illusion*, the criminal in *La Bandéra* and *Pépé-le-Moko*, and the murderer in *Le Jour se Lève*."[22]

A textbook example of what the critics didn't like about Gabin's persona at this point was *La Vérité sur Bébé Donge/The Truth About Bébé Donge* (1951, U.S. release 1952). In this bleak look at marriage in the provinces based on a novel by Georges Simenon, Gabin plays the philandering businessman François Donge. He is in a hospital bed as the film opens, poisoned by his wife, Elisabeth, known as Bébé (Danielle Darrieux). In a series of flashbacks, he reflects on his habitual unfaithfulness and how it hurt Bébé. He dies just as he realizes how much he loved her. She, beyond caring, is charged with murder and led off to jail.

Gabin played second fiddle to Darrieux, a situation that would have been unthinkable before the war. Still, she was generous in praise of his performance: "Jean Gabin is extraordinary," she said in a television interview. "I wouldn't call him an actor, because when you're on the set and he says his lines to you, it's the same as if we were just having a conversation in real life. I've never seen an actor who had so much force, so much *naturel* as Gabin."[23]

Well, we've heard that before, and it's true. But the interest in this instance lies more in the fact that Darrieux, now a first-magnitude star, seems to find it necessary to say something nice about Gabin. Another indication of how low he had fallen was *La Minute de Vérité/The Moment of Truth* (1952, U.S. release 1954), in which he plays Pierre Richard, a doctor cuckolded by his wife, Madeleine (Michèle Morgan). Her lover, a young artist, commits suicide when she won't leave Pierre. They reconcile and become an ordinary middle-class couple, giving the film an unconvincing happy ending, totally at odds with, say, the Gabin-Morgan tragedy of *Le Quai des Brumes.*

Once again, Gabin yields top billing to an actress, this time to the one who owed him her start in pictures. As the unsentimental Morgan put it, "Ours is a cruel profession. The first time I acted opposite Gabin, I was only a beginner and he was the star. Now the situation is different."[24] He would play a loser in a few more films, including a Franco-Italian melodrama, *Fille Dangereuse/Bufere* (1952, literally *The Dangerous Girl*), in which he's a surgeon who leaves his wife and family for the outrageously vamping Italian sex-bomb Silvana Pampanini. The dangerous girl of the title is killed in an accident, his wife wins him back, and the film sinks without a trace.

Now when he played opposite his former partners Danielle Darrieux and Michèle Morgan, or even the newcomer Martine Carole, it was they who got top billing, with his name in increasingly small characters. Gabin's problem stemmed not only from changing tastes in movie stars and the inevitable ups and downs of show business, or even shifting societal mores. It was also the more deep-seated midlife problem of who he was, complicated by his new role as the head of a family he had to support with a reliable income, which inhibited him in experimenting with new characters. His situation was not unlike that of Humphrey Bogart in the mid–1930s, when he rescued his career by changing from the juvenile romantic (one of his memorable early lines was "Tennis, anyone?") to the ruthless Duke Mantee with a grating voice in *The Petrified Forest* (1936).

Before, Gabin had often been the youthful underclass victim of an implacable fate, his struggle against it raising the pictures of his classical period to an aesthetic level approaching tragedy. He could no longer play that role, and directors didn't know quite what to do with him. He who hated makeup even let Micheline try darkening his gray hair with burnt cork. It irritated his scalp and didn't work on film. As director Jacques Becker said when someone suggested Gabin for the lead in a film he was planning, "Gabin? But no one is interested in Gabin."[25]

He had to reinvent Jean Gabin. Or resign himself to the role of gentleman farmer.

19

New Persona

Gabin didn't know it, but he had hit bottom. By 1954 he and a few directors finally figured out what should have been obvious: now arrived at a seasoned middle age, he possessed a natural authority that was being ignored, resulting in miscasting him in passive roles. He had always projected a charismatic, virile dominance in his early films, slapping rivals around with a swift backhand and brooking no insubordination whether in the Casbah, driving a locomotive, or commanding an ocean-going tugboat. In real life he had stood up to Nazi occupiers and their Vichy puppets, and been a tank commander in combat. It was time for another breakthrough film that would let Gabin be Gabin, no longer a pitiable underdog or anybody's fool, no more dying miserably as the word "FIN" fills the screen.

He found it in the adaptation of a novel by Albert Simonin, a master of French crime fiction who knew and used the kind of street talk natural to Jean. In *Touchez pas au Grisbi/Grisbi* (1954, U.S. release 1959, literal translation *Hands off the Loot*), a gangster movie directed by Jacques Becker, he was Max le Menteur, Max the Liar. A respected, graying figure in the Paris underworld who orders champagne by the magnum, drives big American cars, and has mink-wrapped broads for company when he wants them, he has just pulled off the headline-making heist of a dozen gold ingots worth several million dollars at Orly airport. He's getting too old for this business and wants it to be his last job before a respectable bourgeois retirement.

The problem is that his friend and accomplice, Riton (René Dary), has blabbed about the job to a nightclub dancer named Josy (Jeanne Moreau) he's trying to impress. She mentions it to another mobster, Angelo (Lino Ventura), who decides to go after that gold. He kidnaps Riton and demands it as ransom. Out of friendship and respect for the gangland code of honor, Max has to try to save him. In the Chicago-style final shoot-out, Max's gang kills Angelo's, but the gold is lost as his car goes up in flames. Riton is killed, leaving Max without either the gold or his best friend.

Gabin almost didn't get the part that marked the start of his second career with a new persona. Becker wanted the younger stars Daniel Gélin or François Perrier to play Max, but both refused, considering it was a part for an older actor. Gélin suggested his mentor Gabin. In hindsight, it's hard to imagine anyone else, perhaps because he went over the screenplay as he usually did, and made changes to conform to the way he saw his part. The result is a role that fit him perfectly.

The picture is an affecting story of male friendship and aging. For the first time in his 47 films, no love interest is central to the narrative. The main female roles are molls,

Gabin (center) with Lino Ventura and Jeanne Moreau in *Touchez pas au Grisbi*, 1954, Gabin's postwar comeback film. Gabin discovered Ventura, a professional wrestler originally from Italy, and they became close friends. This was the first of many films in which Ventura played an Italian gangster (Collection du Musée Jean Gabin).

showgirls, or secretaries, whose eager bids for attention Max, with a sort of weary, disabused authority, tolerates at best. (Gaby Basset, Jean's first wife, played the wife of the nightclub owner. True to this word, he never forgot her, finding her parts in eight of his films from 1953 to 1959.) No woman excites him, drives him crazy, or makes him suffer.

In a telling nightclub sequence, Riton suggests one more drink before they go, but Max emphatically declines. "After that we'll have to have one with Pierrot [the club's owner], and then the girls will want us to take them out for onion soup, and then we'll have to go to bed with them. And I'm not in the mood. I'm tired." In another, he tells Riton he's too old for chasing girls like Josy. Seizing a mirror, he holds it in Riton's face: "Look at the bags under your eyes. And mine. And this [he pinches his sagging jowls]." Their camaraderie is underlined by a sequence in which they go back to Max's apartment for an improvised dinner of pâté and Muscadet like two old bachelors, with Max digging out two pairs of striped pajamas and letting Riton bed down on the sofa. After Riton is kidnapped, Max, who wanted nothing but to retire from a life of crime, risks everything trying to rescue him.

In addition to his scenes with Riton, Max's age is referred to repeatedly, almost insistently, as if to stress Gabin's new middle-aged persona. At the end, he shows up in a restaurant with a beautiful American girlfriend, Betty (Marylin Buferd, Miss America 1946) on his arm, impressing his friends of the same age with the fact that he can still attract younger women. In a final bit of business, he pulls a pair of glasses from his suit pocket to look up a telephone number in the restaurant, making a point of adjusting them on his nose so the audience can't miss that he's become shortsighted. "This will happen to you too," he tells the restaurant owner when she remarks that it's the first time she's seen him wear them.

The new Gabin had arrived. It won him the Volpi Cup for Best Actor at the 1954 Venice Film Festival. Jean de Baroncelli, the top critic at *Le Monde*, wrote, "In a tailor-made part, we discover the Gabin of the great period, proud and magnificent, amazingly self-assured and calm, with that little spark of feeling burning behind the impassive mask."[1] In America, Kenneth Turan of *The Los Angeles Times* has called the film "a wonderful treasure," noting, "What stays with you most, however, is the poetry of Gabin's face. He's an actor who actually looks like he's lived the life he plays on the screen, and by the closing scenes there's so much of the past in his face—regrets, memories, despair, even a kind of love—that a glance from him is worth an entire performance from lesser actors."[2]

Following his comeback in *Grisbi*, Jean Gabin would do another 48 films over the next 22 years, as many as four or five a year in the 1950s. All would be good entertainment, some worthy of film retrospectives. The settings were nearly always typically French, usually including at least one sequence in a bistro or café, from Paris to Marseille, La Rochelle to Nantes to the Riviera. So would the names of the characters he played—in a dozen films, he was François, Pierre, or Henri; in fully nine, nearly one-tenth of his entire career, his character was named Jean.

The range of roles he played was even greater than his prewar films, a virtual cross section of French social milieux, professions and trades: gangland boss or police commissioner, businessman or lawyer, judge or president, banker, restaurant chef, truck driver, gynecologist, veterinarian, farmer, ex–Foreign Legionnaire, eccentric *clochard* or patriarch of one of France's *grandes familles*. Switching easily from coveralls to business suits, skirting the law or enforcing it, driving a truck or delivering a baby, buying cheese in a street market or quaffing champagne in a swish nightclub, with each succeeding film he became more than ever the actor Frenchmen could identify with.

As the years went by, his films would increasingly reflect, often with undisguised scorn and a certain melancholy, the new, postwar France with its tight social tissue unraveling, the traditional trades vanishing, colorful old neighborhoods being bulldozed to make way for eyesore apartment complexes. Taken together, they form a penetrating portrait of French society during three decades of traumatic change.

Frequently tinctured with French working-class xenophobia, his crime films are peopled with criminals and other undesirables who are Italian, North African, American blacks, anything but French. Like the French themselves, who had to be dragged, kicking and screaming, into the 20th century—not yet the 21st—Gabin's personal conservatism, resistance to change, and skepticism of all forms of modernism were translated into his films. Targets of his scorn ranged from France's New Franc introduced in 1960 to the ersatz New Europe governed from Brussels, to fast, industrialized food and rampant urbanization, along with the whole post–1960s generation of hippies, druggies, hirsute activists and others he considered wackos. Many of his films of this period address these themes directly, giving them an important subtext of social commentary.

Good screenplays were essential to the convincing portrayals of France and its people during this second career, but so was Gabin's own acute observation. "I observe people a lot," he explained in the late 1950s. "That's how I've been able to play a locomotive engineer, a thug, a financier, a bum, and so on. I watch people very carefully. I don't believe in those theories of becoming the character I'm playing, but it's true that the costume I wear makes it easier to get into the part. I think it's the essence of being an actor to try new roles, but it's not easy. I might look very relaxed on the set, but I'm always tense when I'm acting."[3]

He kept Micheline Bonnet as his dresser for most of his career because she knew how to deal with his insecurities and perfectionist temperament. Totally concentrated on his role, he could sit for hours without exchanging a word with her or anyone else on the set. That didn't bother her, but his dislike of the usual obligatory French handshakes and kissing on both cheeks reinforced his reputation for being cranky. The Greco-French director Costa-Gavras graphically described the atmosphere of a Gabin shoot he visited: "When Monsieur Gabin arrived on the set in the morning, you didn't dare shake his hand. It was unthinkable. You kept your distance. In fact, he created the distance. He was a giant, and you don't slap giants on the back."[4]

When he had to play one of his angry outbursts, Gabin started to prepare for it the night before and had already worked himself into a foul mood when he arrived on the set; Micheline warned the cast and technicians beforehand to give him a wide berth. Sometimes he would stand before a mirror and work himself up for a scene. But when the script called for one of his trademark slaps—his arms were too short for realistic punches, but he could slap as fast as a rattlesnake can strike—his partners had little to fear. Annie Girardot, who was 25 when she played opposite him in the gangster film *Le Rouge est Mis* (1957, also known as *Speaking of Murder*), remembered how nervous she was the day she was supposed to receive a Gabin slap. "But it was the most exquisite slap in the world," she said, "a caress, a velvety tap on the cheek that said, 'I like you, kid, did you really think I was going to hurt you?'"[5]

He liked to downplay his tricks of the trade and expressed contempt for method acting, but in fact this was Actors Studio at its instinctive best. His reaction to that suggestion would have been to make light of it, brush it off as pretentious, and say his success was due to luck, or maybe the color of his eyes. He once told his favorite screenwriter, Michel Audiard, with mock seriousness, "I would never have had the career I have if I didn't have blue eyes. Got to have the blue peepers. Look at all those who are successful: Gable, Cooper, Garbo, Morgan, Delon, they've all got light-colored eyes. That's the way it is. Back in the days when I was starting out, all they had to do, in *Le Quai des Brumes*, for example, was focus on my face. I could be thinking about my latest gas bill or the price of endives, it didn't matter."[6]

Henri Decoin, who directed Gabin in two films, *La Vérité sur Bébé Donge* and *Razzia sur la Chnouf*, explained in a documentary,

> It's not the director who directs the film, it's Gabin who tells the director how to do it. For example, he'll go through the script and say, "On page 19 there's a line that doesn't work for me. I'm cutting it." That's Gabin for you. Or the director will say "Jean, now you walk fast to the window, you open it and look down, you close it quickly, the cops are down there." What does he do? He walks slowly across the room, dragging his feet, doesn't open the window, and scratches his neck. That's him all over. His style is a combination of deliberateness, gravity, and interiority, with an economy of gesture and movement that no other actor has.[7]

For him, making films was a job like any other, going to the studio for a shoot was the same as heading to his factory job after he had left home as a teenager. His motto was "On time, makeup done, lines learned," and any actor on the set who didn't follow suit was on the receiving end of his contempt. He insisted on working with directors and technicians he knew and trusted and was faithful to them for years. Besides checking which lens was being used for which shot, he made sure that other technical details reinforced his star status.

He didn't hog the camera, but he always got significantly more close-ups than anybody else, including his most famous leading ladies—in *Martin Roumagnac* he got 55, Dietrich 40, in *En Cas de Malheur*, opposite one of the biggest feminine stars in the world, his face filled the screen 68 times, Brigitte Bardot only 46. As time went on, audiences had to wait longer and longer for his first appearance on the screen: in *Pépé le Moko* in 1936 it was five minutes, in a typical film in the late 1960s it could be up to 15 minutes.[8] The one thing he neglected was pushing his agents to negotiate better fees, finding money talk distasteful. He made an average $200,000 per film during this period, which was not bad, but Dominique was convinced he was worth more and disappointed he didn't insist on it.

I won't attempt to discuss all Jean Gabin's second-career films, only the ones I find most important. A complete list of his movies will be found at the end of the book. For readers interested in more detail, in English there is Charles Zigman's excellent two-volume annotated filmography, *World's Coolest Movie Star*, or in French, Missiaen and Siclier's authoritative *Jean Gabin*, among others.

French Cancan, also known as *Only the French Can* (1955, U.S. release 1956), marked Jean Renoir's return to French filmmaking after some 15 years in California, as well as his reconciliation with Gabin. After their four great films of the 1930s, Gabin wasn't ready to forgive Renoir for remaining in Hollywood during the war and becoming a naturalized U.S. citizen, an *Amérloque* as the French call us when being snarky. Ever the patriot, he felt that the son of a great French artist like Auguste Renoir didn't have the right to abandon his native land voluntarily and let a foreign nation benefit from his talent. Renoir had nothing against Gabin—"I like Gabin and he likes me," he wrote in his memoirs concerning this period—but he was not his first choice for male lead in the film.[9]

Maybe because of ties formed during his Hollywood years, he wanted Charles Boyer to play Henri Danglard, the character representing Charles Zidler, the impresario who created the Moulin Rouge in 1889. But Boyer's fee was too high for the producers, Franco-London Films. Impressed by Gabin's success in *Grisbi*, they told Renoir to take Jean, who was willing to work for less as he climbed out of his career hole. Renoir took him to dinner at a good restaurant, and they warmed over their friendship by discussing recipes the way they used to, Gabin divulging his for hare in mustard sauce and Renoir speaking eloquently about *boeuf mironton*, boiled beef in onion sauce. Once the shoot began they worked together with their old intuitive complicity.[10]

Cancan is Renoir's recreation of the Montmartre of the Belle Epoque and of his own youth when he hung around his father's atelier, getting to know his models and watching him produce luminous paintings celebrating feminine beauty. His screenplay is a conventional, sentimental story of show business ups and downs as Danglard overcomes financial difficulties and his mistress' tantrums to build the Moulin Rouge into a Paris entertainment institution featuring the cancan. (The dancers spent three weeks repeating takes of the film's frenzied finale of flying petticoats and splits.)

Shot in Technicolor, new to France, it was Gabin's first color film. They either got the makeup wrong or slightly botched the processing: his face looks waxy, his lips rouged,

Gabin flanked by dancers (unidentified) in *French Cancan*, his first Technicolor film, 1955. Marking his reconciliation with Jean Renoir, the role furthered his transition to the new persona of his second career (Collection du Musée Jean Gabin).

the eyebrows overdone. Wearing a gray homburg, thumbs stuck in his vest, smoking a large stogie like the typical capitalist as imagined by Comrade Renoir, Gabin is as far from his typical prewar proletarian character as possible. It isn't a very flattering part, it doesn't really use his talent for conveying emotion or developing a three-dimensional character. But by being a completely different kind of role it does help pave the way to his new persona.

Central to the story is the relationship between Gabin and the 24-year-old Françoise Arnoul, who plays Nini, the laundress he makes into a star dancer. When he plucks her from the street and takes her to dancing lessons, she assumes he wants a quid pro quo in bed. He doesn't, then he does and she becomes his new mistress, then it's off again when he tells her the only thing that counts is the show. For the young Arnoul it was a watershed film. "I'd seen all of Gabin's major movies while I was growing up," she told me over drinks at her favorite café near Montparnasse, where she now lives in retirement. "When Renoir asked me to play opposite him, it was like a gift from heaven, I would have done anything for the part. On the set, working a scene with Jean was easy. I was afraid he wouldn't think I was up to it, but he took me under his wing and I felt protected. He probably understood that I was seduced by him, just a little in love. He was a charmer."[11]

Suddenly Gabin was on a roll. Seemingly energized by his newfound domestic happiness, spurred by the need to finance the costly improvements at La Pichonnière and his purchases of racehorses, he did fully a dozen films over the next two years. He played a drug lord, truck driver, restaurant chef in the Les Halles district, successful but cynical artist, gynecologist, *Les Miserables* hero Jean Valjean, and the first of his three performances as Inspector Maigret. Some were potboilers, but many included social commentary on issues rarely treated publicly in France.

In *Chiens Perdus sans Collier/The Little Rebels* (1955) Gabin plays an understanding juvenile court judge who explores the problems of delinquents and tries to help solve them. In *Des Gens sans Importance* (1955, literal translation *Unimportant People*) he is a truck driver who falls in love with a truck-stop waitress. She gets pregnant, has an illegal abortion, and dies as a result. This was the first time a French film dared treat the subject of abortion, which wasn't legalized in Catholic France until 1975. In *Le Cas du Docteur Laurent/The Case of Doctor Laurent* (1957) Gabin is a physician in the French provinces who tries to promote natural childbirth. He is resisted by the local medical establishment and suspicious villagers convinced that it was normal for women to suffer giving birth. He's vindicated when one of his young patients tries it successfully. This was the first commercial film in history to show a human birth in close-up.

Gas-Oil (1955), in which Gabin is again a truck driver, he falls afoul of a criminal gang, only to be saved by his fellow truckers. It's main significance is that it's the first film with dialogue by Michel Audiard. He and Jean would subsequently do 16 pictures together. For a while, they were very close personally and professionally, having been raised in the same Montmartre district, speaking the same *titi parisien* argot, and cultivating the same irreverent provocation.

Some reviewers said Gabin spoke Audiard's slang in those films, but Audiard himself said he used Jean's idiosyncratic expressions in writing his scripts—he once suggested there should be a *Petit Gabin* dictionary to parallel the famous *Petit Larousse*. The team became sure box office, portraying the French in all their truculent, rapid-fire repartee and swaggering arrogance that often covers up a basic timidity. They had a falling out in 1963, when Audiard began to find Gabin too hard to deal with, much to the despair of producers. "Since he started raising racehorses, Old Man Gabin takes himself too seriously," he said.[12] Practically inventing the profession of movie *dialogueiste*, separate from screenwriting, Audiard worked on nearly 100 films and had a Paris square named for him in 1994.

During this most fecund period of Gabin's second career, *La Traversée de Paris/Four Bags Full* (1956, U.S. release 1957) is undoubtedly one of his most controversial films. Contrary to most other movies about the French under Nazi occupation, this one, set in 1943, breaks several taboos by presenting them not as plucky, often unsung heroes of the Resistance. Rather, they are craven collaborators and unscrupulous black marketeers, ready to make a buck any way they can and rat on each other to the Gestapo. Based on a caustic satirical novel by Marcel Aymé and directed by Claude Autant-Lara, Gabin plays the wealthy artist Grandgil. Not knowing who he is, an unemployed taxi driver named Marcel Martin (Bourvil) meets him in a bar and asks his help in carrying four suitcases of black market pork by night across occupied Paris. (Today a café named La Traversée de Paris stands at the spot in the 5th arrondissement where the film begins.)

Martin is doing the job because he needs the money, but Grandgil is cynically going along with it just to have a little adventure. Louis de Funés, in one of his first important roles, is Jambier, the shifty grocer who provides the pork and, in one of the more pitiless depictions of a certain France under the occupation, haggles over the sum he'll pay them to transport it to a black market butcher. The two manage to avoid a pack of hungry dogs

Gabin (left) with Bourvil in *La Traversée de Paris*, 1956. A pitiless look at French behavior under the occupation, it is one of Gabin's most controversial films (Collection du Musée Jean Gabin).

and arrest by the police, but are picked up by German sentries. Their commander, an art lover, recognizes Grandgil and lets him go, but packs Martin off to jail. At film's end, the war is over and Grandgil is taking the train on vacation. Without recognizing him, Martin, now a porter, carries his bags. When Grandgil, leaning from the train window, finally notices him, he gives the working class one final condescending dig: "Well Martin, still carrying bags, I see."

Given his lifelong identification with ordinary Frenchmen, I find this the one of the most astonishing roles in Gabin's repertory, one in which he is spectacularly cast against type and that, for once, few French would want to identify with. Henry Fonda, the perennial good guy, shooting a young boy in cold blood in Sergio Leone's *Once Upon a Time in the West*, is no more surprising than a Gabin excoriating French hypocrisy at this low point in the country's modern history. In scene after scene, he expresses contempt for the working class, the poor—"those bastards, the poor," was one of his lines that shocked audiences—dodgy tradesmen, and the cowardly, hypocritical wartime behavior of his compatriots in general.

Autant-Lara even altered the ending of Aymé's novel to underline the story's bitter tone; in the original, Martin kills Grandgil instead of meekly submitting to his contempt, symbolizing the revenge of the working class over the bourgeoisie. Despite the virulence of many lines and the noir atmosphere of a movie whose action takes place from 7 in the evening to 2 the next morning in several shadowy locales, many reviewers treated this as a comedy, noting only how broadly Gabin played his part. They failed to see how extraordinary it was for Gabin to do a film critical of France, or what an important departure from his usual characters his performance represented. In the summer of 1995, for instance, the Walter Reade Theater at New York's Lincoln Center included it in its festival entitled Classic and Contemporary French Comedies, though the only humor to be found in it is decidedly black.

In July 1957 Gabin began *Maigret Tend un Piège/Inspector Maigret* (1957, U.S. release 1958). Directed by Jean Delannoy, it was the first of his three pictures based on the famous series of thrillers by Georges Simenon featuring Inspector Jules Maigret. In this one and in the two others, *Maigret et l'Affaire Saint-Fiacre/Maigret and the Saint Fiacre Case* (1959) and *Maigret Voit Rouge* (1963, also known as *Maigret Sees Red*), Gabin indelibly imprinted his characterization on Simenon's laconic, pipe-smoking police commissioner who always makes time in the middle of a complex investigation to go home and savor Madame Maigret's cooking.

Many first-rate actors, beginning in 1933 with Harry Bauer and including Charles Laughton, Michel Simon, Albert Préjean, Michael Gambon, and more recently Bruno Cremer and Rowan Atkinson on television, would play Maigret. But none, I think, evoked French village life or the Paris of small shops, convivial cafés, nosy concierges, and the stuffy, smoke-filled atmosphere of police headquarters at 36, Quai des Orfèvres as well

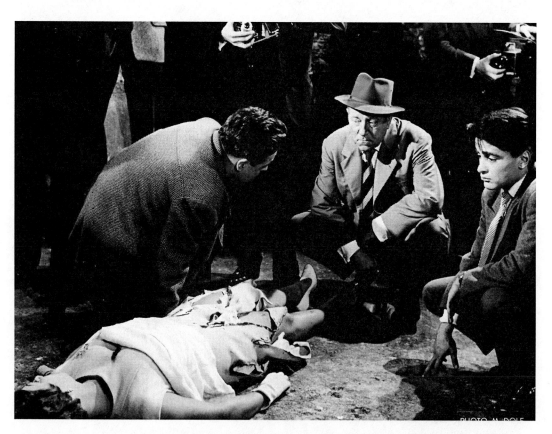

Gabin (center, facing camera) ponders a case as Jules Maigret in *Maigret Tend un Piège/Inspector Maigret*. It was the first of three films in which he memorably incarnated Georges Simenon's famous police inspector. The other actors are unidentified (Collection du Musée Jean Gabin).

as Gabin's Maigret. Simenon himself admired Jean's dense, phlegmatic embodiment of his character, once saying, "I can no longer think of Maigret except through Gabin and Delannoy. It's very annoying. I think they may ask for royalties on my next book."[13] The two became friends. Gabin acted in ten pictures in all adapted from his novels, and Simenon occasionally visited him on the set.

Roger Vadim created Brigitte Bardot in 1956 in his film *Et Dieu … Créa la Femme/…* (*And God Created Woman*), fueling the fantasies of many a young male and turning the

Gabin (right) with Georges Simenon on the set of one of his Inspector Maigret films. Simenon was a fan and friend of Gabin's, who did ten films based on his novels (Collection du Musée Jean Gabin)

homely, unhappy little girl with glasses into an international sex symbol. Initially the film was poorly received in France; it was mainly American audiences that first spawned Bardolatry. In 1957 the film's producer, Raoul Levy, conceived the profitable conceit of bringing together on the same set France's two most popular actors, the *monstres sacrés* Bardot and Gabin. The result was *En Cas de Malheur/Love Is My Profession* (1958). The screenplay was based on a Simenon crime novel in which a successful Paris lawyer jeopardizes his marriage and career by falling for a frivolous, amoral young client.

At first neither of them was enthusiastic about the project. "Gabin?" she joked when Levy mentioned it to her. "You mean that silent movie actor?"[14] In reality, as she recounts in her memoirs, Bardot was terrified at the idea of playing female lead in a film with old pros like Gabin and Edwige Feuillère, an alumna of the Comédie Française with an impressive career on both stage and screen: "It was the first time in my life that I had a part that important in a serious film, with an intransigent director and world-famous actors."[15]

Adding to her emotional state was that she had just fallen in love with the married singer Gilbert Bécaud and was dumping a longtime boyfriend. As for Jean, he was particularly leery of several scenes he considered improper for a 54-year-old man with his new family status. Always prudish, after his marriage he never liked to talk about what he called the "hot scenes" he'd done with some of the world's most beautiful women.[16] He worried that his children would see him kissing "this girl who walks around naked," adding, "Gary Cooper can get away with kissing the young girls, but I can't."[17]

Bardot played Yvette Maudet, an insouciant tart who panics while robbing a neighborhood jewelry store and commits unpremeditated assault and battery. She looks up the famous Paris lawyer André Gobillot (Gabin) and asks him to defend her even though she can't afford his usual fee. He's not interested until she hikes up her skirt in his office to indicate she'll pay in kind. He takes the case and wins it, thanks to illegal witness tampering and a false testimony, and sets Yvette up in a hotel as his mistress. The bar association starts an investigation that might end his career, his wife Viviane (Feuillère) confronts him about the affair, but, in full mid-life crisis, he doesn't care about anything but Yvette and his try for one last fling. Unfortunately her boyfriend, a fiery Italian medical student, does care, and stabs her to death. In a typically bleak Simenon ending, André views her bloody body in the student's sordid hotel room just as the police are about to carry it off into a cold gray morning, leaving him bereft.

The film is, I believe, one of Gabin's best, with its overwhelming pathos and its perceptive portrayal of an aging man suffering the pangs of passion, willing to throw everything over in a desperate attempt to regain his lost youth and start a new life. His minimalist technique shows off his massive, impassive presence at its most powerful. It has now become so subtle that one critic predicted, "Soon he will just sit in a chair, barely open his mouth, move a finger, and open his eyes, and the other actors on the screen will disappear. The miracle happens every time. He fills the screen and dwarfs them all."[18]

He sensed immediately that Bardot was having trouble in her first days on the set. Her tangled love affairs, complicated by excessive use of tranquillizers and Gilbert Bécaud's calling her every night when touring on the road to whisper sweet nothings, left her exhausted. Autant-Lara was a demanding and abrasive director; at one point he requested that a bailiff be on the set to certify that Gabin was, as he always did, altering his lines to suit his style. The two had words several times during the shoot, once nearly coming to blows. But Gabin was protective of Bardot. During her first scene she flubbed her lines

France's two *monstres sacrés*, Jean Gabin and Brigitte Bardot, in *En Cas de Malheur*, 1958. She was terrified of acting opposite him, but it turned out to be one of the best films of her career (Collection du Musée Jean Gabin).

repeatedly and Autant-Lara was ready to blow his top. During the next scene, Jean deliberately muffed his lines, turned to the director and said, "Well, that happens to all of us once in a while."[19] That defused the atmosphere and Bardot, as a fanciful, sloe-eyed beauty in love with love, went on to do a great performance.[20] Gabin later said of her, "She's the most beautiful chick I've ever seen. On the other hand, she's also the only one I've ever seen arrive on the set with pieces of astrakhan fur between her toes."[21]

Bardot now lives reclusively in Paris and Saint Tropez and avoids the media, devoting her time to the Brigitte Bardot Foundation for the protection of animals, which she created in 1986. I managed to establish contact with her and asked what it was like working with Gabin, and what she thought of him in general. Her reply, a handwritten note, was prompt, gracious, and enthusiastic. "With Jean Gabin I did one of the best films of my career," she said. "I was terribly intimidated by him at first, but he hid great kindness behind his gruff exterior, and acting opposite him was enriching—his personality was as powerful as his talent. He had a strong, difficult character, but so did I, and he was a wonderful partner. In general, he represented in many ways the typical Frenchman of the time, very earthy. For me, he remains unique, the actor with a capital 'A' who left his mark on the 20th century. He has never been replaced, and never will be."[22]

Jean Gabin's lifelong ambition of having his own farm in Normandy, where he could cultivate the land and raise cattle and horses, was threatened at 4 a.m. on July 28, 1962. In a well-organized commando-style raid, 700 farmers from the area formed up at three points around La Pichonnière, cut his telephone lines, and marched on his house. Unable to call the local gendarmes, Gabin met with them and heard their complaints: he, a wealthy actor, had bought up 370 acres, including several farms, so he could play at being a gentleman farmer. He didn't need the money, they contended, but he was keeping many young farmers from buying or renting land; that reduced many of them to the status of farm workers instead of farm owners. Gabin countered that he had started out from nothing and was only an entertainer without real financial security. He had bought the land for his three children, and that might be all he would be able to leave them. Having made their point and drawn media attention to their grievances—they wanted the government to restrict the sale of farmland to bona fide farmers—they left. They had scapegoated him to dramatize their situation and get media coverage while the National Assembly was debating an important farm reform bill.[23]

Gabin was shattered. At first he was tempted to leave France for good, feeling that he was insecure in his own home. "I thought I was a farmer, but it seems I'm not," he told *Paris-Match*. "I'm broken-hearted, I have the impression I'm in exile."[24] On second thought, he decided to counterattack, filing a formal complaint against the farmers for breaking and entering and destruction of private property. After he received thousands of letters of encouragement from all over France, he cooled off, withdrew his complaint, and went back to working the farm undisturbed.

But things would never be the same. "It was the greatest disappointment of his life," Dominique said later. "He always liked country people better than city people, and couldn't understand why they didn't accept him as one of theirs. He never got over that."[25] The psychological shock was likely responsible a year later for Gabin's announcement after becoming ill on the set of a film that he would retire from acting for health reasons. He planned, he said, to live full-time at La Pichonnière and devote himself to raising cattle and racehorses.

But he wasn't really ready for retirement and his health was good enough for him to act in another 18 films. Whatever the merits of some of them, critics and film historians generally consider most of these unworthy of him, potboilers to finance his losses at the racetrack, purchases of promising fillies, and the running costs of upkeep and maintaining a large staff at La Pichonnière. To be sure, some of his films of those years were not up to the standard he had set. But I find that many of Gabin's films of the 1960s and '70s were works of full maturity. He had been seasoned by experience and that gave him a density he had not possessed before. There is no longer the romantic self-pity about the unfairness of life and man's inevitable tragic end that forms the undercurrent of his 1930s classics. Many of these, with acting as good as anything he had done before, convey the tough-minded message that there's no happy ending, no salvation through love, no help for pain.

Several were notable for their biting social commentary on the direction society was taking, a direction that took France ever further from his personal humanistic ideals of comradeship, individual responsibility, and attachment to the traditions that made France distinct. It wasn't a question of politics, which Gabin shunned, along with its practitioners, even though he turned in a memorable performance as a Clemenceau-like head of government in *Le Président/The President* (1961). Rather, as Michel Audiard put it, he was basically a man of the left who became so disillusioned with people on the left that he adopted conservative values.

In this country where intellectualized politics is the national pastime discussed morning, noon, and night, his political ideas were simple and straightforward. Notwithstanding his film against the routine death penalty by guillotine—used until 1977—*Deux Hommes dans la Ville*, he stated publicly that criminals guilty of particularly heinous crimes should be put to death. Amid the student-sparked chaos and confusion of France's

Gabin, who personally shunned politics, as the head of government haranguing the National Assembly in *Le President*, 1961. He based his characterization on Georges Clemenceau (Collection du Musée Jean Gabin).

tumultuous year 1968, which horrified him as an attack on France's basic institutions—and, he feared, perhaps on himself and his family; he packed them up and headed to the safety of Deauville until it was over—he told an interviewer, "All that intellectuals and the so-called political elite have done is sow confusion in France. Universal suffrage is a mistake. For that matter, chicks shouldn't have the vote."[26] Statements like that meant the intelligentsia loathed him as reactionary and the average Frenchman loved him all the more. When pollsters asked in the early 1960s which celebrity they would rather resemble, 18 percent answered Charles de Gaulle, 42 percent Jean Gabin.[27]

Time and again, Gabin's second-career pictures deliberately underline the problems of aging, emphasizing rather than minimizing his own age, making an asset of it. In *Un Singe en Hiver/A Monkey in Winter* (1962), in which he and a debutant actor named Jean-Paul Belmondo spend most of their time on screen and off getting plastered, his well-meaning wife, played by Suzanne Flon, asks whether he is happier when drunk. "No," he answers, "what I'm looking for is a little crazyness, something new and unexpected." In other words, what he had when he was young. In 1963 he did *Mélodie en Sous-sol/Any Number Can Win*, a crime film with the young Alain Delon, often considered Gabin's spiritual son due to their closeness and Delon's frequent declarations that Gabin taught him everything he knew about acting. Gabin plays an old con who is the brains behind a robbery at the casino in Cannes, with Delon doing the dirty work. The film is also important as the first of several in which Gabin shows his repugnance, with shots of grim, soulless apartment buildings, at what he considered the inhuman social housing springing up around Paris.

In Le *Pacha/Pacha* (1968), with its snappy underworld dialogue by Michel Audiard and pulsating music by Serge Gainsbourg, he is one of the most authentic, compelling police commissioners in one of the best crime films he ever did. *La Horse/The Horse* (1970) has Gabin as a stubborn, shotgun-wielding family patriarch on a large farm trying to save his grandson from becoming a heroine trafficker, single-handedly taking on a drug gang. Done when he was 66 and looked ten years older, this film is the one where his lifelong attachment to the soil and categorical rejection of the permissive post–1960s values coming into vogue are most plainly on display. As Florence explained to me, "If Papa seemed out of touch with the world around him in later life, it wasn't because he had changed, but because the world had changed. As a man of the 19th-century working class, he held very strict moral values that were no longer adapted to modern society. If he were alive today, he would be completely lost."[28]

His social conscience surfaced again when he and Delon did *Deux Hommes dans la Ville* (*Two Men in Town*) (1973), a critical look at the death penalty, and *L'Affaire Dominici* (*The Dominici Affair*) (1973), based on a controversial 1950s legal case that roiled France for months. In the latter, Gabin again takes on the French justice system, playing Gaston Dominici, an elderly farmer in the South of France who, Gabin believed, was wrongly convicted of murdering an English tourist couple. Dominici was later pardoned by President Charles de Gaulle.

If the distress and torments of aging were the recurrent motif of many of Gabin's best postwar pictures, then I find that *Le Chat/The Cat* (1971, U.S. release 1975) is the high point. It is an unblinking look at the incomprehension and emotional pain of an old couple who can no longer stand to live with, or without, each other in an implacable, grudge-holding, love/hate relationship. Adapted from another Simenon novel, it shows

Gabin (left) with Alain Delon, who said he learned the actor's trade from Gabin, on the set of *Mélodie en Sous-Sol*, **1963 (Collection du Musée Jean Gabin).**

in pitiless detail the daily life of Julien and Simone Bouin, he a retired typographer, she a former circus acrobat crippled by a fall.

They live in a once-attractive suburban neighborhood, now being methodically razed amid clouds of dust by noisy earth-moving equipment, the wrecking ball metaphorically swinging closer and closer to their condemned house. Julien refuses even to acknowledge her existence as they shop at separate times, eat at separate tables, sleep in separate beds. He can't say why, but he doesn't love her any more. What affection he has left, he gives to a stray cat he finds. She kills the cat in a desperate attempt to get him to focus on her, he moves to a louche hotel, she has a fatal heart attack, he stoically commits suicide with a handful of sleeping pills when he discovers her body.

Gabin plays opposite a superb Simone Signoret, who here gives, in my opinion, her most moving performance in a work of almost unbearable poignancy. Though he and she seemed to have little in common—she was active in leftist political causes and read the appropriate newspapers on the set, he despised politics and read the racing form—they enjoyed each other's company and generated surprising synergy. The picture was one of Gabin's all-time favorites. Both he and she won the Silver Bear for best actor and actress at the Berlin International Festival. Taking on the challenge of a difficult, drear subject like this was a testimony to his creative energy in the autumn of his life.

20

Monument

Not everyone liked Jean Gabin, man and actor. He was famously hard to get along with. His obdurate, irascible character led to falling out with friends like Jean Renoir and Michel Audiard, any number of women, and his own children. Directors who worked with him on several films later turned against him.

Jean Delannoy, who directed him six times, praised him to the skies in 1959, saying what he liked about him was that he had retained something of his childhood, and as an actor he was superb at improving dialogue and finding exactly the right gesture to express emotion. But in 1967 he declared he wouldn't work with Gabin any more because, he claimed, he said all his lines the same way and had become a self-caricature.[1] Claude Autant-Lara, despite the triumph of *En Cas de Malheur*, later criticized him harshly, calling him "not an actor, only a celebrity," who treated directors like servants and was more interested in how a film served his interests than in making it a success.[2]

Although Gabin did receive Best Actor awards from the Venice and Berlin film festivals, twice each, Cannes snubbed him, a prophet without honor in his own country. No Best Actor award was ever made to him there to sycophantic applause in the Palais des Festivals, no *hommage* ever dedicated to him for lifetime achievement as the organizers often do after an actor's death. Although he was asked to open the first César Awards ceremony in 1976, the French equivalent of the Oscars, the jury never selected him for the award. To me it's clear that, given the track record of those organizers and their juries of favoring films and actors with a "progressive" slant, Gabin, with his stubbornly anti-modern, traditionalist views, was tacitly persona non grata.

No one ever heard him complain about it. He didn't seek out honors and distinctions. The stuffy *Légion d'Honneur* let it be known in 1954 that he could become a member, but, typically, he found the obligatory request stating his accomplishments demeaning and silly, and refused to send it in. He finally accepted the decoration in 1964 because they told him his refusal was holding up the award for other show business figures that the Legion put in line behind him.

His worst adversaries were *Nouvelle Vague* directors of the 1950s and '60s like François Truffaut and Jean-Luc Godard, who scorned him and the kind of films he did. The feeling was mutual. In their quest for something new and different, the New Wave deconstructed story lines and basic cinema techniques like continuity. They liked to leave actors room to improvise during a shoot, which Gabin was no good at. Everything that came before they castigated as old-fashioned *cinéma de papa*. They usually preferred young, malleable newcomers like Jean-Paul Belmondo and Jean Seberg in *Breathless* (1960).

Truffaut declared in 1959 that he systematically refused to work with stars like Gabin. "They don't hesitate to say who they want in the cast or to refuse certain partners," he complained. "They influence the direction and insist on close-ups. They are ready to sacrifice the film to what they consider their status."[3] In a word, a man who tended to be his own director, who said the key to a good movie was "a good story, a good story, and a good story" was a threat to Truffaut's *auteur* status. Besides, Gabin was the opposite of intellectual, not for him the arty pretensions of Truffaut's *Jules et Jim/Jules and Jim* (1962), or the miasmal maunderings of Alain Resnais' *L'Année Dernière à Marienbad/Last Year at Marienbad* (1961).

Some, like the veteran filmmaker Henri Verneuil, who did four films with Gabin, saw through New Wave pretensions and came to the defense of traditional screenplays and mise en scène. "During my 50 years of making films," he said in his acceptance speech at the French Academy of Fine Arts in March 2000, "I have seen the birth of a form of cinema which often sacrifices instinct and lyricism to narcissistic and cerebral satisfaction. In the absence of talent, some feel they have to be 'intelligent.'"[4]

Though he never said so publicly, Gabin was hurt by their contempt, by the fact that none of them ever asked him to act in one of his films, by the feeling that they had sidelined him as irrelevant to modern cinema. He let it be known that he was ready to help them find producers if they came to him with a decent screenplay, as he had in the past helped Renoir and Carné. None did. In a sense, he had the last word. "I know all about the *nouvelle vague*," he told his friend André Brunelin. "Before the war, it was me."[5] Today, it's his pictures that are most featured on French late-night television and in film festivals around the world. While Truffaut, Goddard, et al. are relegated to a special niche of motion picture history, he has become the undisputed monument of French cinema.

But Jean Gabin never wanted to be a monument. In fact, what he wanted was to disappear from the face of the earth.

The year 1976 got off to a good start. Sergio Leone had approached him with a part in the new film he was planning called *Once Upon a Time in America*, he was starting the shoot for his 95th movie, and he even received a backhanded tribute from the French film Establishment.

For his epic film covering a half-century of organized New York crime from the 1920s to the 1960s, Leone initially considered French actors for the second-lead character Max Bercovicz. He suggested that Gabin take the role of the elder Max, while Gérard Depardieu would be the younger. Jean was dubious about taking on the challenge of an ambitious American movie. In any case, he warned at the outset, don't count on him to make a transatlantic flight. The question became moot as Leone's project dragged on for years, finally being released in 1984, a decade after Gabin's death.[6]

Shooting of *L'Année Sainte* (1976, literally *Holy Year*) began in January. It was a forgettable gangster comedy in which Gabin played an escaped con coincidentally also named Max (and echoing the character he played in his comeback film, *Touchez Pas au Grisbi*). He teams up with a prison mate played by Jean-Claude Brialy to try to recover the considerable loot from a robbery he had stashed in a church in Rome. This being the Jubilee Year proclaimed by Pope Paul VI, they disguise themselves as a bishop (Gabin) and his young secretary making the pilgrimage among millions of other faithful. After a number of droll episodes, including the skyjacking of the plane taking them to Rome, the plan is foiled and crime doesn't pay.

The real interest of the film lies in two facts: this was Gabin's last, and continuity on the set was done by Florence, who had become a professional *script girl* a few years before. It was the only time they worked on the same film, a rare chance for father and daughter to get together during a period of strained relations. Always crazy about horses, she had taken up with a jockey playboy named Christian de Asis-Trem and was living with him in Chantilly, a liaison that Gabin viewed balefully as unworthy of her. Shortly after the shoot ended, he confided to André Brunelin that he hoped it wouldn't be his last movie, as if he had a premonition. When interviewed that spring on television, he had a hacking smoker's cough. He had just finished number 95, would he make it to 100? "You have to be realistic," he replied. "At my age they can't offer me many parts. All I can do is wait."[7]

He returned briefly to singing. He hadn't recorded any songs since his music hall days in the 1920s and '30s, many of which have been reissued and are redolent of the naïve charm of his beginnings. Now he had a text done for him by the writer Jean-Loup Dabadie, a member of the Académie Française. It was a French adaptation of *But Now I Know* by the British composer Philip Green. A moving, bittersweet reflection on the arrogance of youth and the world-weary wisdom of age, Gabin does a gravel-voiced monologue of *Maintenant Je Sais* set to background music. "Now I know, I know that you never know," it concludes. It immediately became a hit on the charts and is still part of the pop-cult baggage of most Frenchmen.

It was clear to Brunelin that Gabin's health was declining, the most obvious symptom being that he had lost his voracious appetite. As far back as the summer of 1954, after finishing *Grisbi* and while Dominique was on a trip, he had secretly checked into the American Hospital in Neuilly for three days of intensive examinations. He never mentioned it to his family, and never told anyone why he had done it or the result of the exams. But it's likely that his heavy smoking—he had smoked an average of three or four packs a day of Craven A and Gauloise cigarettes since youth, starting with his morning coffee, leaving the first two fingers of his right hand permanently stained—and intemperate eating and drinking were taking their toll. In 1973 he had experienced a more serious health episode. A week before beginning *Deux Hommes dans la Ville* with Alain Delon, he had been prostrated at La Pichonnière, unable to get out of bed or take food, barely able to speak to Dominique. The doctor who examined him could find nothing but some hypertension. After three days of that he was back on his feet and able to get on with the film, but pale and visibly having lost weight.

After he had finished *L'Année Sainte*, Gabin was approached by Georges Cravenne, a producer and promoter, who wanted to create the French equivalent of the Oscars. He was getting nowhere with the idea and needed Gabin's help. Would he be willing to serve as honorary president of the opening ceremony? Jean, who had always detested and avoided the *mondanités* of fashionable events, surprised Cravenne by accepting, considering that such an annual event could become a useful promotion for French cinema. Once Gabin's presence was assured, Cravenne easily obtained the necessary support. Jean rehearsed for the nationally-televised ceremony for four days. The evening of April 3, 1976, he took the stage in black tie at Paris' Salle Pleyel to make his opening speech before a Hollywood-style glittering audience of producers, directors, stars and starlets.

In an embarrassing replay of his first speaking role as Marshal Maurice de Saxe at the Folies Bergère in 1922, his mouth went dry in stage fright and he couldn't get a word out. (I can't explain it," he once said, "but I always have the impression that the applause is for someone else.")[8] Jean-Claude Brialy, the bubbly master of ceremonies, tried to break the ice, but it took several minutes of banter to loosen him up enough to say simply, "This evening for the first time, we will award prizes to the French cinema industry. I declare the ceremony open." The situation was saved by the appearance of a still-glamorous, 46-year-old Michéle Morgan to read the name of the winner for Best Film, *Le Vieux Fusil/The Old Gun* (1975) with Philippe Noiret and Romy Schneider.

It was the last time the two old friends and lovers, France's "ideal movie couple," would be together, and they had an emotional reunion there on the stage, exchanging meaningful glances and whispers. After embracing warmly, she opened the envelope and discovered she couldn't read it because she'd forgotten her glasses. In a bit of stage business much appreciated by the audience, he lent her his, and she awarded the César, named for the eccentric sculptor of the same name who created the quirky trophy that looks like it's made of compressed junk. Those few awkward words on stage were Jean Gabin's last appearance in public.

The little world that he had created after the war, from marriage and children to a large spread in Normandy where he raised cattle and racehorses and lived the good life of a gentleman farmer, now began to disintegrate along with his health. With his expensive stable of racehorses, La Pichonnière was costing a fortune to maintain and staff. He realized he could no longer make enough income from films to sustain it and properly support his family. Whatever was eating away at him—due to his refusal to change his living habits and to obey doctors' orders after his rare check-ups, only too late was it discovered to be leukemia—made him increasingly secretive, distrustful, and antisocial.

It wasn't only physical. The basic anxiety that had gnawed at him all his life now began to dominate his outlook, making life painful for him and impossible for those around him. It was especially hard on Dominique. "It's difficult for me to admit it," she told Brunelin, "but although I lived with Jean for 27 years, he remained an enigma to me. He underwent a slow, progressive change of character. Fortunately, that worry he had wasn't permanent. He always managed to have moments when he was relaxed, cheerful, and charming, but at the least upset he closed in on himself or exploded in anger, often for no reason. For us, he became incomprehensible."[9]

His relation with her was still solid, though periodically punctuated by her escape to a hotel for a few days when she couldn't stand any more of his highs and lows and mulish crotchets. His son Mathias, with whom he was close, had pleased him by doing his military service in the navy, and was ready to take over La

Gabin and Morgan at the Césars ceremony, 1976. It was his last public appearance (Collection du Musée Jean Gabin).

Pichonnière. But he got along with his headstrong daughters less and less. The adventurous Valérie was always off in America, or Asia, or maybe Egypt, and he feared increasingly that she would come to no good. As for Florence, she not only refused his demand that she end her relation with the playboy "gentleman rider," but that summer announced she would marry him. At that, he blew up—did a Gabin, some would say—and declared he wouldn't attend the wedding. "Subconsciously, he would have liked us not to grow up at all," Mathias later said, "or at least manage us and decide whom his daughters would marry."[10] The stubborn old man wouldn't yield. Lino Ventura, one of his few remaining close friends, stood in for him at the wedding in Deauville on August 19, 1976, and gave the bride away. "This time, you're going too far," he told Jean.[11] The marriage was the first of the two emotional shocks that rocked him during this cruel year.

The other was France's agricultural crisis provoked by the worst drought in a century. There had been little rain all winter and spring. Summer crops shriveled beneath cloudless skies and record temperatures—for normally temperate northern France—of 90-plus degrees day after day. Prodded by France's powerful agricultural union, the FNSEA, the government imposed a special drought tax to finance subsidies for stricken farmers and cattlemen. With his 300 head, Gabin could normally expect to receive a subsidy of around $2,000. But when the FNSEA president announced the subsidies with fanfare during a television interview in early October, he made a point of mentioning the gentleman farmer who had been a favorite whipping boy since his property was attacked in 1962. "Jean Gabin will receive not a cent," he replied to the interviewer's question. Mathias recalled in a documentary how the news was received at La Pichonnière: "We were watching television when the president of the FNSEA was asked how much financial relief farmers would receive due to the drought. When Papa heard he had been singled out to receive nothing, he looked over at Maman and burst into tears. He finally realized he would never be accepted as a real farmer. I'd never seen Papa cry. The next day he announced he was selling La Pichonnière."[12] His lifelong, Mériel-born dream ended that day. Men's hearts have broken for less.

A month later, Gabin lost it, wandering around the farm in a stupor. On November 9 they decided to return to their Paris apartment on rue Raymond-Poincaré. Dominique drove them back in their Mercedes, and as they approached the city he asked her to go by the Eiffel Tower for a good look. Over the next few days he weakened. They cancelled the gala dinner where he was to be promoted to the rank of officer in the Legion of Honor.

Doctors had him transported to the American Hospital at 7 p.m. on November 14. Told he was resting calmly and in no immediate danger, Dominique returned to the apartment. At 6 the next morning, a phone call from the hospital informed her that he was dead. (Today it tastelessly lists Jean Gabin among the famous who have died there, after Aristotle Onaissis and ahead of François Truffaut.) His last recorded words were "*Maman! Maman!*" Was he calling for Dominique? Or had his failing mind placed him back in the Mériel of his childhood, seeking the mother whose kisses he had missed?

Messages of condolences poured in. Jean Renoir said he had lost his brother, Lino Ventura declared he would miss his father. Alain Delon sent a wreath emblazoned "To Jean from The Kid." Georges Simenon declared he was "crushed" by the loss of one of his best friends, while President Valéry Giscard d'Estaing expressed his "deep emotion at the death of this great artist." The two women with whom he had been most passionately and painfully involved reacted in typically different ways. Her husband Rudi having died shortly before Marlene Dietrich learned of Gabin's death, she said with her usual flair for the melodramatic, "I'm a widow for the second time."[13] Michèle Morgan, more detached and coolly perceptive, later wrote in her memoirs, "He left us too early, much too early. He didn't have time to rid himself of that little sorrow that was within him, that he always lived with, the dissatisfaction, the permanent melancholy that nagged him. He never lived totally involved in life, never really felt it."[14]

Located on the eastern edge of Paris, the Père Lachaise cemetery is the resting place of French culture heroes from Molière to Marcel Proust, Sarah Bernhardt to Honoré de Balzac, not to mention Edith Piaf. It was created by Napoleon in 1804 as the world's first municipal garden cemetery, and is traditionally where France's great national funerals are held.

In the gloom of a chill, damp morning on November 17, a crowd began gathering outside its monumental gates. Their number had grown steadily, mutely, since early morning, ordinary men and women from Paris and all over France. "I loved him and I'm saddened that he is no longer with us," one lady in dark glasses told a television reporter. "I've come all the way from Villeneuve-sur-Lot, Monsieur," said a frail, elderly woman in a beret, visibly proud that she had made the 400-mile train trip from the southwestern region of Perigord. "So you can see how much he meant to me." Also among them, wearing his Fusiliers beret and campaign medals as part of the honor guard, was Raymond Thiébault, Gabin's driver on *Souffleur II*.

At 2:30 p.m. Jean Gabin's coffin, draped in ceremonial black velvet trimmed with white, arrived in a hearse and was placed on a catafalque. On it was set a cushion pinned with his official decorations—the Croix de Guerre 1939–1945, the Ordre National du Mérite, the Légion d'Honneur—tokens of recognition from the nation he loved and served in his own way. After a respectful pause, the crowd began filing slowly past it, then unexpectedly stopped. Those at the head of the line wanted to pause to reflect on the 45-year career, the 95 films that had given them such pleasure. On the man with whom, off-screen and on, they had felt a tacit kinship. On the symbol of a France that they felt was disappearing.

Those at the back, thousands, pushed forward to have their turn, creating havoc. In the Gallic shoving and jostling, tempers flared, insults were exchanged, bouquets dropped. The police, in kepis, ceremonial red fourragères, and white gloves, lost control. With difficulty they managed to wheel the coffin into the cemetery entrance. As the crowd began to drain away into the city, most didn't notice the thin stream of smoke rising from the neo-byzantine crematorium. By eerie coincidence, a Paris theater was running a three-week retrospective of 21 of his films, "*Gabin le Magnifique.*"

The funeral was broadcast live for two hours on French national television, unprecedented coverage for those days, followed that evening by commentary. "Alexis Moncorgé is dead," the 8 o'clock news began. "We knew him under the name of Jean Gabin, the tough guy with a soft heart of French cinema. What people will remember is that amazing face of a man in whom the French recognized themselves: a man of stubborn strength, peasant cunning, shy pride, and great sensitivity. The example of a certain love of life. Gabin, *quoi.*"[15]

Organizing the coverage was a challenge in those still-early days of French television, when only a few channels existed and the technical means of covering live news were basic. "It wasn't easy, because we knew very well what was going to happen," Paul Lefèvre, the anchorman who handled it, later explained to a reporter. "We had to respect the family's privacy, but we could feel an enormous, very emotional public reaction. Gabin had been nothing less than a monument for them, something like de Gaulle. He was their father, grandfather, friend, brother, lover. His death shocked France because everybody thought Jean Gabin was immortal. They refused to accept that he was dead because in a way, he was us."[16]

The mass-circulation weekly picture magazine *Paris Match* quickly put out an 18-page souvenir photo album, "The last *monstre sacré* of French cinema." Its caption beneath a full-page photo of a tousled young Gabin attempted to speak for the nation: "We loved this very average Frenchman."[17] It also published deathbed photos of him and the French adventurer, novelist, and all-purpose intellectual André Malraux, who died shortly after Gabin, calling them both "great men of our century."[18] (The family sued over that photo, and the magazine was fined $1,200 for invasion of privacy.) All of France's newspapers and magazines published special features and supplements saying more or less the same thing as the weekly newsmagazine *Le Point*: "Through his films, he had become the patriarch of our cinema, the incarnation of our history and traditions."[19]

Jean Gabin didn't ask to be cremated. But he had visited the tomb of his friend Fernandel in the Passy cemetery of Paris and heard remarks by visitors he found offensive. He told Dominique he didn't want that to happen to him after his death, people coming to see his tomb and commenting on his life and his roles. As Mathias recalled, "Papa told Maman, 'When I die, you'll throw me overboard. I want to finish in the sea. I want to be with my pals, my real friends of the navy.'"[20] The quandary the family faced was that burial at sea is against French law. The only way they could respect his last wish was cremation and then depositing his ashes in the sea.

At 9:30 on the morning of November 19, Dominique, Florence, and Mathias—Valérie was in Cairo, where she learned of her father's death only when she spotted a German newspaper with the headline "*Jean Gabin ist tot*"—plus the devoted Alain Delon, boarded the 264-foot, missile-armed French patrol boat *Détroyat* in the port of Brest. Sailing west toward the Celtic Sea, they carried with them the funeral urn, a wooden box with Jean Gabin's name graven on a bronze plaque. Military honors by the *Marine Nationale* had been authorized exceptionally by President Giscard d'Estaing in view of Gabin's wartime service in the navy. With the boat 20 nautical miles off Brest, the ship's six officers, in full dress uniform, carried the urn to the afterdeck and turned it over to the captain. While the 82-man crew presented arms, he dropped the closed urn from the stern into the sea. Florence and Mathias tossed bouquets of violets, Jean's favorite flower, after it.

"It's a way of keeping him alive," Dominique said. "He wouldn't have admitted it, but he would have been secretly flattered."[21] She was attending the grand opening of the Musée Jean Gabin on September 26, 1992. It was just down the street from the house at 61 Grande Rue in Mériel, where the young Jean Alexis watched the trains go by from his bedroom window and longed to drive one. Created at the initiative of the family and overseen by Mathias, with support from close friends like André Brunelin, it offers an extensive collection of memorabilia donated by Dominique. Financed by dues from the Friends of the Jean Gabin Museum and municipal and regional authorities, it is one of the few museums in the world dedicated to a single movie star, the other main one being the Jimmy Stewart Museum in Indiana, Pennsylvania. Outside the museum, in the middle of Place Jean Gabin, stands a six-foot stele topped with a bust of Gabin carved by his friend and fellow actor Jean Marais.

By special authorization from President Valéry Giscard d'Estaing, the French Navy renders military honors before depositing Gabin's ashes in the sea off Brest. At lower left are Mathias and Florence (Collection du Musée Jean Gabin).

Besides posters and clips of most of his films, visitors can see a folding studio chair with his name on the back, many of the hats and cloth caps he wore during his Inspector Maigret and other movies, his racetrack binoculars and racing silks, and the fetish accordion that made the trip to Hollywood and back. In the archives is a trove of letters, press clippings, and official documents like passports, his union card, and his never-used 1943 State Department authorization to re-enter the U.S., along with photos from his films and private life.

In a history-proud city where the great and good, from kings, presidents, and generals to artists and writers, have streets, boulevards, avenues and squares named for them, it took the Paris city fathers a long time to get around to it. But on May 16, 2008, the Place Jean Gabin was inaugurated in the heart of Montmartre, not far from the elementary school where he pretended to study and cheated his way to a diploma, and that today dignifies his time there with a plaque. The locals drop in for a drink at the café Le Gabin on the square and look over the stills from his movies that line the walls. In 2016 the French Mint issued silver and gold ten-euro commemorative coins with a tousled Gabin on one side, a puffing steam locomotive, much like the one he drove in *La Bête Humaine*, leaving the Gare Saint Lazare on the other. In its official notice, the mint noted that some 161 million persons had seen his films during his career.

Judging by the frequency with which his films are broadcast on television and featured in film festivals, the French still have an insatiable appetite for Gabin. They seemingly

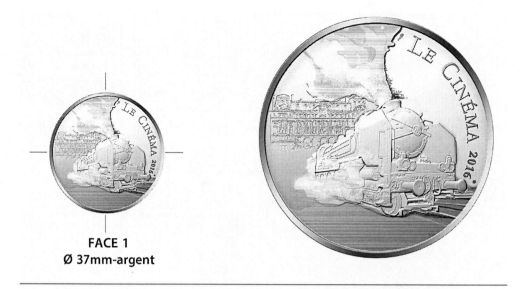

FACE 1
Ø 37mm-argent

REVERS 1
Ø 37mm-argent

The 10-euro silver coin produced by the French mint in 2016 to commemorate the 40th anniversary of his death. The locomotive leaving the Gare Saint Lazare refers to his great role in *La Bête Humaine* in 1938 (© Monnaie de Paris).

seek the France he evoked: a distinctive, special land with a peculiar pungency that existed before globalization and its handmaiden, the European Union, began systematically effacing their national characteristics. Scarcely a week goes by without a dose of prime-time Gabin on a television channel looking to improve its ratings with a sure-fire audience-builder. Any pretext is good for a major retrospective of his movies. One of the more ambitious recent ones was put on by France's national Cinémathèque in 2016, the 40th anniversary of his death. Held in the eccentric building on Paris' Quai de Bercy originally designed in 1993 by Frank Ghery to serve as the short-lived American cultural center, it ran on for ten weeks, with fully 50 Gabin films and three recondite hour-long lectures explicating various aspects of his career and his importance to French motion picture history. He was, said the program, "more than just a great popular actor, an icon whose career was exemplary, incarnating the evolution of French cinema."

During the rare droughts when no Gabin picture is scheduled in an art cinema or on television, and no film festival is offering a selection of his work, the public can fall back on the frequent 90-minute documentaries on his life. The titles of a few reveal what he means to the French public in general and Gabinophiles in particular: *Intimate Jean Gabin, Aristocrat and Peasant; Jean Gabin, A French Soul; The Hidden Face of Jean Gabin.* "There's something of Jean Gabin in all of us," François Aymé, who co-wrote the television documentary *A Frenchman Named Gabin* in 2017, told me. "He embodies the history of France and the French people during the 20th century."[22]

Our perception of France is colored and shaped by the 95-film mosaic of it this Gallic Everyman left us. For many of us who seek through the distancing lens of foreign eyes one of the best vestiges of this idiosyncratic nation caught in a time warp—a France that was, is no more, and will never be again—Jean Gabin, because of his films and because of his very authenticity, was France itself.

Filmography

Jean Gabin's films are listed in chronological order according to initial release date, with the director's name following. If it was not released in the U.S. but had a generally recognized worldwide title, I have labeled it "Also known as." In cases where there was no recognized English title, I have given my own translation in parentheses. When the title is a proper noun, no translation is necessary.

1930

Chacun sa chance (*Everybody Wins*). Directors René Pujol and Hans Steinhoff.
Méphisto. Directors Henri Debain and Nick Winter.

1931

Paris Béguin (Also known as *The Darling of Paris*). Director Augusto Génina.
Tout ça ne vaut pas l'amour (*All That's Not Worth Love.*) Director Jacques Tourneur.
Coeur de Lilas (*Lilac*). Director Anatole Litvak.
Pour un Soir (*For an Evening*). Director Jean Godard.
Coeux Joyeux (*Happy Hearts*). Directors Hans Schwartz and Max de Vaucorbeil.
Gloria (*Glory*). Directors Hans Behrendt and Yvan Noé.

1932

Les Gaîtés de l'Escadron (*The Joys of the Army*). Director Maurice Tourneur.
La Belle Marinière (*The Beautiful Sailor Shirt*). Director Harry Lachmann.
La Foule Hurle/The Crowd Roars. Directors Howard Hawks and Jean Daumery.

1933

L'Étoile de Valencia/The Star of Valencia. Director Serge de Poligny.
Adieu les Beaux Jours/Happy Days in Aranjuez. Directors Johannes Meyer and André Beucler.
Le Tunnel (*The Tunnel*). Director Kurt Bernhardt.
Du Haut en Bas (Also known as *High and Low*). Director G. W. Pabst.

1934

Zouzou/Zou Zou. Director Marc Allégret.
Maria Chapdelaine. Director Julien Duvivier.

1935

Golgotha/Behold the Man. Director Julien Duvivier.
Variétés (*Variety Show*). Director Nicolas Farkas.
La Bandéra/Escape from Yesterday. Director Julien Duvivier.

1936

La Belle Équipe/They Were Five. Director Julien Duvivier.
Les Bas-Fonds/The Lower Depths. Director Jean Renoir.
Pépé le Moko. Director Julien Duvivier.

1937

La Grande Illusion/Grand Illusion. Director Jean Renoir.
Le Messager (Also known as *The Messenger)*. Director Raymond Rouleau.
Gueule d'Amour (Also known as *Lady Killer*). Director Jean Grémillon.

1938

Le Quai des Brumes/Port of Shadows. Director Marcel Carné.
La Bête Humaine/The Human Beast. Director Jean Renoir.

1939

Le Récif de Corail (Also known as *Coral Reefs*). Director Maurice Gleize.
Le Jour se Lève/Daybreak. Director Marcel Carné.

1941

Remorques/Stormy Waters. Director Jean Grémillon.

1942

Moontide/La Péniche de l'Amour. Director Archie Mayo.

1944

The Impostor/L'Imposteur. Director Julien Duvivier.

1946

Martin Roumagnac/The Room Upstairs. Director Georges Lacombe.

1947

Miroir (*Mirror*). Director Raymond Lamy.

1948

Au-Delà des Grilles/The Walls of Malapaga. Director René Clément.

1950

La Marie du Port/Marie of the Port. Director Marcel Carné.
Pour l'Amour du Ciel (*For the Love of Heaven*). Director Luigi Zampa.

1951

Victor. Director Claude Heymann.
La Nui est Mon Royaume/The Night is My Kingdom. Director Georges Lacombe.
La Vérité sur Bébé Donge/The Truth about Bébé Donge. Director Henri Decoin.

1952

Le Plaisir (Pleasure). Director Max Ophüls.
La Minute de Vérité/The Moment of Truth. Director Jean Delannoy.
Fille Dangereuse/Bufere (*Dangerous Girl*). Director Guido Brignone.

1953

Leur Dernière Nuit/Their Last Night. Director Georges Lacombe.
La Vierge du Rhin (*Rhine Virgin*). Director Gilles Grangier.

1954

Touchez pas au Grisbi/Grisbi. Director Jacques Becker.
L'Air de Paris (*The Air of Paris*). Director Marcel Carné.
Napoléon. Director Sacha Guitry.
Le Port du Désir/House on the Waterfront. Director Edmond T. Gréville.

1955

French Cancan/French Cancan. Director Jean Renoir.
Razzia sur la Chnouf/Razzia. Director Henri Decoin.
Chiens Perdus sans Collier (Also known as *The Little Rebels*). Director Jean Delannoy.
Gas-Oil (Also known as *Hijack Highway*). Director Gilles Grangier.

1956

Des Gens sans Importance (Also known as *People of No Importance*). Director Henri Verneuil.
Voici le Temps des Assassins/Deadlier than the Male. Director Julien Duvivier.
Le Sang à la Tête (*Also known as Blood to the Head*). Director Gilles Grangier.
La Traversée de Paris/Four Bags Full. Director Claude Autant-Lara.
Crime et Châtiment/Crime and Punishment. Director Georges Lampin.

1957

Le Cas du Docteur Laurent/The Case of Doctor Laurent. Director Jean-Paul Le Chanois.
Le Rouge est Mis (Also known as *Speaking of Murder*). Director Gilles Grangier.
Les Miserables/Les Miserables. Director Jean-Paul Le Chanois.
Maigret Tend un Piège/Inspector Maigret. Director Jean Delannoy.

1958

La Désordre et la Nuit/The Night Affair. Director Gilles Grangier.
En Cas de Malheur/Love is My Profession. Director Claude Autant-Lara.
Les Grandes Familles/The Possessors. Director Denys de la Patellière.

1959

Archiméde le Clochard/The Magnificent Tramp. Director Gilles Grangier.
Maigret et l'Affaire Saint-Fiacre/Maigret and the Saint Fiacre Case. Director Jean Delannoy.
Rue des Prairies/Rue de Paris. Director Denys de la Patellière.

1960

Le Baron de l'Écluse (Also known as *The Baron of the Locks*). Director Jean Delannoy.
Les Vieux de la Vielle (Also known as *The Old Guard*). Director Gilles Grangier.

1961

Le Président (Also known as *The President*). Director Henri Verneuil.

Le Cave se Rebiffe/The Counterfeiters of Paris. Director Gilles Grangier.

1962

Un Singe en Hiver/A Monkey in Winter. Director Henri Verneuil.
Le Gentleman d'Epsom/The Gentleman from Epsom. Director Gilles Grangier.

1963

Mélodie en Sous-Sol/Any Number Can Win. Director Henri Verneuil.
Maigret Voit Rouge (Also known as *Maigret Sees Red*). Director Gilles Grangier.

1964

Monsieur (Also known as *Monsieur*). Director Jean-Paul Le Chanois.
L'Age Ingrat (*The Awkward Age*.) Director Gilles Grangier.

1965

Le Tonnerre de Dieu (Also known as *God's Thunder*). Director Denys de la Patellière.

1966

Du Rififi à Paname/The Upper Hand. Director Denys de la Patellière.
Le Jardinier d'Argenteuil (*The Gardner of Argenteuil*). Director Jean-Paul Le Chanois.

1967

Le Soleil des Voyous/Action Man. Director Jean Delannoy.

1968

Le Pacha (Also known as *Pacha*). Director Georges Lautner.

Le Tatoué/The Tatoo. Director Denys de la Patellière.

1969

Sous le Signe du Taureau (Also known as *Under the Sign of the Bull*). Director Gilles Grangier.
Le Clan des Siciliens/The Sicilian Clan. Director Henri Verneuil.

1970

La Horse (Also known as *The Horse*). Director Pierre Granier-Deferre.

1971

Le Chat/The Cat. Director Pierre Granier-Deferre.
Le Drapeau Noir Flotte sur La Marmite (Also known as *The Black Flag Flies over The Scow*). Director Michel Audiard.

1972

Le Tueur (Also known as *Killer*). Director Denys de la Patellière.

1973

L'Affaire Dominici (Also known as *The Dominici Affair*). Director Claude Bernard-Aubert.
Deux Hommes dans la Ville/Two Men in Town. Director José Giovanni.

1974

Verdict/The Verdict. Director André Cayatte.

1976

L'Année Sainte (*Holy Year*). Director Jean Giraud.

Chapter Notes

André Brunelin, a French screenwriter and film critic who died in 2005, was a close friend and colleague of Jean Gabin for some 30 years. He was privy to his reminiscences as was no other French source. Gabin's children consider his biography of their father, titled simply *Gabin* and published in 1987, to be the most accurate, reliable, and objective document concerning his life. It is the inevitable starting point, especially about his early years, for any effort to understand him.

Introduction

1. John L. Hess, "Jean Gabin, 72, French Film Star Who Played Hero-Victim, Is Dead," *The New York Times*, November 16, 1976.
2. Edward Baron Turk, *Child of Paradise: Marcel Carné and the Golden Age of French Cinema* (Cambridge: Harvard University Press, 1989), 120.
3. Nicholas MacDonald, *In Search of La Grande Illusion: A Critical Appreciation of Jean Renoir's Elusive Masterpiece* (Jefferson, NC: McFarland, 2014), 1.
4. Alain Paucard, interview with the author, Paris, April 18, 2016.
5. Konstantinos Costa-Gavras interview in "Jean Gabin, une âme Française," December 25, 2015, 52 min. 3 sec., Cinétévé, Institut national de l'audiovisuel. http://www.ina.fr/video/CPD15007941/jean-gabin-une-ame-francaise-video.html, retrieved March 3, 2016.
6. Colin Crisp, *Classic French Cinema, 1930–1960* (Bloomington: Indiana University Press, 1993), 273.
7. André Bazin, *What Is Cinema?* (Berkeley: University of California Press, 1971), Vol. 2, 177.
8. Claude Gauteur and Ginette Vincendeau, *Jean Gabin: Anatomie d'un mythe* (Paris: Nouveau Monde Editions, 2006), 79.
9. Bosley Crowther, "Moontide" (review), *The New York Times*, May 2, 1942.
10. David Kehr, "France's Sad-eyed Cagney," *The New York Times*, June 23, 2002.
11. "Jean Gabin: Everybody's Star" (program), The Film Society of Lincoln Center, June 27, 2002.
12. Colleen Kennedy-Karpat, *Rogues, Romance, and Exoticism in French Cinema of the 1930s* (Madison, NJ: Fairleigh Dickinson University Press, 2013), 18.
13. Gauteur and Vincendeau, *Anatomie*, 50.
14. *Ibid.*, 29.
15. Steven Bach, *Marlene Dietrich, Life and Legend* (London: HarperCollins, 1992), 318.

Chapter 1

1. André Brunelin, *Gabin* (Paris: Robert Laffont, 1987), 32.
2. Charles Braibant, *Histoire de la Tour Eiffel* (Paris: Librairie Plon, 1964), 18.
3. Joseph Harriss, *The Tallest Tower: Eiffel and the Belle Epoque* (Boston: Houghton Mifflin, 1975), 7.
4. Jacques Rougerie, *Paris insurgé: La Commune de 1871* (Paris: Gallimard, 2012), 264–270.
5. Brunelin, *Gabin*, 31.
6. William Shirer, *The Collapse of the Third Republic: An Enquiry into the Fall of France in 1940* (New York: Simon & Schuster, 1969), 35.
7. Jean Gabin, "Quand Je Revois Ma Vie," *Pour Vous*, September 5, 1935, et seq.
8. Brunelin, *Gabin*, 46.

Chapter 2

1. Brunelin, *Gabin*, 57.
2. Jean Gabin, "Quand Je Revois Ma Vie," *Pour Vous*, September 5, 1935, et seq.
3. Brunelin, *Gabin*, 47.
4. Leon Surmelian, "The Love Dilemma of Jean Gabin," *Photoplay*, July 1942, 66 et seq.
5. Brunelin, *Gabin*, 56.
6. Jean Gabin, *Confidences*, unpublished, undated document in archives of the Musée Jean Gabin, Mériel.
7. Brunelin, *Gabin*, 72.
8. *Ibid.*, 75.
9. *Ibid.*, 76.
10. *Ibid.*, 81–82.
11. *Ibid.*, 82.
12. *Ibid.*, 89.

Chapter 3

1. Brunelin, *Gabin*, 99.
2. Charles Castle, *The Folies Bergere* (London: Methuen, 1984), 16.
3. *Ibid.*, 25.
4. *Ibid.*, 38.
5. Jacques Damase, *Les Folies du Music-Hall: A History of the Paris Music-Hall from 1914 to the Present Day* (London: Anthony Blond, 1962) 6.
6. Castle, *The Folies Bergere*, 134.
7. *Ibid.*, 136.
8. *Ibid.*, 142.
9. Brunelin, Gabin, 100.
10. *Ibid.*, 105.
11. Philppe Huet and Marie-France Coquart, *Mistinguett: La Reine des Années Folles* (Paris: Albin Michel, 1996), 223.
12. Brunelin, *Gabin*, 109.
13. Jeanne Karr, "First Love," *Modern Screen* 24, no. 3 (February 1942): 32 et seq.
14. Brunelin, *Gabin*, 110–111.
15. *Ibid.*, 111.
16. Louis Paraz, writer, "Gabin Intime: Aristocrate et Paysan," documentary DVD produced by Ciné-Développement/SND, Paris, 2006.

Chapter 4

1. Brunelin, *Gabin*, 113.
2. *Ibid.*, 115.
3. *Paris Match* 1435 (November 26, 1976). "Jean Gabin: L'Album Souvenir du Dernier Monstre Sacré de Notre Cinéma," 56; Brunelin, *Gabin*, 118.
4. Brunelin, *Gabin*, 117.
5. *Trois Jeunes Filles ... Nues!* (theater program), Théatre des Bouffes-Parisiens, Les Publications Willy Fischer, 1925–26.
6. Brunelin, *Gabin*, 120–121.
7. CGT union card no. 4,185 in the archives of Le Musée Jean Gabin, Mériel.
8. Marcel Dalio, *Mes Années Folles* (Paris: J.-C. Lattès, 1976), 49.
9. Huet and Coquart, *Mistinguett*, 216.
10. Bruno Fuligni, *Dans les archives inédites des services secrets: Un siècle d'histoire et d'espionnage français (1870–1989)* (Paris: Folio, 2014). See chapter "Mistinguett, un cœur au service de la france."
11. Huet and Coquart, *Mistinguett*, 220.
12. Jacques Pessis and Jacques Crépineau, *Le Moulin Rouge* (Paris: Hermé, 1989). 12.
13. David Price, *Cancan!* (Madison, NJ: Farleigh Dickinson University Press, 1998), 2–3.
14. *Ibid.*, 14.
15. Pessis and Crépineau, *Le Moulin Rouge*, 117 et seq.
16. Damase, *Les Folies du Music-Hall*, 26.
17. Huet and Coquart, *Mistinguett*, 218.
18. Brunelin, *Gabin*, 130.
19. *Ibid.*, 131
20. Huet and Coquart, *Mistinguett*, 224.
21. Brunelin, *Gabin*, 132–133.

Chapter 5

1. Brunelin, *Gabin*, 135.
2. Jean-Jacques Jelot-Blanc, *Jean Gabin Inconnu* (Paris: Flammarion, 2014), 28; *Paris Match* 1435 (November 26, 1976), 56.
3. Brunelin, *Gabin*, 137.
4. Florence Moncorgé-Gabin, *Quitte à avoir un père, autant qu'il s'appelle Gabin* (Paris: Le Cherche-Midi, 2003), 38.
5. Brunelin, *Gabin*, 142–143.
6. *Ibid.*, 139.
7. Jelot-Blanc, *Jean Gabin Inconnu*, 31.
8. Brunelin, *Gabin*, 147.
9. Patrick Glâtre and Sylvain Palfroy, "Jean Gabin, Une Âme Française" DVD produced by Cinétévé, Paris, 2015.
10. Brunelin, *Gabin*, 149.
11. *Ibid.*, 150–152.
12. *Ibid.*, 156.
13. *Ibid.*

Chapter 6

1. Colin Crisp, *Classic French Cinema, 1930–1960* (Bloomington: Indiana University Press, 1993), 171.
2. Charles Zigman, *World's Coolest Movie Star: The Complete 95 Films (and Legend) of Jean Gabin* (Los Angeles: Allenwood Press, 2008), Vol. 1, xlix.
3. Alan Williams, *Republic of Images: A History of French Filmmaking* (Cambridge: Harvard University Press, 1992), 184.
4. Paraz, writer, "Gabin Intime," documentary DVD.
5. Jeffrey Meyers, *Gary Cooper, American Hero* (New York: William Morrow, 1998), 130.
6. Pierre Tchernia interview with Gabin, February 22, 1970, 8 min. 43 sec. http://www.ina.fr/video/I00010319, retrieved March 19, 2016.
7. Jelot-Blanc, *Jean Gabin Inconnu*, 41.
8. Marc Lemonnier, *Jean Gabin dans le Siècle* (Paris: City Editions, 2006), 35.
9. Brunelin, *Gabin*, 161–162.
10. *Paris Match* 2262 (October 1, 1992). Interview with Dominique Gabin, 35 et seq.
11. Toby Cole and Helen Krich Chinoy, eds., *Actors on Acting* (New York: Crown, 1970), 24.
12. Jean Renoir, *Ma vie et mes films* (Editions Flammarion, 1974, Edition corrigée, 2005), 118.
13. Jean-Marie Coldefly, producer, "Michèle Morgan: Anecdote dans la scène du baiser de *Quai des brumes*," June 9, 1956, 2 min. 22 sec, Cinétévé, Institut national de l'audiovisuel. http://www.ina.fr/video/I06248804/michele-morgan-anecdote-dans-la-scene-du-baiser-de-quai-des-brumes-video.html, retrieved February 1, 2017.
14. James Curtis, *Spencer Tracy* (New York: Alfred A. Knopf, 2011), 795.
15. Brunelin, *Gabin*, 156–157.
16. Turk, *Paradise*, 120.
17. Didier Goux in interview with the author, Paris, August 21, 2016.
18. Françoise Arnoul, interview with the author, Paris, September 22, 2016.
19. Marcel Carné, *La Vie à Belles Dents* (Paris: Editions Jean-Pierre Ollivier, 1975), 94.
20. Brunelin, *Gabin*, 168–169.
21. Louis Paraz, writer, "Gabin Intime: Aristocrate et Paysan," documentary DVD produced by Ciné-Développement/SND, Paris, 2006.
22. Jean-Claude Baker and Chris Chase, *Josephine: The Hungry Heart* (New York: Random House, 1993) 183.

23. Josephine Baker and Jo Bouillon, *Josephine* (London: W. H. Allen, 1978), 94.

24. *Ibid.*, 75.

Chapter 7

1. Voltaire (François-Marie Arouet) in *Candide.*

2. Yves Desrichard, *Julien Duvivier: Cinquante ans de noirs destins* (Paris: BiFi/Durante, 2001) 37.

3. Julien Duvivier Retrospective (program notes), Museum of Modern Art, New York, May 1–28, 2009, organized by Joshua Siegel, associate curator, Department of Film, and Lenny Borger, film historian.

4. Jean Tulard, *Dictionnaire du cinéma—Les réalisateurs* (Éditions Bouquins, 2002), 283.

5. Brunelin, *Gabin*, 173.

6. Maurice Tillier, *Le Figaro Littéraire*, June 11, 1964.

7. Jean Gabin, "Quand je revois ma vie," *Pour Vous* 359 (October 3, 1935).

8. Marcel Carné, *La Vie à Belles Dents* (Paris: Editions Jean-Pierre Ollivier, 1975), 96.

9. Alastair Phillips, and Ginette Vincendeau, eds., *Journeys of Desire: European Actors in Hollywood* (London: British Film Institute, 2006) 162.

10. Jean Gabin discusses the filming of *Varietés* in his article "Quand je revois ma vie."

11. Yves Desrichard, *Julien Duvivier*, 14.

12. Paraz, writer, "Gabin Intime," documentary DVD, 2006; Brunelin, *Gabin*, 176.

13. Gabin, "Quand je revois ma vie."

14. "Moi, Ponce Pilate," *Paris-Soir*, October 6, 1934.

15. *Ibid.*

16. Desrichard, *Julien Duvivier*, 38–39.

17. Gauteur and Vincendeau, *Anatomie*, 141.

18. Pierre Mac Orlan, "Autour de la Bandéra," *Pour Vous*, July 11, 1935, 3 et seq.

19. Odile Cambier, *Cinémonde*, September 19, 1935.

20. John Martin, *The Golden Age of French Cinema 1929–1939* (Boston: Twayne, 1983) 56.

21. Pierre Mac Orlan, "Autour de la Bandéra."

22. David Slavitt, "Jean Gabin: A Screen Image," *The Hopkins Review* 1, no. 2 (Spring 2008, New Series): 275–293.

23. Gabin, "Quand je revois ma vie."

24. Brunelin, *Gabin*, 205.

25. Gabin, *Confidences*, unpublished, undated document in archives of the Musée Jean Gabin, Mériel.

26. Colleen Kennedy-Karpat, *Rogues, Romance, and Exoticism*, 16; Helmut Gruber, "Jean Gabin: Doomed Worker-Hero of a Doomed France," *International Labor and Working-Class History* 59 (April 1, 2001): 15–35.

27. Gruber, *Doomed Worker*, 15–35; Turk, *Child of Paradise*, 112.

28. Kennedy-Karpat, *Rogues, Romance, and Exoticism*, 18.

29. *The New York Times*, November 16, 1976.

30. Jean Fayard, "On demande *un cinéma virile*," *Pour Vous*, July 11, 1935.

31. Turk, *Child of Paradise*, 112, 120.

32. Jean Fayard, *Candide*, September 26, 1935.

33. Alexandre Arnoux, *Les Nouvelles Littéraires*, September 28, 1935.

34. André Bazin, *What Is Cinema?* 177.

35. Gabin, "Quand je revois ma vie."

36. *Cinémonde*, December 1, 1937.

37. Brunelin, 186–187.

38. Crisp, *Classic French Cinema*, 361.

39. Gabin, "Quand je revois ma vie."

Chapter 8

1. Crisp, *Classic French Cinema*, 213.

2. *Ame Française* documentary.

3. Macdonald, *In Search of La Grande Illusion*, 8.

4. Gabin interview in *Pour Vous*, October 11, 1935.

5. http://www.sainte-gemme-moronval.fr/decouvrir.php?men=1&rub=2, retrieved February 6, 2018.

6. Statement filed in June 1946 requesting compensation for wartime damage to his house and furnishings. Archives of Musée Jean Gabin, Mériel.

7. Alan Riding, *And the Show Went On: Cultural Life in Nazi-Occupied Paris* (New York: Alfred A. Knopf, 2010), 3–4, 14.

8. Eugen Weber, *The Hollow Years: France in the 1930s* (New York: W.W. Norton, 1994), 9.

9. *Ibid.*, 8, 7.

10. Riding, *Show*, 14.

11. Weber, *Hollow Years*, 247.

12. *Ibid.*, 142.

13. *Ibid.*, 19.

14. Riding, *Show*, 11.

15. Weber, *Hollow Years*, 240.

16. Riding, *Show*, 11.

17. Weber, *Hollow Years*, 33–49.

18. James Vernon. *Hunger: A Modern History* (Cambridge: The Belknap Press, 2007), 56, 296.

19. Julian Jackson, *The Popular Front in France: Defending Democracy 1934–1938* (Cambridge: Cambridge University Press, 1990) 1.

20. Jackson, *Popular Front*, 176.

21. *Ibid.*

22. Weber, *Hollow Years*, 157.

23. Jackson, *Popular Front*, 13; Riding, *Show*, 19.

24. Martin, *Golden Age*, 112.

25. *Ibid.*, Foreword; Turk, *Paradise*, 1–2.

26. Brunelin, *Gabin*, 193–195.

27. David Kehr, *The New York Times*, June 23, 2002.

28. Desrichard, *Julien Duvivier*, 42.

29. Brunelin, *Gabin*, 195.

30. Leo Braudy, *Jean Renoir: The World of His Films* (New York: Doubleday & Co., 1972) 204; Alexander Sesonske, *Jean Renoir: The French Films, 1924–1939* (Cambridge: Harvard University Press, 1980), 258.

31. Sesonske, 258.

32. Brunelin, *Gabin*, 199.

33. Jean Renoir interview with Michel Gorel, *Cinémonde*, October 15, 1936.

34. Brunelin, *Gabin*, 199.

35. Brunelin interview with Charles Spaak in *Gabin*, 198; Patrick Glâtre and Olivier Millot, *Jean Gabin: La traversée d'un siècle* (Paris: Creaphis, 2004), 16.

36. Braudy, *Renoir*, 205.

Chapter 9

1. Dudley Andrew, *Mists of Regret: Culture and Sensibility in Classic French Film* (Princeton: Princeton University Press, 1995), 6.

2. Bazin, *What Is Cinema?* 177.

3. Turk, *Paradise*, 174.

4. Slavitt, *A Screen Image*, 284.

5. Gauteur and Vincendeau, *Anatomie*, 32.

6. Andrew, *Mists*, 225.

7. See Amanda J. Field, "Impeccably Dressed: How Costume in Pépé-le-Moko Constructs Jean Gabin as Object of the Erotic Gaze," *Short Takes Film Studies* (Luton: Andrews UK, 2015).

8. Brunelin, *Gabin*, 208.

9. Denis Marion, *La Nouvelle Revue Française*, April 1937.

10. Jean-Claude Missiaen cited in Brunelin, *Gabin*, 204.

11. Pauline Kael, *5001 Nights at the Movies* (New York: Holt, Rinehart and Winston, 1982), 454.

12. Kenneth Turan, "'Pépé le Moko' Prowls the Casbah Again," *The Los Angeles Times*, April 19, 2002.

13. Slavitt, *A Screen Image*, 284.

14. Ruth Barton, *Hedy Lamarr: The Most Beautiful Woman in Film* (Lexington: University Press of Kentucky [Screen Classics Series], 2010) 70.

15. Stephen Michael Shearer and Robert Osborn, *Beautiful: The Life of Hedy Lamarr* (New York: Saint Martin's Griffin, 2013), Kindle edition.

16. Bosley Crowther, *The New York Times*, November 16, 1976.

17. Renoir, *Ma Vie*, 128.

18. Sesonske, *Renoir*, 287.

19. Nicholas Macdonald, *In Search of La Grande Illusion*, 1.

20. Janet Maslin, *The New York Times*, August 6, 1999.

21. Jean Renoir, "M. Renoir Speaks of War," *The New York Times*, October 23, 1938.

22. Ronald Bergan, *Jean Renoir: Projections of Paradise* (London: Bloomsbury, 1992), 178.

23. Sesonske, *Renoir*, 282.

24. Macdonald, *Grande Illusion*, 1.

25. Georges Simenon, *Mes Dictées: Au Delà de Ma Porte-Fenêtre* (Paris: Presses de la Cité, 1979), 17.

26. Kael, *5001 Nights*, 227.

27. Renoir, *Ma Vie*, 145; Arthur Lennig, *Stroheim* (Lexington: University Press of Kentucky, 2000), 365–370.

28. Brunelin, *Gabin*, 219.

29. *Ibid.*, 225.

Chapter 10

1. Carné, *La Vie*, 100.

2. Turk, *Paradise*, 97.

3. Carné, *La Vie*, 96–98.

4. Glâtre and Millot, *Gabin*, 18.

5. Riding, *Show*, 35.

6. Brunelin, *Gabin*, 233.

7. Michele Morgan, *Avec ces yeux-là* (Paris: Robert Laffont, 1977), 108–110; Turk, *Paradise*, 124.

8. Morgan, *Avec ces yeux-là*, 108; Jean-Marie Coldefly, producer, "Michèle Morgan: Anecdote dans la scène du baiser de *Quai des brumes*," June 9, 1956, 2 min. 22 sec. Cinétévé, Institut national de l'audiovisuel. http://www.ina.fr/video/I06248804/michele-morgan-anecdote-dans-la-scene-du-baiser-de-quai-des-brumes-video.html.

9. Morgan, *Yeux*, 94; Brunelin, *Gabin*, 236–237.

10. *Ibid.*, 102.

11. *Ibid.*, 104.

12. Anita Gates, "Michèle Morgan, the First 'Best Actress' at Cannes, Dies at 96," *The New York Times*, December 23, 2016.

13. Brunelin, *Gabin*, 243.

14. Turk, *Paradise*, 114.

15. Carné, *La Vie*, 117.

16. Turk, *Paradise*, 114; Brunelin, *Gabin*, 249.

17. *Ibid.*, 122.

18. "Jean Gabin: Everybody's Star" (program), The Film Society of Lincoln Center, June 27, 2002.

19. Kael, *5001 Nights*, 466.

20. Undated French newspaper profile entitled "Mme Jean Gabin" in archives of Musée Jean Gabin. Reference no. 305016GAB "Vie Privée."

21. "Hard-Boiled Egg, French Style," *The New York Times*, May 22, 1938; *Pour Vous*, September 29, 1937.

22. *Pour Vous*, September 29, 1937.

23. *Ibid.*

24. Sesonske, *Renoir*, 355.

25. Jean Gabin. *Confidences*, unpublished, undated document in archives of the Musée Jean Gabin, Mériel.

26. *Cinémonde*, December 7, 1938.

27. Interview with the author, June 15, 2016.

28. Renoir, *Ma Vie*, 124.

29. *Ibid.*

30. *Ibid.*, 125.

31. *Journal de la Société des Amis du Musée Jean Gabin* (May 1994): 7.

32. Glâtre and Millot, *Gabin*, 18.

33. *Variety*, December 31, 1938.

34. Frank S. Nugent, *The New York Times*, February 20, 1940.

35. Dudley Andrew, *Mists*, 304.

36. Bosley Crowther, *The New York Times*, August 7, 1954.

37. Crisp, *Classic French Cinema*, 365.

38. *Ibid.*, 274.

39. Kael, *5001 Nights*, 293.

40. Carné, *La Vie*, 143.

41. *Ibid.*, 148.

42. Brunelin, *Gabin*, 262; Jeanne Witta (who did continuity for *Le Jour se Lève*), *Ciné-Club*, April 1954.

43. Bazin, *What Is Cinema?* 177.

44. Brunelin, Gabin, 262.

45. Martin, *Golden Age*, 127; Gauteur interview with the author, March 23, 2016.

46. Turk, *Paradise*, 159–160.

Chapter 11

1. Turk, *Paradise*, 175.

2. Lemonnier, *Gabin dans le Siècle*, 50.

3. Carné, *La Vie*, 152.

4. Dominique Maillet, "Dernier sursaut du Front Populaire," supplement to DVD of *Le Jour Se Lève*.

5. Kenneth Turan, *The Los Angeles Times*, November 13, 2014.

6. *The Daily Telegraph*, January 6, 2011; *Variety*, September 2008.

7. Turk, *Paradise*, 175.

8. *Ibid.*.

9. Curtis, *Spencer Tracy*, 372–373; *Pour Vous*, May 1939.

10. Weber, *Hollow Years*, 260.

11. Riding, *Show*, 26.

12. *Ibid.*, 39–40.

13. *Ibid.*, 27.

14. *Ibid.*, 34; Harriss, *Tallest Tower*, 182.

15. Brunelin, *Gabin*, 238.

16. Morgan, *Yeux*, 116.

17. *Ibid.*, 117.

18. *Ibid.*, 125–126.

19. *Ibid.*, 127–129.

20. *Ibid.*

21. *Ibid.*

22. *Ibid.*, 130.
23. *Ibid.*, 133.
24. *Ibid.*, 135.
25. *Ibid.*, 136.
26. "Quel est ce matelot?" *France Magazine* 30 (October 24, 1939).
27. Patrick Glâtre, *Gabin-Dietrich: Un Couple dans la Guerre* (Paris: Robert Laffont, 2016), 27.
28. Morgan, *Yeux*, 141.
29. Brunelin, *Gabin*, 273.
30. Riding, *Show*, 39.
31. *Ibid.*, 38.
32. Weber, *Hollow Years*, 5.

Chapter 12

1. Riding, *Show*, 44–45.
2. Morgan, *Yeux*, 142.
3. Glâtre, *Gabin-Dietrich*, 29–31. Brunelin, *Gabin*, 274–278; Paraz, *Gabin Intime* documentary.
4. Riding, *Show*, 50–51.
5. *Ibid.*
6. Williams, *Republic of Images*, 256.
7. Riding, *Show*, 64.
8. *Ibid.*, 65.
9. *Ibid.*, 191.
10. *Ibid.*
11. *Ibid.*, 334.
12. *Ibid.*, 58.
13. *Ibid.*
14. Morgan, *Yeux*, 146.
15. *Ibid.*, 149–150.
16. Wilbur Morse, Jr., "Escape from the Nazis" *Photoplay*, July 1941, 36; Patrick Glâtre, *Jean Moncorgé Gabin Acteur de la Liberation de Royan* (Vaux-sur-Mer: Editions Bonne-Anse, 2015), 16.
17. Morgan, *Yeux*, 150; Brunelin, *Gabin*, 285.
18. Brunelin, *Gabin*, 286.
19. *Ibid.*, 288.
20. *The New York Herald-Tribune*, March 26, 1944.
21. Wilbur Morse, Jr., *Photoplay*, July 1941, 36.
22. Robert Chaza, French television interview with Jean Gabin about his career, 8 min. 54 sec. December 6, 1970. Institut National de l'Audiovisual. https://www.ina.fr/video/I00010383/jean-gabin-a-propos-de-sa-carriere-d-acteur-video.html, retrieved February 8, 2017.
23. Morse, *Photoplay*, 36.
24. *Ibid.*
25. Thomas M. Pryor, "By Way of Report," *The New York Times*, March 6, 1941.

Chapter 13

1. Brunelin, *Gabin*, 293–294.
2. Phillips and Vincendeau, *Journeys*, 85.
3. John Baxter, *The Hollywood Exiles* (London: MacDonald and Jane's, 1976), 231.
4. Phillips and Vincendeau, *Journeys*, 86.
5. Glâtre, *Gabin-Dietrich*, 135; Brunelin, *Gabin*, 295.
6. Baxter, *Exiles*, 128.
7. Maria Riva, *Marlene Dietrich* (New York: Alfred A. Knopf, 1993), 509.
8. Marcel Dalio, *Mes Années Folles* (Paris: J.-C. Lattès, 1976), 187.
9. *Ibid.*, 187–188.
10. Drake Hunt, "Imported Idol," *Hollywood* 31, no.

1 (January 1942): 18; Harry Brand, director of Publicity, 20th Century–Fox, "Vital Statistics on Moon Tide [sic]," undated; Maude Cheatham, "Gabin Looks at the Girls!" *Screenland* (May 1942): 50.
11. Morgan, *Yeux*, 184.
12. Glâtre, *Gabin-Dietrich*, 304.
13. Maude Cheatham, "Gabin Looks at the Girls!" *Screenland* (May 1942): 50.
14. Bosley Crother, "Moontide" (review), *The New York Times*, May 3, 1942.
15. Leon Surmelian, "The Love Dilemma of Jean Gabin," *Photoplay*, July 1942, 66 et seq.
16. Baxter, *Exiles*, 12.
17. Showman's campaign for *Deadlier Than The Male* (New York: Continental Distributing, n.d.).
18. Morgan, *Yeux*, 158.
19. *Ibid.*, 157.
20. Cheryl Cheng, "Michele Morgan, French Actress in 'The Fallen Idol,' Dies at 96," *The Hollywood Reporter*, December 20, 2016.
21. Morgan, *Yeux*, 222–223.
22. *Ibid.*, 156.
23. *Ibid.*, 174.
24. Robert Sklar, *City Boys: Cagney, Bogart, Garfield* (Princeton: Princeton University Press, 1992), 76.
25. Cal York, "Cal York's Inside Stuff," *Photoplay*, July 1941, 8.
26. Cheatham, *Screenland*.
27. George Benjamin, "Who Is This Great Lover?" *Modern Screen* (July 1941): 42 et seq.
28. Harry Brand, "Vital Statistics."
29. Georges Magnane, *L'Ecran Français* 18 (October 29, 1945).
30. Cheatham, *Screenland*; Surmelian, *Photoplay*, July 1942.
31. Morgan, 182–183; Brunelin, 295–296.
32. Glâtre, *Gabin-Dietrich*, 55.
33. Stefan Kanfer, *Tough Without a Gun: The Life and Extraordinary Afterlife of Humphrey Bogart* (New York: Knopf, 2011) 94.
34. Glâtre, *Jean Moncorgé Gabin*, 10; Brunelin, *Gabin*, 328.
35. Brunelin, *Gabin*, 303.
36. Morgan, *Yeux*, 161.
37. *Ibid.*, 163.
38. *Ibid.*
39. Ginger Rogers, *Ginger: My Story* (New York: HarperCollins, 1991), 231.
40. Steven Bach, *Marlene Dietrich, Life and Legend* (London: HarperCollins Publishers, 1992), 311.
41. *Ibid.*, 263.
42. Eon Wood, *Dietrich: A Biography* (London: Sanctuary, 2002), 249.
43. Winthrop Sergeant, "Dietrich and Her Magic Myth," *Life* (August 18, 1952): 86.
44. Peter B. Flint, "Marlene Dietrich, 90, Symbol of Glamour, Dies," *The New York Times*, May 7,1992.
45. Charles Higham, *Marlene: La Vie d'Une Star* (Paris: Calmann-Lévy, 1978), 17.
46. Marlene Dietrich, *Marlene* (New York: Grove Press, 1989), 137–142.
47. Riva, *Marlene Dietrich*, 504.

Chapter 14

1. Riva, *Marlene*, 504.
2. *Ibid.*

3. Wood, *Dietrich*, 202.

4. Donald Dewey, *James Stewart: A Biography* (Atlanta: Turner, 1996), 184.

5. Norma Bosquet and Michel Rachline, *Marlene Dietrich: Les Derniers Secrets* (Paris: Nouveau Monde Éditions, 2007), 16.

6. Scott Eyman, *John Wayne: The Life and Legend* (New York: Simon & Schuster, 2014), 109.

7. Marc Eliot, *American Titan: Searching for John Wayne* (New York: Dey Street Books, 2014), 111.

8. Eyman, *John Wayne*, 110.

9. Dietrich, *Marlene*, 132.

10. Wood, *Dietrich*, 199.

11. Dietrich, *Marlene*, 137.

12. Steven Bach, *Marlene Dietrich, Life and Legend* (London: HarperCollins, 1992), 318.

13. Brunelin, *Gabin*, 301.

14. Riva, *Marlene*, 517.

15. Bach, *Marlene Dietrich*, 311.

16. Dalio, *Folles*, 188.

17. Brunelin, *Gabin*, 304.

18. Riva, *Marlene*, 514.

19. *Ibid.*, 516.

20. *The New York Times*, March 9, 1942.

21. Riva, *Marlene*, 516.

22. Wood, *Dietrich*, 203.

23. Dietrich, *Marlene*, 132.

24. Harry Brand, "Vital Statistics."

25. *Ibid.*

26. "Reviewing Movies of the Month," *Photoplay*, July 1942, 6.

27. *The New York Herald-Tribune*, May 3, 1942.

28. Bosley Crowther, *The New York Times*, May 3, 1942.

29. Rogers, *Ginger*, 231.

30. Leon Surmelian, "The Love Dilemma of Jean Gabin," *Photoplay*, July 1942, 66 et seq.

31. *Ibid.*

Chapter 15

1. Surmelian, "The Love Dilemma."

2. Glâtre, *Gabin-Dietrich*, 128–129.

3. *Ibid.*, 130.

4. *Ibid.*

5. "Memorandum for the Director," Federal Bureau of Investigation, May 13, 1942. Retrieved from FBI Records: The Vault, March 16, 2017.

6. Naomi Blumberg, "Mabel Walker Willebrandt, American Lawyer," *Encyclopaedia Britannica* online; Dorothy M. Brown, "Willebrandt, Mabel Walker," *American National Biography* online; Mabel Walker Willebrandt, *The Inside of Prohibition* (Indianapolis: Bobbs-Merrill, 1929).

7. Letter dated May 16, 1942, from John Edgar Hoover to Special Agent in Charge, Los Angeles, California, R.B. Hood. Retrieved from FBI Records: The Vault, March 16, 2017.

8. All information cited in these pages concerning the FBI investigation of Marlene Dietrich and Jean Gabin is publicly available in the 60-page Bureau file entitled "Marlene Dietrich" available in FBI Records: The Vault. https://vault.fbi.gov/Marlene%20Dietrich%20/Marlene%20Dietrich%20Part%201%20of%205/view#document/p2.

9. Glâtre, *Gabin-Dietrich*, 134.

10. Brunelin, *Gabin*, 308.

11. Bosley Crowther, "The Imposter" (movie review), *The New York Times*, March 27, 1944.

12. Phillips and Vincendeau, *Journeys*, 116.

13. *Ibid.*

14. *Ibid.*, 120.

15. Reproduction of order by Bureau de New York de la Mission Militaire Française aux Etats-Unis. In Patrick Glâtre, *Jean Moncorgé Gabin, Acteur de la Libération de Royan* (Editions Bonne-Anse, 2015), 34.

16. *Ibid.*, 29.

17. Reproduction of telegram from the French Naval Mission in Washington to the New York Mission outlining Gabin's options. In Glâtre, *Gabin-Dietrich*, 164.

18. Riva, *Marlene Dietrich*, 528.

19. Brunelin, *Gabin*, 311–312.

Chapter 16

1. Dietrich, *Marlene*, 136.

2. Glâtre, *Gabin-Dietrich*, 167.

3. Brunelin, *Gabin*, 314–315.

4. Dietrich, *Marlene*, 137.

5. Bach, *Marlene Dietrich*, 291.

6. Glâtre, *Gabin-Dietrich*, 192.

7. *Ibid.*, 209–211.

8. Riva, *Marlene Dietrich*, 580.

9. "Jean Gabin's Films Barred in France," *The New York Times*, May 8, 1944.

10. Film clip from the Institut national de l'audiovisuel: http://www.ina.fr/video/I00012416, retrieved June 15, 2017 (author's translation).

11. Author's interview with Florence Moncorgé-Gabin, August 14, 2016.

12. Glâtre, *Gabin-Dietrich*, 212.

13. "La face Cachée de Jean Gabin," 4 min., FR2. Magneto Presse. http://www.magnetotv.com/un-jour-un-destin/saison-3/jean-moncorge-la-face-cachee-de-jean-gabin/, retrieved March 20, 2017.

14. *Ibid.*

15. Riding, *Show*, 331–334.

16. Glâtre, *Royan*, 55–60.

17. Riva, *Marlene Dietrich*, 542.

18. Glâtre, *Gabin-Dietrich*, 256–257.

19. Glâtre, *Royan*, 76; Glâtre, *Gabin-Dietrich*, 244–253.

20. Glâtre, *Gabin-Dietrich*, 312.

21. Paraz (writer), "Gabin Intime," documentary DVD.

Chapter 17

1. Brunelin, *Gabin*, 332–333.

2. Glâtre, *Gabin-Dietrich*, 206, 238.

3. Brunelin, *Gabin*, 326.

4. *Ibid.*

5. Le Minotaure, *L'Ecran Français*, November 27, 1946.

6. "Qui etait Jean Gabin?" interview with Leon Zitrone in 1960. https://www.youtube.com/watch?v=idBQKXAzss8, retrieved February 12, 2017.

7. Riva, *Marlene Dietrich*, 558–559.

8. *Ibid.*

9. *Ibid.*, 567.

10. *Ibid.*, 571.

11. Baker and Chase, *Josephine*, 263.

12. Riva, *Marlene Dietrich*, 560.

13. David Bret, *Marlene, My Friend* (London: Robson, 1993), 125; Turk, *Paradise*, 351; Brunelin, *Gabin*, 337–345; Bach, *Marlene Dietrich*, 312–315; Glâtre, *Gabin-Dietrich*, 281–284; Bosquet and Rachline, *Marlene Dietrich*, 58; Wood, *Dietrich*, 247.

14. Brunelin, *Gabin*, 344.

15. Riva, *Marlene Dietrich*, 575.

16. Wood, *Dietrich*, 253.

17. *Ibid.*, 249.

18. Riva, *Marlene Dietrich*, 583.

19. Wood, *Dietrich*, 250.

20. Riva, *Marlene Dietrich*, 584.

21. Glâtre, *Gabin-Dietrich*, 294.

22. *Ibid.*, 296.

23. *Mon Film*, February 5, 1947, 8–9.

24. Glâtre, *Gabin-Dietrich*, 298.

25. Higham, *La Vie*, 160.

26. Bach, *Marlene Dietrich*, 328.

27. Jean-Jacques Debout, "Comment Gabin a brûlé la dernière letter de Marlene," *Nice-Matin Week-end*, 16–18.

28. Morgan, *Yeux*, 311.

29. Glâtre, *Gabin-Dietrich*, 302.

Chapter 18

1. Brunelin, *Gabin*, 366.

2. *Ibid.*, 358.

3. *Ibid.*, 360.

4. Francis Ambrière, "La Soif" (review), *Opéra*, February 16, 1949.

5. Lucien Guitry, "La Soif" (review), *Vogue*, April 1949.

6. Kael, *5001 Nights*, 365.

7. "Jean Gabin," *France-Dimanche*, September 28, 1947; Brunelin, *Gabin*, 371–372.

8. "Madame Gabin Raconte Gabin," *Paris-Match* 1972 (March 13, 1987): 83.

9. Author's interview with Florence Moncorgé-Gabin, August 14, 2016.

10. *Ibid.*

11. "Interview with Dominique Gabin," *Paris Match* 2262 (October 1, 1992), 35 et seq.

12. Television interview of Jean Gabin by Jean Delannoy, 8 avril 1958, 2 min. 50 sec. http://www.ina.fr/video/I000100DONE61/jean-delannoy-et-jean-gabin-video.html, retrieved October 19, 2016.

13. Author's interview with Florence Moncorgé-Gabin, August 14, 2016.

14. Paraz, writer, "Gabin Intime," documentary DVD.

15. Author's interview with Florence Moncorgé-Gabin, August 14, 2016.

16. *Ibid.*

17. *Ibid.*

18. *Ibid.*

19. *The New York Times*, May 17, 1964.

20. Author's interview with Florence Moncorgé-Gabin, August 14, 2016.

21. Brunelin, *Gabin*, 410.

22. *Ibid.*, 381.

23. Danielle Darrieux in television interview about acting with Gabin in *La vérité sur Bébé Donge*, February 23, 1957. https://www.ina.fr/video/I00010041/danielle-darrieux-sur-jean-gabin-video.html, retrieved February 13, 2018.

24. Morgan, *Yeux*, 311.

25. Nicholas Hewitt, "Gabin, Grisbi and 1950s France," *Studies in French Cinema* 4, no. 1 (2004): 66.

Chapter 19

1. Hewitt, *Gabin, Grisbi*, 68.

2. Kenneth Turan, "Darkness in the City of Light," *The Los Angeles Times*, September 5, 2003.

3. Gabin interview broadcast November 15, 1976, on French television channel Antenne2. https://www.youtube.com/watch?v=7cgvbsX5B2A, retrieved May 15, 2017.

4. Konstantinos Costa-Gavras interview in "Jean Gabin, une âme Française," December 25, 2015, Cinétévé, Institut national de l'audiovisuel. http://www.ina.fr/video/CPD15007941/jean-gabin-une-ame-francaise-video.html, retrieved March 3, 2016.

5. "Annie Girardot fut giflé par Jean Gabin," *Vanity Fair* (French edition), March 20, 2014.

6. "Michel Audiard vous raconte Gabin, dit 'Pépé-la-sentence,'" *Paris-Match* 1074 (December 6, 1969): 122.

7. "Henri DECOIN parle de Jean Gabin," https://www.ina.fr/video/I00010102/henri-decoin-sur-jean-gabin-video.html, retrieved April 3, 2017.

8. Gauteur and Vincendeau, *Anatomie*, 163.

9. Renoir, *Ma Vie*, 250.

10. Claude Gauteur, interview with the author, March 23, 2016.

11. Françoise Arnoul, interview with the author, Paris, September 22, 2016.

12. "La Brouille Gabin-Audiard Désespère les Producteurs," *Paris-Match* 735 (May 11, 1963): 123 et seq.

13. Georges Simenon, *Mes Dictées: Au Delà de Ma Porte-Fenêtre* (Paris: Presses de la Cité, 1979), 308.

14. Jelot-Blanc, *Jean Gabin Inconnu*, 279.

15. Brigitte Bardot, *Initiales B.B* (Paris: Bernard Grasset, 1996), 161.

16. "Madame Gabin Raconte Gabin," *Paris-Match* 1972 (March 13, 1987): 82.

17. Zigman, *World's Coolest Movie Star* 2, xxi.

18. *Le Canard Enchaîné*, April 22, 1964, 6.

19. Bardot, *Initiales*, 165.

20. *Ibid.*, 161.

21. Florence Moncorgé-Gabin, *Quitte à avoir un père*, 71.

22. Handwritten note to the author, March 20, 2017.

23. Robert Collin, "Jean Gabin le dur a choisi les sabots," *Paris-Match* 786 (May 2, 1964).

24. Raphaël Tarnowski, "Gabin 'Le Cumulard' s'explique," *Paris-Match* 696 (August 11, 1962): 24–31.

25. "Madame Gabin Raconte Gabin," *Paris-Match* 1972 (March 13, 1987): 83.

26. Gauteur and Vincendeau, *Anatomie*, 90–91.

27. François Aymé and Yves Jeuland, "Un Français Nommé Gabin," documentary broadcast on France 3 television, April 28, 2017.

28. Author's interview with Florence Moncorgé-Gabin, August 14, 2016.

Chapter 20

1. Gauteur and Vincendeau, *Anatomie*, 59.

2. Claude Autant-Lara, *Les Cahiers de la Cinémathèque* 9, 10, 11, Perpignan, Summer–Fall 1973.

3. François Truffaut, *Arts* 720 (April 29, 1959).

4. Barbara Giudice, "French pic acad taps Verneuil," *Variety*, December 10, 2000.

5. Brunelin, *Gabin*, 485–486.

6. Zigman, *World's Coolest Movie Star* 2, xxvi.

7. Gabin's last interview (Youtube): Institut national de l'audiovisuel, https://www.youtube.com/watch?v=4yNK51TC7xo,
http://www.ina.fr/video/CPA7605622201/hommage-a-jean-gabin-video.html

8. Brunelin, *Gabin*, 19.

9. *Ibid.*, 410–411.

10. *Ame Française* documentary.

11. *Ibid.*; "Gabin, sa fille et le gentleman rider," *Paris-Match* 1372 (September 13, 1975): 21; "Pour Gabin, le gentleman rider qui veut épouser sa fille ne fait pas le poids," *Paris-Match* 1409 (May 29, 1976): 8–9.

12. *Ame Française* documentary.

13. Bret, *Marlene, My Friend*, 213; Bach, *Marlene Dietrich*, 328.

14. Morgan, *Yeux*, 151.

15. Paul Lefevre, Antenne 2, November 17, 1976. https://www.ina.fr/video/CAB7600935701.

16. Paul Lefevre in *Ame Française* documentary.

17. "L'Album souvenir du dernier monstre sacré de notre cinéma," *Paris-Match* 1435 (November 26, 1976).

18. "En France, deux masques réunis par le destin," *Paris-Match* 1442 (January 14, 1977): 38–39.

19. *Le Point*, November 22, 1976.

20. *Ame Française* documentary.

21. *Paris Match* 2262 (October 1, 1992). Interview with Dominique Gabin, 35 et seq.

22. Interview with the author, May 3, 2017.

Bibliography

Books on Jean Gabin

Andreu, Guillaume, and Frédéric Menant. *Les mots de Gabin*. Paris: Philippe Rey, 2005.

Barbier, Philippe, and Jacques Moreaux. *Jean Gabin, Gentleman du Cinéma*. Paris: Editions Dualpha, 2007.

Brieu, Jean-François. *Jean Gabin*. Paris: Albin Michel, 2001.

Brunelin, André. *Gabin*. Paris: Robert Laffont, 1987.

Dureau, Christian. *Jean Gabin: Le monument du cinéma Français*. Paris: Editions Didier Carpentier, 2009.

Field, Amanda J. "Impeccably Dressed: How Costume in Pépé-le-Moko Constructs Jean Gabin as Object of the Erotic Gaze." *Short Takes Film Studies*. Luton: Andrews UK, 2015.

Gauteur, Claude, and Ginette Vincendeau. *Jean Gabin: Anatomie d'un mythe*. Paris: Nouveau Monde Editions, 2006.

Gauteur, Claude. *Gabin: Ou, les Avatars d'un Mythe*. Paris: Pac, 1976.

Gauteur, Claude. *Jean Gabin, du livre au mythe*. Paris: LettMotif, 2015.

Glâtre, Patrick. *Gabin-Dietrich: Un Couple dans la Guerre*. Paris: Robert Laffont, 2016.

Glâtre, Patrick. *Jean Moncorge Gabin Acteur de la Libération de Royan*. Vaux-sur-Mer: Editions Bonne-Anse, 2015.

Glâtre, Patrick, and Patrick Millot. *Jean Gabin: La traversée d'un siècle*. Paris: Creaphis, 2004.

Glâtre, Patrick, ed. *Jean Gabin*. Paris: Créathis, 2004.

Jelot-Blanc, Jean-Jacques. *Jean Gabin Inconnu*. Paris: Flammarion, 2014.

Lemonnier, Marc. *Jean Gabin dans le Siècle*. Paris: City Editions, 2006.

Missiaen, Jean-Claude, and Jacques Siclier. *Jean Gabin*. Paris: H. Veyrier, 1977.

Moncorgé-Gabin, Florence. *Quitte à avoir un père, autant qu'il s'appelle Gabin*. Paris: Le Cherche-Midi, 2003.

Moncorgé-Gabin, Florence and Mathias. *Gabin hors champ*. Paris: Michel Lafon, 2004.

Paucard, Alain. *La France de Jean Gabin*. Sion, Switzerland: Editions Xenia, 2016.

Zigman, Charles. *World's Coolest Movie Star: The Complete 95 Films (and Legend) of Jean Gabin*. 2 vols. Los Angeles: Allenwood Press, 2008.

Books for Context

Abecassis, Michael, ed. *French Cinema in Close-up*. Dublin: Phaeton, 2015.

Andrew, Dudley. *Mists of Regret: Culture and Sensibility in Classic French Film*. Princeton: Princeton University Press, 1995.

Arnoul, Françoise. *Animal doué de Bonheur*. Paris: Belfond, 1996.

Assouline, Pierre. *Simenon*. New York: Alfred A. Knopf, 1997.

Ayers, Andrew. *The Architecture of Paris*. Fellbach: Edition Axel Menges, 2003.

Bach, Steven. *Marlene Dietrich, Life and Legend*. London: HarperCollins, 1992.

Baker, Jean-Claude, and Chris Chase. *Josephine: The Hungry Heart*. New York: Random House, 1993.

Baker, Josephine, and Jo Bouillon. *Josephine*. London: W. H. Allen, 1978.

Bakshy, Alexander. "The Theater of Max Gorky," in *The Lower Depths and Other Plays*. New Haven: Yale University Press, 1945.

Bardot, Brigitte. *Initiales B.B.* Paris: Bernard Grasset, 1996.

Barrot, O. *Inoubliables! Visages du cinéma français, 1930–1950*. Paris: Calmann-Levy, 1986.

Barton, Ruth. *Hedy Lamarr: The Most Beautiful Woman in Film*. Lexington: University Press of Kentucky (Screen Classics Series), 2010.

Baxter, John. *The Hollywood Exiles*. London: MacDonald and Jane's, 1976.

Bazin, André. *What Is Cinema?* Berkeley: University of California Press, 1971. Vol. 2.

Bergan, Ronald. *Jean Renoir: Projections of Paradise*. London: Bloomsbury, 1992.

Bosquet, Norma, and Michel Rachline. *Marlene Dietrich: Les Derniers Secrets*. Paris: Nouveau Monde Éditions, 2007.

Boulanger, Pierre. *Le Cinéma Colonial*. Paris: Seghers, 1975.

Braibant, Charles. *Histoire de la Tour Eiffel*. Paris: Librairie Plon, 1964.

Braudy, Leo. *Jean Renoir: The World of His Films*. New York: Doubleday & Co., 1972.

Bret, David. *Marlene, My Friend*. London: Robson, 1993.

Buchsbaum, Jonathan. *Cinema Engagé: Film in the Popular Front*. Champaign: University of Illinois Press, 1988.

Caine, Michael. *Acting in Film: An Actor's Take on Movie-making*. New York: Applause Theater Book Publishers, 1990.

Cameron, Ian, ed. *The Movie Book of Film Noir*. London: Studio Vista, 1992.

Carné, Marcel. *La Vie à Belles Dents*. Paris: Editions Jean-Pierre Ollivier, 1975.

Castle, Charles. *The Folies Bergere*. London: Methuen, 1984.

Clair, René. *Cinema Yesterday and Today*. New York: Dover Publications, 1972.

Cole, Toby, and Helen Krich Chinoy, eds. *Actors on Acting*. New York: Crown Publishers, 1970.

Conard, Mark T., ed. *The Philosophy of Film Noir*. Lexington: University Press of Kentucky, 2007.

Crisp, Colin. *Classic French Cinema, 1930–1960*. Bloomington: Indiana University Press, 1993.

Crisp, Colin. *Genre, Myth, and Convention in the French Cinema, 1929–1939*. Bloomington: Indiana University Press, 2002.

Curtis, James. *Spencer Tracy*. New York: Alfred A. Knopf, 2011.

Dalio, Marcel. *Mes Années Folles*. Paris: J.-C. Lattès, 1976.

Damase, Jacques. *Les Folies du Music-Aall: A History of the Paris Music-Hall from 1914 to the Present Day*. London: Anthony Blond, 1962.

DeMaio, Patricia A. *Garden of Dreams: The Life of Simone Signoret*. Jackson: University Press of Mississippi, 2014.

Desrichard, Yves. *Julien Duvivier: Cinquante ans de noirs destins*. Paris: BiFi/Durante, 2001.

Dewey, Donald. *James Stewart: A Biography*. Atlanta: Turner, 1996.

Dickos, Andrew. *Street with No Name: A History of the Classic American Film Noir*. Lexington: University Press of Kentucky, 2013.

Dietrich, Marlene. *Marlene*. New York: Grove Press, 1989.

Dimendberg, Edward. *Film Noir and the Spaces of Modernity*. Cambridge: Harvard University Press, 2004.

Eliot, Marc. *American Titan: Searching for John Wayne*. New York: Dey Street Books, 2014.

Eyman, Scott. *John Wayne: the Life and Legend*. New York: Simon & Schuster, 2014.

Fuligni, Bruno. *Dans les archives inédites des services secrets: Un siècle d'histoire et d'espionnage français (1870–1989)*. Paris: Folio, 2014.

Gabin, Jean. *Confidences*. Unpublished, undated document in archives of the Musée Jean Gabin, Mériel.

Gauteur, Claude. *D'après Simenon, du cinema à la television*. Les Amis de Georges Simenon, 2012.

Harriss, Joseph. *The Tallest Tower: Eiffel and the Belle Epoque*. Boston: Houghton Mifflin, 1975.

Harriss, Joseph. *About France*. Lincoln: iUniverse, 2005.

Hayward, Susan, and Ginette Vincendeau, eds. and introd. "The Fleeing Gaze: Jean Renoir's La Bête humaine (1938)" in *French Film: Texts and Contexts*, 42–62. London; Routledge, 2000.

Higham, Charles. *Marlene: La Vie d'Une Star*. Paris: Calmann-Lévy, 1978.

Hillier, Jim, ed. *Cahiers du Cinéma, Vol 1. The 1950s: Neo-Realism, Hollywood, New Wave*. London: Routledge, 1985.

Huet, Philppe, and Marie-France Coquart. *Mistinguett: La Reine des Années Folles*. Paris: Albin Michel, 1996.

Jackson, Julian. *The Popular Front in France: Defending Democracy 1934–1938*. Cambridge: Cambridge University Press, 1990.

Jeancolas, J.-P. *15 ans d'année trente: le cinéma des Français, 1929–1944*. Paris: Nouveau Monde Editions, 2005.

Kael, Pauline. *5001 Nights at the Movies*. New York: Holt, Rinehart and Winston, 1982.

Kanfer, Stefan. *Tough Without a Gun: The Life and Extraordinary Afterlife of Humphrey Bogart*. New York: Knopf, 2011.

Kennedy-Karpat, Colleen. *Rogues, Romance, and Exoticism in French Cinema of the 1930s*. Madison, NJ: Fairleigh Dickinson University Press, 2013.

Lannoy, François de. *Les Régiments de Chars de la 2e DB*. Paris: Editions Techniques pour l'Automobile et l'Industrie, 2014.

Lennig, Arthur. *Stroheim*. Lexington: University Press of Kentucky, 2000.

Macdonald, Nicholas. *In Search of La Grande Illusion: A Critical Appreciation of Jean Renoir's Elusive Masterpiece*. Jefferson, NC: McFarland, 2014.

Maillot, Pierre. *Les fiancés de Marianne: la société française à travers ses grands acteurs*. Paris: Éditions du Cerf, 1996.

Malraux, André. *Esquisse d'une psychologie du cinema*. Paris: Nouveau Monde Editions, 2003.

Martin, John. *The Golden Age of French Cinema 1929–1939*. Boston: Twayne, 1983.

Meyers, Jeffrey. *Gary Cooper, American Hero*. New York: William Morrow, 1998.

Morgan, Michele. *Avec ces yeux-la*. Paris: Robert Laffont, 1977.

O'Connor, Patrick. *Dietrich: Style and Substance*. New York: Dutton, 1992.

O'Connor, Patrick. *Toulouse Lautrec: The Nightlife of Paris*. London: Phaidon, 1991.

Pessis, Jacques, and Jacques Crépineau. *Le Moulin Rouge*. Paris: Hermé, 1989.

Phillips, Alastair, and Ginette Vincendeau, ed. *Journeys of Desire: European Actors in Hollywood*. London: British Film Institute, 2006.

Powell, Dilys. *The Golden Screen*. London: Headline, 1990.

Price, David. *Cancan!* Madison, NJ: Farleigh Dickinson University Press, 1998.

Renoir, Jean. *Ma vie et mes films*. Editions Flammarion, 1974 (Edition corrigée, 2005).

Renoir, Jean, and Olivier Curchod. *La Grande Illusion*. Paris: Armand Colin, 2005.

Riding, Alan. *And the Show Went On: Cultural Life in Nazi-Occupied Paris*. New York: Alfred A. Knopf, 2010.

Riva, Maria. *Marlene Dietrich*. New York: Alfred A. Knopf, 1993.

Rogers, Ginger. *Ginger: My Story*. New York: HarperCollins, 1991.

Rougerie, Jacques. *Paris insurgé: La Commune de 1871*. Paris: Gallimard, 2012.

Sadoul, Georges. *French Film*. London: Falcon Press, 1953.

Sesonske, Alexander. *Jean Renoir: The French Films, 1924–1939*. Cambridge: Harvard University Press, 1980.

Shearer, Stephen Michael, and Robert Osborn. *Beautiful: The Life of Hedy Lamarr*. New York: St. Martin's Griffin, 2013 (Kindle edition).

Shirer, William. *The Collapse of the Third Republic: An Enquiry into the Fall of France in 1940*. New York: Simon & Schuster, 1969.

Simenon, Georges. *Mes Dictées: Au Delà de Ma Porte-Fenêtre*. Paris: Presses de la Cité, 1979.

Sklar, Robert. *City Boys: Cagney, Bogart, Garfield*. Princeton: Princeton University Press, 1992.

Temple, Michael, and Michael Witt, eds. *The French Cinema Book*. London: British Film Institute, 2004.

Tuchman, Barbara. *The Proud Tower: A Portrait of the World Before the War, 1890–1914*. New York: The Macmillan Co., 1966.

Tulard, Jean. *Dictionnaire du cinéma—Les réalisateurs*. Paris: Éditions Bouquins, 2007.

Turk, Edward Baron. *Child of Paradise: Marcel Carné and the Golden Age of French Cinema*. Cambridge: Harvard University Press, 1989.

Vernon, James. *Hunger: A Modern History*. Cambridge: The Belknap Press, 2007.

Vincendeau, Ginette. *Stars and Stardom in French Cinema*. London: Bloomsbury Academic, 2000.

Weber, Eugen. *The Hollow Years: France in the 1930s*. New York: Norton, 1994.

Willebrandt, Mabel Walker. *The Inside of Prohibition*. Indianapolis: Bobbs-Merrill, 1929.

Williams, Alan. *Republic of Images: A History of French Filmmaking*. Cambridge: Harvard University Press, 1992.

Wood, Eon. *Dietrich: A Biography*. London: Sanctuary, 2002.

Periodicals

Ambrière, Francis. "La Soif" (review). *Opéra*, February 16, 1949.

"Annie Girardot fut giflé par Jean Gabin." *Vanity Fair* (French edition), March 20, 2014.

Autant-Lara, Claude. *Les Cahiers de la Cinémathèque*, 9, 10, 11, Perpignan, Summer-Fall 1973.

Benjamin, George. "Who Is This Great Lover?" *Modern Screen* (July 1941): 42 et seq.

Billard, Pierre. "Gabin: Les Deux Mythes." *Le Point* 218 (November 22, 1976): 163–165.

Bourdet, Maurice. "Les Gaietés de L'Escadron." *Vu* 236 (September 21, 1932): 1523.

Brest, René. "'Hollywood? Très Peu pour Moi!' dit Jean Gabin." *Pour Vous*, September 29, 1937: 11.

"La Brouille Gabin-Audiard Désespère les Producteurs." *Paris-Match* 735 (May 11, 1963): 123 et seq.

Cambier, Odile. *Cinémonde*, September 19, 1935.

Cheatham, Maude. "Gabin Looks at the Girls!" *Screenland*, May 1942: 50.

Cheng, Cheryl. "Michele Morgan, French Actress in 'The Fallen Idol,' Dies at 96." *The Hollywood Reporter*, December 20, 2016.

Collin, Robert. "Jean Gabin le dur a choisi les sabots." *Paris-Match* 786 (May 2, 1964).

Crowther, Bosley. "Moontide" (review). *The New York Times*, May 3, 1942.

Debout, Jean-Jacques. "Comment Gabin a brûlé la dernière letter de Marlene." *Nice-Matin Week-end* (May 5, 2017): 16–18.

"En France, deux masques réunis par le destin," *Paris-Match* 1442 (January 14, 1977): 38–39.

Farber, Manny. "Gabin in Hollywood." *The New Republic* 106, no. 19 (May 11, 1942): 639–640.

Fayard, Jean. "On demande un cinéma virile." *Pour Vous*, July 11, 1935.

Gabin, Jean. "Quand Je Revois Ma Vie." *Pour Vous* 5, 12, 19, 26 September, 3 October 1935: 3 et seq.

"Gabin, sa fille et le gentleman rider." *Paris-Match* 1372 (September 13, 1975): 21.

Gates, Anita. "Michèle Morgan, the First 'Best Actress' at Cannes, Dies at 96." *The New York Times*, December 23, 2016.

Giudice, Barbara. "French pic acad taps Verneuil." *Variety* (December 10, 2000).

Green, Graham. "The Cinema." *The Spectator* (April 22, 1937): 15.

Gruber, Helmut. "Jean Gabin: Doomed Worker-Hero of a Doomed France." *International Labor and Working-Class History* 59 (April 1, 2001): 15–35.

Guitry, Lucien. "La Soif" (review). *Vogue*, April 1949.

"Hard-Boiled Egg, French Style." *The New York Times*, May 22, 1938.

Hess, John L. "Jean Gabin, 72, French Film Star Who Played Hero-Victim, Is Dead." *The New York Times*, November 16, 1976.

Hewitt, Nicholas. "Gabin, Grisbi and 1950s France." *Studies in French Cinema* 4, no. 1 (2004): 65–75.

Hunt, Drake. "Imported Idol." *Hollywood* 31, no. 1 (January 1942): 18.

"Interview with Dominique Gabin." *Paris Match* 2262 (October 1, 1992): 35 et seq.

"Jean Gabin's Films Barred in France." *The New York Times*, May 8, 1944.

Karr, Jeanne. "First Love." *Modern Screen* 24, no. 3 (February 1942): 32 et seq.

"Jean Gabin: L'Album Souvenir du Dernier Monstre Sacré de Notre Cinéma." *Paris Match* 1435 (November 26, 1976): 51–69.

Journal de la Société des Amis du Musée Jean Gabin (May 1994): 7.

Kehr, David. "France's Sad-eyed Cagney." *The New York Times*, June 23, 2002.

"L'Album souvenir du dernier monstre sacré de notre cinéma," *Paris-Match* 1435 (November 26, 1976).

Mac Orlan, Pierre. "Autour de la Bandéra." *Pour Vous*, July 11, 1935: 3 et seq.

"Madame Gabin Raconte Gabin." *Paris-Match* 1972 (March 13, 1987): 77 et seq.

Magnane, Georges. *L'Ecran Français* 18 (October 29, 1945).

Marguy, Paule. "Maria Mauban Nous Dit la Vérité." *Mon Film* 28 (February 5, 1947): 8–9.

"Michel Audiard vous raconte Gabin, dit 'Pépé-la-sentence.'" *Paris-Match* 1074 (December 6, 1969): 122.

Morse, Wilbur Jr. "Escape from the Nazis." *Photoplay*, July 1941: 36.

"Pour Gabin, le gentleman rider qui veut épouser sa fille ne fait pas le poids." *Paris-Match*, No. 1409, May 29, 1976: 8–9.

Pryor, Thomas M. "By Way of Report," *The New York Times*, March 6, 1941.

"Quel est ce matelot?" *France Magazine* 30 (October 24, 1939).

Renoir, Jean. "M. Renoir Speaks of War." *The New York Times*, October 23, 1938.

Sergeant, Winthrop. "Dietrich and Her Magic Myth." *Life*, August 18, 1952: 86.

Slavitt, David. "Jean Gabin: A Screen Image." *The Hopkins Review* 1, no. 2 (Spring 2008, New Series): 275–293.

"La Soif" (supplement) *France Illustration* 70 (November 11, 1950).

Sorrento, Matthew. "La Bête humaine: Unquiet Desperation." *Senses of Cinema* 69 (December 2013): 24–24.

Surmelian, Leon. "The Love Dilemma of Jean Gabin." *Photoplay*, July 1942, 66 et seq.

Tarnowski, Raphaël. "Gabin 'Le Cumulard' s'explique." *Paris-Match* 696 (August 11, 1962): 24–31.

Thomson, David. "The Grand Illusion." *The New Republic* 245, no. 12 (July 14, 2014): 56–58.

Tillier, Maurice. "Jean Gabin." *Le Figaro Littéraire*, June 11, 1964.

Truffaut, François. *Arts* 720 (April 29, 1959).

Turan, Kenneth. "Darkness in the City of Light." *The Los Angeles Times*, September 5, 2003.

Turan, Kenneth. "'Pépé le Moko' Prowls the Casbah Again." *The Los Angeles Times*, April 19, 2002.

Vincendeau, Ginette. "Community, Nostalgia and the Spectacle of Masculinity." *Screen* 26, no. 6 (Nov./Dec. 1985): 18–38.

Vincendeau, Ginette. "Grand Illusion." *Sight & Sound* 22, no. 5 (May 2012): 40–42.

Wahl, Lucien. "Gueule d'Amour." *Pour Vous* 462 (September 23, 1937): 7.

York, Cal. "Cal York's Inside Stuff." *Photoplay*, July 1941, 8.

Documentaries

Buckard, Christian, and Daniel Guthmann. "Jean Gabin und Marlene Dietrich." DVD produced by WDR Mediagroup, Cologne, Germany, 2011.

Glâtre, Patrick, Sylvain Palfroy, and René-Jean Bouyer. "Jean Gabin, Une Âme Française." DVD produced by Cinétévé, Paris, 2015.

Maillet, Dominique. "Dernier Sursaut du Front Populaire." Supplement to DVD of *Le Jour Se Lève*.

Paraz, Louis, writer. "Gabin Intime: Aristocrate et Paysan." DVD produced by Ciné-Développement/ SND, Paris, 2006.

Tavernier, Bertrand. *Voyage à Travers le Cinéma Français.* DVD produced by Little Bear-Gaumont Pathé, Paris, 2017.

Thisse, Simon, and Laurent Delahousse. "Jean Moncorgé, la Face Cachée de Jean Gabin." June 2010. A Magneto Presse production for the France 2 Télévision program *Un Jour/Un Destin*, broadcast October 26, 2010. (Unavailable online, DVD by request from France 2 Télévision, Paris.)

Theater Programs

Trois Jeunes Filles. Nues! Théatre des Bouffes-Parisiens. Published by Les Publications Willy Fischer, 1925–26.

Julien Duvivier Retrospective (program notes). Museum of Modern Art, New York. May 1–28, 2009. Organized by Joshua Siegel, associate curator, Department of Film, and Lenny Borger, film historian.

Publicity

Brand, Harry, director of Publicity, 20th Century–Fox. "Vital Statistics on Moon Tide [sic]." Undated.

Audio-Visual

Ardisson, Thierry. Interview with Florence Moncorgé Gabin about her book *Un père qui s'appelle Jean Gabin*. 20 min. 36 sec. January 11, 2003. YouTube June 23, 2014. Archive INA (Institut National de l'Audiovisual). https://www.youtube.com/watch?v=2o61PfzNqpI, retrieved February 25, 2016.

Aymé, François, and Yves Jeuland. "Un Français Nommé Gabin." 1 h. 44 min. 54 sec. Broadcast on France 3 Télévision, April 28, 2017. Archive INA. http://www.ina.fr/video/5961890_001, retrieved May 2, 2017.

Chancel, Jacques. "Michel Audiard, le maître du dialogue." Radio interview with Michel Audiard. 57 min. 19 sec. Radioscopie, Grandes Heures Radio France. YouTube April 6, 2015. https://www.youtube.com/watch?v=sqI2-wjkBtk, retrieved January 17, 2016.

Chazal, Robert. French television interview with Jean Gabin about his career. 8 min. 54 sec. December 6, 1970. Archive INA. https://www.ina.fr/video/I000 10383/jean-gabin-a-propos-de-sa-carriere-d-acteur-video.html, retrieved February 8, 2017.

Coldefly, Jean-Marie (producer). "Michèle Morgan: Anecdote dans la scène du baiser de *Quai des brumes*. June 9, 1956. 2 min. 22 sec. Cinétévé, Institut national de l'audiovisuel. http://www.ina.fr/video/I06248804/ michele-morgan-anecdote-dans-la-scene-du-baiser-de-quai-des-brumes-video.html, retrieved October 15, 2016.

Costa-Gavras, Konstantinos. Interview in "Jean Gabin, une Âme Française." December 25, 2015. 52 min. 3 sec. Cinétévé, Institut national de l'audiovisuel. http://www.ina.fr/video/CPD15007941/jean-gabin-une-ame-francaise-video.html, retrieved February 10, 2017.

Darrieux, Danielle. Interview about acting with Gabin in *La vérité sur Bébé Donge*. 1 min. 16 sec. February 23, 1957. "Gros Plan," Office National de Radiodiffusion et Television. https://www.ina.fr/video/I000 10041/danielle-darrieux-sur-jean-gabin-video.html, retrieved July 14, 2016.

Decoin, Henri. Talk about directing Jean Gabin. 3 min. 21 sec. June 4, 1960. "Gros Plan," Office National de Radiodiffusion et Television. https://www.ina.fr/video/I00010102/henri-decoin-sur-jean-gabin-video.html, retrieved May 14, 2016.

De la Patellière, Denys. Interview about directing Jean Gabin and Louis de Funès. 2 min. 23 sec. April 25, 1968. Published YouTube November 14, 2006. https://www.youtube.com/watch?v=rBNFajKFkN8, retrieved January 10, 2016.

Delannoy, Jean. "Les Joie de la Vie," interview with Jean Gabin. 2 min. 50 sec. April 8, 1958. Archive INA. http://www.ina.fr/video/I000100DONE61/jean-delannoy-et-jean-gabin-video.html, retrieved March 19, 2016.

"La dernière interview de Jean Gabin" 5 min. 46 sec. YouTube August 26, 2015. Archive INA. https://www.youtube.com/watch?v=4yNK5ITC7xo http://www.ina.fr/video/CPA7605622201/hommage-a-jean-gabin-video.html, retrieved May 12, 2016.

Durieux, Christian, and Alain Chaboud. "Gabin à Coeur Ouvert." 9 min. 17 sec. September 6, 1965, published YouTube November 26, 2014. https://www.youtube.com/watch?v=MnDKHbuqiGg, retrieved May 12, 2016.

Gabin, Jean. "Pourquoi j'ai tourné 'l'Affaire Dominici." 6 min. 8 sec. March 2, 1973. YouTube August 26, 2015. Archive INA. https://www.youtube.com/watch?v=HdEnS0cRI7M, retrieved April 7, 2016.

Gabin, Jean. Sings *Maintenant Je Sais*, 1974. 3 min. 14 sec. YouTube August 4, 2011. https://www.youtube.com/watch?v=Gl8AFljtG7U, retrieved April 2, 2016.

"Jean Gabin est Mort." French television reports Gabin's death. 36 min 12 sec. November 15, 1976. Antenne 2, Archive INA. https://www.youtube.com/watch?v=7cgvbsX5B2A, retrieved December 2, 2016.

"Obsèques Jean Gabin." Le Journal Antenne 2. 2 min. 8 sec. November 17, 1976. Archive INA. https://www.ina.fr/video/CAB7600935701, retrieved May 9, 2016.

"Pour le Cinéma." Interviews with Jean Gabin and others involved in filming *Le Chat*. 18 min. 55 sec. December 6, 1970. "Office National de Radiodiffusion et Television. Archive INA. http://www.ina.fr/video/I05044066/jean-gabin-sur-le-tournage-du-film-le-chat—video.html, retrieved February 14, 2015.

Roche, France, and Daniel Cazal. Interviews with Gabin's dresser, Micheline Bonnet, screenwriter Michel Audiard, and his notary, Maître Naveau. 4 min 54 sec. November 15, 1976. *Le Journal*, Antenne 2. Archive INA. http://www.ina.fr/video/CAB7601257001, retrieved March 24, 2017.

Ruggieri, Eve. "Gabin et Belmondo parlent Audiard." 7 min. 31 sec. March 25, 1980. Archive INA. YouTube December 14, 2014. https://www.youtube.com/watch?v=fEisUWlriLI, retrieved April 29, 2017.

Serillon, Claude. "Entretien avec Michèle Morgan sur le célèbre baiser donné à Jean "Gabin dans le film *Quai des brumes*." 1 min. 36 sec. December 1, 1987. Antenne 2, *Les Dossiers de l'Ecran*. Archive INA. http://www.ina.fr/video/I15174996/michele-morgan-sur-le-baiser-avec-jean-gabin-video.html, retrieved April 15, 2016.

Simenon, Georges. Discusses his admiration for Jean Gabin. 4 min. 21 sec. November 15, 1976. TF1 Actualités. Archive INA. https://www.ina.fr/video/I00010364/temoignage-sonore-de-georges-sur-jean-gabin-video.html, retrieved February 10, 2017.

Tchernia, Pierre. Interview with Jean Gabin. 8 min. 43 sec. February 22, 1970. Cinétévé, Institut national de l'audiovisuel. http://www.ina.fr/video/I00010319, retrieved June 9, 2016.

Welles, Orson. *L'Affaire Dominici*. 51 min. 46 sec. 1955. Published YouTube September 4, 2013. https://www.youtube.com/watch?v=vGzFzqQfI9Y, retrieved October 13, 2016.

Zitrone, Léon. Interview in "Qui etait Jean Gabin?" 5 min. 18 sec. December 3, 1959. Archive INA. YouTube August 26, 2015. https://www.youtube.com/watch?v=idBQKXAzss8, retrieved May 14, 2016.

Index

Numbers in *bold italics* indicate pages with illustrations